Pragmatic Muslim Politics

Andreas Johansson

Pragmatic Muslim Politics

The Case of Sri Lanka Muslim Congress

 Springer

Andreas Johansson
Swedish South Asian Studies Network (SASNET)
Lund University
Lund, Sweden

ISBN 978-3-030-12788-6   ISBN 978-3-030-12789-3   (eBook)
https://doi.org/10.1007/978-3-030-12789-3

Library of Congress Control Number: 2019933329

This Springer imprint is published by the registered company Springer Nature Switzerland AG.
The registered company address is: Gewerbestrasse 11, 6330 Cham, Switzerland

Contents

1	**Introduction**	1
	Historical Background	3
	Pre-Colonial and Colonial Times	3
	The Origins of the Civil War	8
	The Impact of da'wa Movements	14
	The Twenty-First Century and Post-Conflict Sri Lanka	16
	An Introduction to the Sri Lanka Muslim Congress	18
	State, Nation, and Ethnicity	22
	Muslim Politics – Behind the Ethnic Marker	24
	Material	26
	Parliamentary Speeches	27
	The SLMC's Official Documents	28
	Interviews	29
	References	30
2	**Official Documents**	35
	The Constitution of the Sri Lanka Muslim Congress	35
	Code of Conduct	39
	Convention Speeches	42
	The Party on the Internet and in "Public Spaces"	45
	The Tree as a Public Symbol	52
	Analysis	54
	References	57
3	**Narratives of the Party**	61
	The Genesis of the Party	61
	Organization	64
	Women in the Party Organization	66
	Being Muslim	67
	The Current Situation in Sri Lanka	69
	Islam	72
	Scripture and Law	72

        Majlis-e-shoora and Shura 76
    Analysis.. 79
    References.. 82

4   Ashraff in Parliament 1989–1992 85
    The Civil War 85
        The Indo-Lankan Accord 85
        Jihad and the Aftermath of the Indo-Sri Lankan Peace Accord........... 88
    The Nation 93
        Democracy 94
    Education 98
    Islamic Economics 104
    Public Morals... 106
    Islamic Laws 108
    Foreign Policy 109
    Analysis... 112
    References.. 117

5   Hakeem in Parliament 2006–2011 121
    The Civil War... 121
        Tamil Militant Movements... 121
        The Government 125
    Additional Issues... 131
    Analysis... 133
    References.. 135

6   Concluding Remarks – Pragmatic Muslim Politics............................ 137
    References.. 143

Appendices.. 145

Abbreviations

BBS	Bodu Bala Sena
CVF	Civil Volunteer Force
EPRLF	Eelam People's Revolutionary Liberation Front
EROS	Eelam Revolutionary Organisation of Students
ESLMUF	East Sri Lanka Muslim United Front
GoSL	Government of Sri Lanka
IDP	Internally Displaced Person
IPKF	Indian Peace Keeping Force
JHU	Jathika Hela Urumaya
JVP	Janatha Vimukthi Peramuna
LTTE	Liberation Tigers of Tamil Eelam
MEP	Mahajana Eksath Peramuna
MULF	Muslim United Liberation Front
MSGR	Muslim Self-Governing Region
NUA	National United Alliance
PA	People's Alliance
PLOTE	People's Liberation Organisation of Tamil Eelam
SLFP	Sri Lanka Freedom Party
SLMC	Sri Lanka Muslim Congress
TELO	Tamil Eelam Liberation Organization
TNA	Tamil National Alliance
TULF	Tamil United Liberation Front
UNF	United National Front
UNP	United National Party
UPFA	United People's Freedom Alliances

Chapter 1
Introduction

Abstract This chapter introduces the main purpose of this book. It also gives the historical background of the Muslim community in Sri Lanka. It explains the diversity within the Tamil community in Sri Lanka and how Muslims started to identify themselves as Moors. This chapter also gives an introduction to pre-colonial times and colonial times in Sri Lanka. From the perspective of the Muslim community in Sri Lanka, this chapter also gives the reader an introduction to the civil war and post-war conflicts involving the Sri Lankan community. This chapter also has an introduction to the political party that this book analyzes, namely, the Sri Lankan Muslim Congress. In this chapter the reader will also get an introduction to some or the theoretical points of departure in this book. The chapter ends by discussing the source material upon which this study is based as well as how it is analyzed. The three types of sources are: interviews, parliamentary speeches, and official documents from the SLMC. They will be analyzed separately in the following chapters and will then be compared in the final chapter. The different forms of source material not only give a widespread empirical base but also correspond to the overall aim and questions posed by me in this book.

Keywords Muslim politics · Islam · Muslims · Sri Lanka · Sri Lanka Muslim Congress

> OK, I don't quote the Qur'an and the Sunna, but occasionally I refer to the Qur'an and various other things […] I am careful in a multiethnic society, that even Mr. Ashraff in the latter part of his political career, even attempted to rebrand the SLMC, under a new […] name, which has its own rationale. He founded the National Unity Alliance […] We had a discussion on reinventing the idea so we don't impose the Muslim element or the Muslim factor, and to rebrand in such a way that it would be more acceptable and also attract the non-Muslims to the political movement, and we will try to be a little more diverse in our composition.[1]

This book investigates the use of religious terms and symbols in politics. More specifically, it investigates Muslim politics. When scholars of Islamic Studies and the

---

[1] Rauff Hakeem, 2013-02-24.

© Springer Nature Switzerland AG 2019
A. Johansson, *Pragmatic Muslim Politics*,
https://doi.org/10.1007/978-3-030-12789-3_1

study of religion research Muslim political parties, they generally focus on Islamist or post-Islamist politics, even though the world of Muslim politics is much wider. When political scientists analyze political parties, religious features are often brushed aside even though they are presented as crucial by the parties themselves. Many books and articles about Muslim political parties consequently deal superficially with Islamic terminology and its meaning. The aim of this book is therefore to analyze the role of religious terms and symbols within a non-fundamentalist political party, namely, the Sri Lanka Muslim Congress (SLMC), a Muslim political party that has been part of the democratic process in Sri Lanka since the 1980s. Thereby, I hope to broaden the research on political parties founded on religious ideologies.

There exist several important academic studies that focus on ethnic conflict in Sri Lanka. Many, however, mention Muslims only in passing.[2] One reason is most probably that Muslims did not participate in the civil war as an organized group. Muslim Sri Lankans were, however, clearly affected by the conflict and were even directly targeted by non-Muslim Tamil and Sinhalese activists.[3] There are furthermore a few other studies that concern the rise of SLMC, but they do not address the issue of religion.[4]

This book analyzes the official documents and parliamentary speeches (1989–1992 and 2006–2011) of the SLMC, as well as interviews conducted with SLMC High Command, which is the highest decision-making body in the SLMC.[5]

This book is organized around the key argument that the SLMC's use of religious terms and symbols has been pragmatic and changed depending on context and a shifting political landscape. More specifically, the book presents two main findings. The use of religious symbols and terms in the SLMC differs in internal party documents (such as member guidelines) from publically visible documents (such as parliamentary speeches and public posters). In internal party documents, Islamic symbols and terms are used to delimit Muslims as a specific group in the political context of post-colonial Sri Lanka. In public documents, on the other hand, we see a significant historical change. Between 1989 and 1992 these documents reveal a use of Islamic terms and symbols as parts of solutions to social problems. Such a use changed following the post-9/11 anti-Muslim that emerged across the globe. The SLMC responded by more or less refraining from using Islamic terms and symbols in parliament, and using inclusive terms to attract non-practicing Muslims and differentiating itself from openly Islamist parties and movements. The quote above, which is a statement from SLMC party leader Rauff Hakeem, captures precisely this

---

[2] For some examples, see Wickramasinghe 2006, Warnapala 2001, and Meyer 2001.

[3] For example, see Abdullah 2004, Ali 2004, 2014, Brune 2003, De Munk 2005a, b, Gaasbeek 2010, Haniffa 2013, Imtiyaz, 2005, 2009, Imtiyaz and Iqbal 2011, Mahroof 1990, McGilvray 1974, 1991, 1998, 2001, 2004, 2011b, 2014, Mohan 1987, Shukri 1986, Walker 2013, Zackariya and Shanmugaratnam 2003, and Klem 2011.

[4] For examples, see Alif 2012, Gosh 2003: 237–242, and De Silva 1998: 251–271.

[5] The fieldwork upon which this book is based was concluded in 2013, and the political narrative concludes with the election of 2012.

major change. However, even though the SLMC's symbolic politics exhibit these different uses and changes, there is also a continuity: both the internal and public documents are clearly premised on an essentialist idea that Sri Lankan Muslims are a distinct race that share a religion because, they claim, they are descendants of Arab merchants who arrived in the seventh century.

It is understandable from a strategic point of view that the SLMC would change its rhetoric so as not to be framed as Islamists in a country where Muslims are a minority and where suspicions of political Islam exist, and spread wider after 9/11. However, this strategy has not fully succeeded in rebranding the SLMC as an inclusive and multiethnic party in the eyes of their political opponents and public discourse, where an ethnic Muslim label is used to describe the SLMC's identity and politics.

Historical Background

Overviews of the communities in Sri Lanka generally categorize its inhabitants as Sinhalese, Tamil, or Muslim. Although this categorization is a simplification, it is a useful beginning. The majority population of Sri Lanka consider themselves to be Sinhalese and are predominantly Buddhist (74%). The major minority groups are Tamils, who are predominantly Hindu (15%), and Muslims, who then are categorized solely by religious affiliation (9.7%).[6] The thorny issue of the categorization of the population will be addressed below (Illustration 1.1).

Pre-Colonial and Colonial Times

The origins of Sri Lanka's Muslim community may be traced back to the trade that occurred between South and Southeast Asia and the Middle East. Traders from the Middle East (that is, Arabs and Persians) first had commercial interests in the south of India in the seventh century, and this interest also spread to Sri Lanka.[7] The merchants from the Middle East married Tamil and Sinhalese women and settled in the

---

[6] See McGilvray 2015. Christians can also be counted among the Sinhalese and Tamil populations (7.4%). There are also other minorities in the country, such as the Vedda people and burghers, who are self-identifying communities. See McGilvray 2008: 47–49, 174–175, 181–182. For a detailed table of the Muslim population in each province, see Ameerdeen 2006: 29. Muslims are traditionally seen as traders, although most Muslims work in the service industry or in agriculture. In the east, Muslims are farmers and fishermen and own 50% of the paddy land in the Trincomalee and Batticaloa districts. For more information about the legislative council, see Ameerdeen 2006: 62f, and for a detailed table of information regarding current Muslim employment, see Ameerdeen 2006: 53.

[7] Shukri 1986: 337 and McGilvray and Raheem 2007: 4.

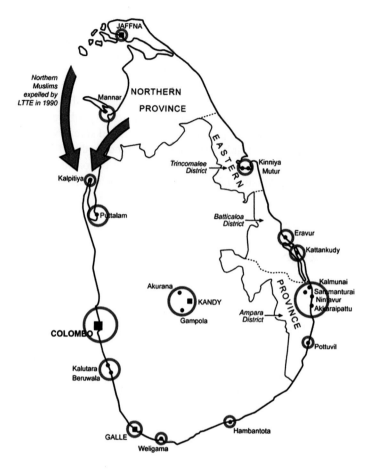

Illustration 1.1 Map of important sites for the Muslim population of Sri Lanka. (Published with the permission from the authors McGilvray and Raheem 2007: 5)

east around the area of Batticaloa and Ampara.[8] Most of the Muslims in Sri Lanka have Tamil as their mother tongue and display clear traits of Tamil culture and, to some degree, Tamil social structure: "the Sri Lankan Muslims also preserve matri-lineal and matrilocal family patterns" that have "shaped Tamil social structure".[9] The Buddhist and Hindu kingdoms in Sri Lanka allowed the Muslims to continue trading, and soon these kingdoms assumed a powerful role as an international trading community.[10]

In the early sixteenth century, the Portuguese colonized the island, which they controlled from 1502 until 1638. At this time, Muslim inhabitants dominated the

---

[8] For more detailed information about Arab/Persian history in Sri Lanka, see Dewaraja 1994.

[9] McGilvray and Raheem 2007: 5.

[10] McGilvray and Raheem 2007: 4.

trading business, both internationally and within Sri Lanka. The Portuguese strove to end Muslim domination in this area because of their trading ambitions.[11] Though the Portuguese did not manage to monopolize the trading, the colonizers put restrictions on indigenous groups, including Muslim traders.[12] Muslims hence lost their dominant trading position, and the main reason for it was their inability to respond to the Portuguese naval power. This weakness was also one of the key factors that enabled other European powers, especially the Dutch and the British, to further encroach upon areas like trade that previously had been in the hands of Muslims.[13]

The European powers brought Christianity to Sri Lanka and established Christian institutions.[14] The Portuguese used the term "Moor" for the Muslims of the island (as they did for other Muslim communities they encountered throughout the world).[15] As a consequence, a local "Moorish" identity was established. Stories about Arabic merchants settling down in Sri Lanka "became the official rationale for treating 'Moors' as 'racially' distinct from Tamils in late nineteenth century colonial sociology".[16] The Moorish label developed into a self-definition for Muslims in Sri Lanka in the early twentieth century, beginning with the elite, who promoted it as a unique racial identity which they labeled "Ceylon Moors". The Ceylon Moor identity referred to those with a presumed Arab origin, which distinguished them mainly from the local Tamils.[17] In the history of the political identification of Muslims, some of the Muslim political leaders emphasized a difference between Ceylon Moors and Coast Moors, arguing that the Ceylon Moors had Arabic ancestors and that the Coast Moors were of Indian origin.[18] Muslim political leaders have continued to promote a "Moorish" identity, with the focus on a collective Arab "blood connection", pointing out that Muslims are not bound to any specific language (even though most of them speak Tamil).[19] This is very important in the case of Sri Lanka compared to that of Muslims in Tamil Nadu, who sees themselves as Tamils who adhere to the Islamic faith.

After the Portuguese, the Dutch, who held power between 1638 and 1796, began to colonize the island. The new colonizers treated Muslim inhabitants as the Portuguese had done, which forced Muslims to move from the east coast to other places in the country. Local Sinhalese kings assisted in these resettlements.[20]

---

[11] McGilvray and Raheem 2007: 6.

[12] De Silva, C.R. 1986: 159.

[13] De Silva, C.R. 1986: 160.

[14] See Mahroof 1990.

[15] McGilvray and Raheem 2007: 9.

[16] Spencer 2014: 4.

[17] McGilvray and Raheem 2007: 9.

[18] O'Sullivan 1999a: 57. Like the Muslims, the Tamil community has also been constructed throughout history. For a discussion on how the Tamil identity was constructed and how it included Muslims, see O'Sullivan 1999a: 150f. A detailed discussion of the cultural and linguistic affinities of the Sri Lankan Muslims can be found in McGilvray 1998 and McGilvray 2016.

[19] McGilvray and Raheem 2007: 10.

[20] Nuhman 2002: 33.

Muslims now had to turn to new occupations besides trade, such as fishing and weaving, and were accepted in Sinhalese kingdoms.[21] With the Dutch came a new group of Muslims to the island, the Malays, who had their own distinct language and culture.[22]

Later, the British came to power in Sri Lanka in 1796 and ruled until 1948. Muslims once again found themselves in a new situation because the trade policy of the British towards the Muslims differed from that of earlier colonizers. The British were more tolerant of Muslims' involvement in trade.[23] Muslims also became more active in politics as a distinct group. They established, for example, Shari'a courts. Most of the Muslims in Sri Lanka today belong to the Shafi'i school of law, *madhhab,* as did the first Muslims who came to the island.[24] As will be discussed below, from 1880 onwards there were Muslim representatives in the all-island council, which meant that Muslims had a political voice. It has been argued that it was the British who helped Muslims to formulate their own identity.[25]

Under British rule (1796–1948), there were also several new Muslim newspapers published. They reported on events occurring in the Muslim world at large. These newspapers were moreover printed in various languages, for example, Arabic Tamil (Tamil written in Arabic script).[26] A common religious identity was shaped at this point by the Muslim elite. The narratives of the Muslim elite regarding the history of Muslims are rather focused on the Arabic (male) merchants, and not the Persians who also arrived in the country at that time. Women were mostly excluded: "It would appear that Arab men gave birth, by themselves, to the Sri Lankan Muslim social formation".[27] Not only was Arabic heritage important, but some also emphasized that these early Muslims descended from the *Banu Hashim,* the clan of the prophet Muhammad.[28]

The first legislative council, which was instituted by the British, was held in 1833 and in it a Tamil-speaking member represented the Muslims. That a Hindu represented Muslims prompted the Muslim political elite to demand their own representative, and it took them over 50 years to succeed in achieving this goal.[29] In the 1880s a Muslim politician claimed that Tamils and Muslims are separate groups and should be treated as equals, for example, regarding the recognition of their own

---

[21] Goonewardena 1986: 225.

[22] McGilvray and Raheem 2007: 6. It is possible that the Malay culture has a longer history in Sri Lanka; for an introduction to the Malay language and history in Sri Lanka, see Mahroof 1992. For an "insider's" narrative of being Malay in Sri Lanka, see Saldin 2003.

[23] Ali 1986: 236.

[24] There is also the practice of the Hanafi School in Sri Lanka. For an introduction to the different Sunni schools of law, see Hallaq: 1997.

[25] O'Sullivan 1999a: 50.

[26] Arabic Tamil is not recognized by the state. See Ahmad 2012: 276.

[27] Ismail 1995: 75. The focus on Arab merchants is still current. For an example, see Hussein 2011.

[28] Ismail 1995: 65.

[29] Ameerdeen 2006: 61.

laws.[30] A Muslim identity was formally institutionalized when a Muslim member was elected into the legislative council in 1889.[31] The British, in a "crucial sense, thus helped 'create' a Muslim identity".[32]

In 1887 an event that contributed further to the establishment of Tamil and Muslim as distinct emic groups, despite the fact that most Muslims spoke Tamil, was a famous speech made by the politician Ponnambalam Ramanathan in which he stated "that the Moors were simply Muslim members of the Tamil 'race'" because both had the Tamil language in common.[33] This classification of Muslims as Tamils affected, among other things, the area of education. In Tamil-dominated areas, there were only Hindu and Christian schools.[34] The lack of Muslim schools led to a boycott in the early 1900s by Muslim inhabitants, and the education level among Muslim youths dropped as a result. The matter of Muslims schools started to gain more attention. Later, Muslim schools and Islamic schools flourished, and the first school for Muslim girls was started.[35]

Another incident that symbolizes the strengthening of a Muslim identity at this time was "the fez cap incident", which took place in 1905.[36] It occurred when a chief justice of the Supreme Court objected to the wearing of fezzes in court, which resulted in massive demonstrations that spread around the island.[37] One of the explanations for why the Muslim elite started to wear fezzes is attributed to Arabi Pasha, an Egyptian in exile and a person who inspired Muslim activists throughout the country at this time.[38]

Later in the 1900s, another incident would further the notion of Muslims as a group distinct from other groups. In 1915, riots, or, as some would like to call it, organized violence, took place in Sri Lanka between Sinhala Buddhists and Muslim communities.[39] The riots began with events that took place in connection with the Vesak festival, when police changed the original route of the celebrating Buddhists in order to prevent them from passing a mosque. In combination with the mockery from Muslims, this sparked violence between the two communities in various parts of the country.[40] Twenty-five Muslims were killed, around 200 were injured, Muslim women were raped, 17 mosques were damaged, and many businesses belonging to Muslims were destroyed.[41] According to political scientist Meghan O'Sullivan, certain Sinhala politicians started to express anti-Muslim statements, claiming that

[30] Uyangoda 2001: 120.
[31] Haniffa 2013: 175.
[32] Ismail 1995: 74.
[33] McGilvray and Raheem 2007: 9.
[34] Wimalratne 1986: 428.
[35] O'Sullivan 1999a: 53.
[36] Ahmad 2012: 277.
[37] Ahmad 2012: 277.
[38] Ismail 1995: 73.
[39] Ismail 1995: 86.
[40] O'Sullivan 1999a: 60.
[41] O'Sullivan 1999a: 60.

Muslims were not Sri Lankans and stating that these two communities never could get along.[42] However, the event did bring the British and the Muslims closer together. As a result, the Sinhalese anti-colonization movement came to consider Muslims to be loyal supporters of the British.[43]

From an outside perspective, the Sri Lankan Muslims of today do not constitute a homogenous group language-wise, culturally, or even denominationally. They belong to different subgroups, such as Sri Lankan Moors, Malays, Bohras, and Memons.[44] The majority are Sunni even though the Bohras, for example, are a part of a Shi'a (Ismaili) tradition. The Sunni-Shi'a divide is, however, not of major importance in Sri Lanka.[45] The greatest concentration of Muslims is to be found in the eastern part of the country.[46] As pointed out earlier, the majority of Tamils are Hindus. In some other countries, such as India, the Tamil cultural and social connections have led to divisions among Muslims in a caste-like fashion; this caste-like division does not occur among Tamil-speaking Muslims in Sri Lanka, however.[47]

The Ampara district has the highest concentration of Muslims, that is, around 42%. The east coast Muslims represent one-third of the country's Muslim population. A large number of the remaining two-thirds lives on the southwestern coast of the country. These are Sinhalese-dominated areas, including the largest city, Colombo.[48]

The Origins of the Civil War

Before introducing the Sri Lanka Muslim Congress and Muslim political activism, it is necessary to introduce some organizations and events in relation to the civil war. These events and organizations are crucial for understanding the context of the SLMC. After the British left (1948), the United National Party (UNP) dominated the Sri Lankan government (GoSL) in the first election. The UNP had a nationalistic agenda that was inclusive towards all of the island's different communities. The first Prime Minister, D.S. Senanayake, emphasized the common interests of the island's various groups. The GoSL had as its basis an acceptance of a pluralistic society mirroring the reality of the island and sought the reconciliation of the legitimate

---

[42] O'Sullivan 1999a: 62 and Ismail 1995: 87.

[43] De Silva K.M. 1986: 457.

[44] Bohras, Memons, and Afghans came to the island at the end of the nineteenth century. Afghans are considered to be fully integrated through intermarriage. For more details, see O'Sullivan 1999a.

[45] McGilvray and Raheem 2007: 12.

[46] For an overview of the demographic changes of the Muslim population (1881–1981), see Marga Institute 1988.

[47] McGilvray and Raheem 2007: 7. For a detailed overview of the history of Muslims in Tamil Nadu, see More 2004.

[48] McGilvray and Raheem 2007: 7.

interests of the majority and minorities within the context of an all-island policy.[49] This pluralistic view of nationalism seemed to be a viable alternative to ideas about narrower communalism that were beginning to develop in the country. One important group, led by Buddhist monks, expressed that it felt left out of this political process. Anthropologist Jonathan Spencer states that: "from the early 1940s on, [...] one vociferous group of Buddhist monks had been calling for the right to participate in national politics".[50] According to Buddhist activists, the UNP was unsympathetic to the religious, linguistic, and cultural ideals of Buddhism, and this neglect of Buddhism was one of the reasons why the elections of 1956 had a different outcome than the elections immediately after independence.[51]

In the election of 1956, Solomon Bandaranaike of the Sri Lankan Freedom Party (SLFP) became prime minister, and a new Sinhala nationalistic era began. The "Sinhala only" project then started, a project which sought to make Sinhalese the only official language.[52] It had a linguistic nationalist agenda and was a reaction to the colonial era from which the Sinhalese-oriented groups wanted to distance themselves.[53] There were other focal points in the project as well: the new government emphasized the uniqueness of the Sinhalese past and focused on Sri Lanka as the land of the Sinhalese and the country in which Buddhism in its purest form was to be found.[54] As the majority of the Tamil population were, and still are, Hindu, the reaction from the Tamil part of the country was massive and protests erupted.[55]

During the first years of the post-colonial era, issues dear to the Muslim population were completely neglected by Sinhalese governance. This state of affairs led to clashes between Sinhalese groups, and groups formed around a common Muslim identity in the 1970s.[56]

In the 1970s, Tamil separatists started to emerge, and these separatists went on a collision course with the GoSL. The two major points of disagreement were language and religion. The disagreement began with the formulation of a new constitution in 1972, which stated that: "Accordingly it shall be the duty of the state to protect and foster Buddhism while assuring to all religions the rights secured [...]".[57] This new constitution additionally changed the name of the country from Ceylon to Sri Lanka. In doing so, the ruling government tried to distance itself from its colonial heritage.[58]

---

[49] De Silva K.M. 2005: 609.

[50] Spencer 2012: 727.

[51] De Silva K.M. 2005: 627.

[52] De Silva K.M. 2005: 628.

[53] De Silva K.M. 2005: 629.

[54] De Silva K.M. 2005: 673.

[55] Tamils are of course not a homogenous group; there are differences in caste, nation (Sri Lankan, Indian), religion (Christian, Hindu), region (east, north), politics, and class; see Wilson 2000: 23. For more details about Muslims' interactions with the Tamils, see McGilvray 2008.

[56] De Silva K.M. 2005: 628.

[57] De Silva K.M. 2005: 674.

[58] Spencer 2012: 727.

Tamil groups at this time claimed that the new constitution assigned the Tamils a position as second-class citizens. Tamils henceforth started to organize themselves, and the biggest Tamil political party in the parliament was the Tamil United Liberation Front (TULF), which first ran for election in 1977.[59]

Two specific events spurred Tamil reactions. The first was an incident in 1974 in which police were said to have assaulted without provocation Tamils who were at a meeting of the International Conference of Tamil Research. Some years later, in 1981, a Sinhala mob burned down the library in Jaffna, the so-called "capital" of the Tamil community in the north. More than 97,000 books were destroyed. This later event triggered a Tamil military uprising.[60]

Several different militant organizations were active during the civil war. The Liberation Tigers of the Tamil Eelam (LTTE) was one of those that would change the political environment. The LTTE stemmed from a student group called the Tamil Students Federation, and it was renamed the LTTE in 1975. The LTTE had a strict Tamil-nationalistic ideology, and its goal was to create a separate Tamil state. It had a Marxist outlook, but much of its rhetoric was based on traditional Tamil and Hindu narratives, with some Christian references. Historian of religions Peter Schalk claims that from the start the LTTE rhetoric was "rich in religious terms – in a completely secular context".[61] The symbol of the LTTE, a tiger, was chosen because it was the "royal mark of the Chola Kings who oversaw the expansion of Hinduism as well as the Tamil language and culture in Sri Lanka".[62] In 1978, the LTTE was banned from parliament.[63]

The LTTE was not the only armed group at the time, but it became the main military resistance to the regime.[64] In addition to the LTTE, there were essentially four other organizations that had to be reckoned with. The first was the People's Liberation Organization of Tamil Eelam (PLOTE), which broke away from the LTTE in 1981. The PLOTE followed a Marxist-Leninist ideology and became infamous for kidnappings and bank robberies. The PLOTE was not particularly successful for very long and lost its influence after 1985. When its leader was assassinated in 1989, the PLOTE disappeared for good.[65] The second organization was the Tamil Eelam Liberation Organization (TELO), which had a separate military branch. After years of fighting with the LTTE, the armed part of the TELO disappeared and transformed into a pro-LTTE party in parliament.[66] The third organization was the Eelam People's Revolutionary Liberation Front (EPRLF), a Marxist-Leninist

---

[59] It was formerly known as the Tamil United Front (formed in 1972) but later changed its name to the TULF (in 1976) to emphasize a more radical role. See Wilson 2000: 108.

[60] De Silva K.M. 2005: 681f.

[61] Schalk 1997: 80. For more examples, see Natali 2008.

[62] O'Sullivan 1999a: 210.See also O'Sullivan 1999b.

[63] Wickramasinghe 2006: 284.

[64] There might have been as many as 37 different militant Tamil groups at this point. See Wilson 2000: 126.

[65] Wilson 2000: 127.

[66] Wilson 2000: 128.

organization based in the eastern part of the country, mainly in Batticaloa. In the 1970s and 1980s, the EPRLF was the only Tamil organization that advocated treating Muslims as a separate community (that is, not as part of the larger Tamil group). Today, the organization is a party with representation in parliament, but the EPRLF was long regarded as primarily a military organization, one that performed such actions as kidnappings. The party claimed to fight for the people, the poor, and those from a lower caste.[67] The last and the smallest of organizations alongside the LTTE was the EROS, or the Eelam Revolutionary Organization of Students. The EROS became part of the LTTE in 1990, but before that the organization had carried out a series of attacks in its own name against the Sri Lankan government. In 1989, the EROS ran for election, and 13 of its candidates were elected.[68] Most of the other Tamil opposition groups were eliminated by the LTTE, which lay claim to being the only fighting force of the Tamil independence struggle. In 1987, after an internal battle between different Tamil groups, the LTTE became the dominant Tamil militant group in the north.[69]

In 1983, an attack by the LTTE on the government led to the biggest anti-Tamil riots in recent history. This event and the impact it had are usually considered as being the triggers behind the civil war even though violence between the government and Tamil groups had occurred earlier. The LTTE killed 13 soldiers in an ambush and claimed that the attack was a response to the killing of a number of LTTE representatives and a gang rape of a Tamil girl by government soldiers.[70] The Sri Lankan army quickly responded by attacking Tamils in the area, and when the bodies of the dead soldiers were brought back to Colombo, an angry Sinhalese mob rioted against local Tamils. The riots spread all over the island, and many Tamils were killed. Tamil leaders accused the government of being passive in their response to the riots. Tamils were raped and murdered. Several shops and buildings owned by Tamils were destroyed. The Sri Lankan government's lack of intervention upset Tamil organizations.

In the face of continued discrimination, many Tamils came to view parliamentary procedure as no longer a real option. Just before July of 1983, the Tamil population was, despite military factions, a fairly unified force when it came to which candidate they supported in the struggle for a separate state. One of these leaders at this time was Appapillai Amirthalingam (All-Ceylon Tamil Congress, later TULF), who had the explicit aim of creating a separate Tamil state by peaceful means.[71]

At the same time, there were similar developments in the Sinhalese left-wing movements in the country. The Sinhalese movement called the Janatha Vimukthi Peramuna (JVP) started a militant campaign against the minorities (especially Tamils) and the government in the 1970s. The JVP fostered an ideology that has

[67] Wilson 2000: 128.
[68] Wilson 2000: 129.
[69] Wilson 2000: 123.
[70] Arena 2006: 177.
[71] Wilson 2000: 113.

been described as a caricature of Marxism (with roots in a Maoist group) or, by other commentators, as an indigenous variant of Marxist patriotism.[72] The JVP put forward the mythological idea that Ruhuna, an area between Hambantota and Potuville in the southern part of the island, was the historical center of Sri Lanka, the site of the mythic battle between King Ruhuna and the king of the Tamils.[73] The JVP tried to revive the spirit of Ruhuna for modern times.[74] The movement also tried to overthrow the government in 1971 because, as it explained, of the government's lack of reforms and lack of appreciation for Sinhalese tradition. This attempt failed.[75]

In the so-called Indo-Sri Lankan Peace Accord of July 1987, it was agreed that the Sri Lankan army would withdraw from the northeast and be replaced by an Indian peacekeeping force (IPKF). This accord led to a merger of the northern and eastern provinces, which meant that the Muslim population, which was in greater number in the eastern province, now got a smaller percentage of the total population in the new northeastern province. The LTTE was not a part of this accord and refused to comply.[76]

Indian involvement in Sri Lankan conflicts has a longer history than that of India's intervention in 1987. Some of India's Tamil population compelled the leaders in the Indian province of Tamil Nadu to support both the Tamil United Liberation Front and the military branches of the Tamil population in Sri Lanka. Meetings between the Sri Lankan government, India, and the Tamil groups were common in the mid- 1980s. After the riots of 1983, India, led by President Indira Gandhi, began its involvement in Sri Lanka. India supported the TULF as the voice of the Tamil community. A meeting held in Thimphu in 1985 ended with the two sides being unable to agree upon Tamil autonomy or self-government in the north and the east. A few months later, another meeting was held, but again it ended in bitterness. Muslims were not represented as a separate group in any of the meetings.[77]

The failed negotiations between the government and the Tamil groups led to the former president Junius Richard Jayewardene (UNP) turning to India and suggesting that an Indian peacekeeping force should come to Sri Lanka. The LTTE accused the GoSL of trying to buy time in order to mobilize militarily. India's role was controversial; there were reports of military training camps for Tamils throughout all of India, especially in the province of Tamil Nadu.[78]

India wanted to consolidate its role as a major player in the region, and the Indian president Rajiv Gandhi saw this opportunity as a good time to do so. Gandhi wanted to accelerate the process of an Indian intervention and ignored the Tamil demand for

---

[72] For further reading on the JVP, see Kapferer 2001.

[73] Wickramasinghe 2006: 244.

[74] Wickramasinghe 2006: 244.

[75] Wickramasinghe 2006: 234.

[76] De Silva K.M. 2005: 701.

[77] Wilson 2000: 137f.

[78] Wilson 2000: 147.

a separate state.[79] One suggestion from India at this point was to make the northern and eastern regions of Sri Lanka part of India. Gandhi wanted to meet the TULF's demand that the eastern and northern provinces in Sri Lanka be merged into one. The merger also became a reality when India officially intervened with its peace-keeping force in the country. India's interference led to a political power struggle between the governments. The Sri Lankan army marched towards Jaffna, where the LTTE had its base. The Indian president threatened Sri Lanka, stating that if the army attacked Jaffna, India would take action, that is, the Indian army would invade northeastern Sri Lanka or even the whole country. India started sending supplies by air and by sea to northern Sri Lanka. India's aid to northern Sri Lanka was done without the authorization of the Sri Lankan government.[80]

The Indian government negotiated with the different Tamil groups. It was mainly the LTTE that opposed the proposal that came from the Sri Lankan government. In this proposal, there were two main points that the LTTE opposed, namely, turning in its weapons and holding a referendum on the merger of the northern and eastern provinces.[81]

While India continued to declare the TULF as the voice of the Tamils, in reality it was the LTTE who held power.[82] India's support to the TULF led to violence between the IPKF and the LTTE, and, consequently, the peacekeepers became com-batants.[83] The IPKF at first consisted of 5000–7000 soldiers, but after the LTTE and the peacekeeping forces began to attack each other, India sent more soldiers and had at one point as many as 100,000 soldiers serving as peacekeepers in Sri Lanka. The LTTE could no longer view India as a potential alliance partner. The IPKF captured Jaffna and imposed a curfew.[84]

In the absence of the IPKF, Tamil activists and parts of the Muslim community came into conflict. The conflict reached a critical point in 1990, when approxi-mately 75,000 Muslims from the north were forced by the LTTE to leave their homes.[85] The LTTE gave an ultimatum to the Muslim inhabitants of the north according to which they had 48 h to leave or else they would be killed. This event is described as having come as a surprise to the people who lived in the affected area.[86] Exactly why the people were forced to leave their homes is unclear, but in 1990 a

---

[79] Wilson 2000: 148. The Indian intervention that began in 1987 and ended in 1990 led not only to former president Jayewardene's downfall but later also to India's prime minister Rajiv Gandhi being assassinated by the LTTE through a suicide bombing in 1991. Before that, he had lost his post as prime minister, and his successor, V. P. Singh, ordered the withdrawal of the IPKF. In the political power vacuum, Muslims found themselves in a vulnerable position.

[80] Wilson 2000: 151.

[81] Wilson 2000: 153–4.

[82] De Silva 2005: 697–8.

[83] De Silva 2005: 698–9.

[84] De Silva 2005: 701.

[85] Brune 2003: 119. See also Thiranagama 2011, especially chapters 3 and 4, which deal with the conditions of the Muslim refugees. For a more recent study on how Muslim women struggle in these camps, see Zackariya and Shanmugaratnam 2003.

[86] Brune 2000: 2.

number of conflicts between Tamil activists and members of Muslim communities took place, and many within the latter, over 50,000 people, ended up in the north-western province near Puttalam.[87] Some of these Internally Displaced Persons (IDP) still live in refugee camps in other parts of the country while others have returned to their homes. Moreover, the LTTE also confiscated Muslim farmers' land in the east and gave it to non-Muslim Tamils.[88] Before these incidents occurred, Tamil-speaking Muslims had been a part of the LTTE, and as late as in 1989 the LTTE sent two Muslim representatives to the peace talks with the government.[89]

As a consequence of the events of 1990, an increased number of Muslim activists organized themselves politically as Muslims. To organize under the label of Muslims, however, was not something entirely new. There were initiatives in this direction already in the late 1970s and early 1980s. Two of the largest Muslim orga-nizations were the Sri Lanka Muslim Congress (SLMC) and the Muslim United Liberation Front (MULF). The MULF was involved in Tamil politics and M.H.M. Ashraff, the former leader of the SLMC, was at first part of the MULF as a legal adviser, and he even ran for a seat in parliament for the MULF.[90]

The Impact of da'wa Movements

In the 1970s, the term "Moor" (*sonahar* in Tamil) as a designation for Sri Lanka Muslims had become "out of date". Instead, "Muslim" became the preferred descriptive term.[91] One of the reasons for this change was the arrival of international *da'wa* movements, that is, Muslim missionary groups.[92] The tendency to adapt to homogenizing terminology exemplifies the global Islamization of the 1970s.[93] Organizations with roots in the Indian subcontinent, such as Jamaat-e-Islami and Tablighi Jamaat, were, and still are, important organizations in the Sri Lankan Muslim context. During the last few decades, these organizations have had a huge

---

[87] Brune 2003: 120.

[88] Lewer and Ismail 2011: 124.

[89] McGilvray and Raheem 2007: 20.

[90] SLMC: "Our History", retrieved, 2013-04-02.

[91] Another term that was used for Muslims in the Sri Lankan census in the 1970s was Lanka Yonka; see McGilvray 1998.

[92] McGilvray and Raheem 2007: 11. Another factor that is sometimes used to explain the strength-ening of the Muslim identity in the 1970s is that many Sri Lankan citizens got the opportunity to work in the Middle East, primarily the Arabian Peninsula. This resulted in an increasing number of educated Muslims and their economic status rose. See O'Sullivan 1999a: 256 and Zackariya, and Shanmugaratnam 2003.

[93] See Nuhman 2002. McGilvray (1998) argues that this conflict started much earlier, that is, well before Ceylonese independence in 1948. It was reflected in the rivalry between the Ceylon Moors Association and the Ceylon Muslim League. (See McGilvray 1998: 452.)

impact on the process of Islamization in the country, building mosques and Muslim schools, for example.[94]

Traditionally in Sri Lanka, religious scholars have been divided into several categories: a *moulavi* is an Islamic religious expert who has studied at a religious college registered with the government; an *'alim* is someone who is attributed with extensive knowledge of Islam but who could be self-taught; and, finally, a *lebbe* (in Arabic *labbaik*) could be a man or a woman (*lebbemma*) without any formal theological training but who still teaches different Islamic practices (sometimes going from house to house offering his or her services). This latter term is also used to designate the imam of a mosque in eastern Sri Lanka.[95]

The Islamic revival that reached Sri Lanka in the 1970s in the form of *da'wa* groups strengthened the notion of the Muslim *umma*, the unified community, and hence influenced the development of a Muslim identity, with political consequences.[96] Over 50 mosques and Arabic colleges were built, and Muslim orphanages were funded with money from Saudi Arabia, Bahrain, and Qatar.[97]

But the arrival of *da'wa* movements also led to conflicts between different Muslim groups, such as in one case that occurred at the end of the 1970s, when Abdul Rauf, a Sufi leader, stated that "Islam allowed the practice of respecting and worshipping Muslim saints" and preached that Allah could be seen as embodied in nature.[98] The focus on Muslim saints was fiercely rejected by Muslim reformists (sometimes referred to as Salafism).[99] Sufism has long had a strong foothold in Sri Lanka, and some of the Sufi movements in Sri Lanka had transnational connections with similar movements in Tamil Nadu and Kerala.[100]

The emergence of the term "Muslim" in political discourse as a label for a distinct group could similarly be seen as a result of a debate among Muslim politicians and theologians in the 1970s. Before the 1970s and the civil war, Muslim and non-Muslim Tamils had much in common. Besides the language, there were also, for example, religious connections, such as shared religious festivals.[101] In the 1970s, Muslim political activists changed their rhetoric. Tamil-speaking Muslims were not to be seen only as a part of the larger Tamil community but also as a distinct group

---

[94] Ali 2001: 7.

[95] Mahroof 1990: 27–28.

[96] *Da'wa movements* are not exclusively found on the Indian subcontinent; the phenomenon is worldwide. For other examples on how these movements have had an impact on the Asian context, see Mutalib 1990 and Knoerzer 1998: 154.

[97] O'Sullivan 1999a: 104–7.

[98] Hasbullah and Korf 2013: 39.

[99] In Sri Lanka it is common to equate Sufism with saint-worshipping and Hindu culture. See Hasbullah and Korf 2013: 39. The term "reformists" is sometimes used to describe movements or individuals that propagate an Islamic revival. For a discussion on the term "reformist" in South Asia, see Osella and Osella 2013: xii. For a discussion on the term "salafist", see Meijer 2009.

[100] McGilvray 1998: 443. See also McGilvray, 2004, 2011a and 2013.

[101] See McGilvray 1974.

within it.[102] On the other side, non-Muslim Tamil militants produced pamphlets that spoke about the riots between the Sinhala and Muslim communities in the southwest and the "suffering of the Muslims under Sinhalese governments".[103] After the riots that took place in 1983, in the period leading up to the civil war, the Tamil-speaking community became increasingly divided into Muslims and Hindus.[104] In the mid-1980s, clashes between the groups worsened, mostly due to the development of the armed Tamil activists.[105] The Tamil militants and the government of Sri Lanka portrayed the violence as religious in nature, and at the same time the government downplayed the religious factor in the Sinhalese-Muslim conflict in the southwest.[106] For example, in 1985 there were clashes between non-Muslim Tamils and Muslims in the towns of Kalmunai, Eravur, Ottamavadi, Valaichchenai, Mutur, and Kinniya, which resulted in 55 deaths and the displacement of over 35,000 people.[107]

The Twenty-First Century and Post-Conflict Sri Lanka

In the beginning of the twenty-first century, the participants of the civil war were engaged in a peace process; this process, led by Norway, was not successful.[108] As the Sinhalese left wing and the GoSL were fighting Tamil militants, Buddhist monks began to justify the war. There were, of course, diverse opinions for and against the war to be found throughout the communities, but during this period there was a tendency among Buddhist monks to exploit the war.[109] The idea of a righteous war was quite contrary to a Buddhist doctrine of pacifism.[110] Buddhist religious justifications often appeared in the media and were specifically aimed at the LTTE. The Jathika Hela Urumaya (JHU) that had emerged from the Sinhala Heritage Party was active in promoting these ideas. The JHU's rhetoric was originally directed towards the Tamil community as a whole but came to be directed more specifically towards the LTTE. The aim was to strengthen the Sinhala Buddhist community by targeting other religious communities. The focus on the Sinhala Buddhist community created a clear politicization of religion in Sri Lanka, not least through the active participation of Buddhist monks.[111]

---

[102] O'Sullivan 1999a: 164.

[103] O'Sullivan 1999a: 211.

[104] Ismail et al. 2004: 163.

[105] For a general example, see McGilvray and Raheem 2007: 20.

[106] O'Sullivan 1999a: 224.

[107] McGilvray and Raheem 2007: 21 and O'Sullivan 1999a: 221.

[108] See Goodhand and Walton 2009, Höglund and Svensson 2009.

[109] J.P. Pathirana quoted in Bartholomeusz 2002: 84.

[110] Bartholomeusz 2002: 167.

[111] Helbardt et al. 2013: 44.

Similar to the period between 1970 and the 1990, this stretch of time was not free from violence between Tamil activists and Muslim groups. The violence was, however, concentrated to the east.[112] There were also reports of a growing militant activism among Muslims in the east.[113]

In 2004, an Indian Ocean earthquake created a tsunami that hit the island, which resulted in more than 30,000 lost lives and destruction to buildings and the infrastructure, which displaced many from their homes. As the tsunami struck the eastern part of the country, many Muslims living in the area were affected.[114] When the war ended in 2009, after a huge military operation against the LTTE, the Sri Lankan government came under investigation for war crimes due to the massive loss of civilian lives.[115] This investigation is still ongoing.

The conflicts in Sri Lanka are still ongoing. Sinhala colonization in the east and north has triggered protests among the Muslim population.[116] This issue not only concerns land-grabbing but also the setting up of new Buddhist temples. Moreover, there is a new wave of Buddhist nationalism targeting Muslims as a group. One of the frontrunners in these confrontations is an organization called the Bodu Bala Sena (BBS). It is responsible for mass-producing anti-Muslim propaganda. Its public meetings have often ended in violence directed towards Muslims.[117] Muslim activists accuse the government of being too passive in dealing with this sort of anti-Muslim activism.

But Muslims, like before, are not a homogenous group. There is internal diversity and conflict regarding religious matters, a continuation of the conflict that began in the 1970s. For example, the town of Kattankudy is described as a location where there is an ongoing radicalization of segments of the Muslim population.[118] It is also claimed by Buddhist nationalists that some of the Islamic schools (*madrasas*) in Sri Lanka have direct connections to movements and organizations in the Middle East that promote radical Islam.[119] In 2006, the internal conflicts and divisions on religious matters among Sri Lankan Muslims in Kattankudy became evident.[120] A Sufi leader, Abdullah Payilvan, claimed that Muslims did not have to adhere to the five pillars of Islam in order to "achieve high spiritual levels".[121] Instead, contact with the divine could be achieved through meditation. That statement led to a controversy between Sufi-oriented Muslims and non-Sufi Muslim activists. The conflict

---

[112] Goodhand et al. 2009: 686.

[113] Imtiyaz 2005: 15.

[114] For further reading on the discussion about Muslim politicians and the effects of the tsunami, see Haniffa 2005 and Hasbullah and Korf 2009.

[115] See Amarasingam and Bass 2015.

[116] For one example, see Klem 2014.

[117] See Haniffa 2015, Holt 2016, and Samaratunge and Hattotuwa 2014.

[118] Hasbullah and Korf 2013: 34.

[119] Hasbullah and Korf 2013: 34.

[120] For an historical overview of Kattankudy religious diversity, see Ali 2009 and Spencer et al. 2014.

[121] Hasbullah and Korf 2013: 38.

reached its peak in an attack on a new meditation center set up by the Sufi group in question. The attack was carried out following the funderal that was held for Abdullah Payilvan at the center and resulted in two deaths (of Payilvan's followers). The meditation center, which also served as a mosque, was partly destroyed.[122] Other violent incidents have also occurred between Muslim groups having different theological orientations in the country.[123] A non-violent conflict has arisen due to internal dissention within the *da'wa* movement concerning women's issues. Al Muslimaat is a *da'wa* group that runs Islamic nursery schools and distributes free *hijabs* and has become a target for criticism from other groups within the larger *da'wa* movement.[124]

An Introduction to the Sri Lanka Muslim Congress

In this melting pot of civil war, natural disasters, external hostility, and internal intra-Muslim conflict, several groups and individuals claim to represent Muslims politically. The largest political party harboring such claims is the main focus of this book, namely, the Sri Lanka Muslim Congress (SLMC). In the early 1980s, the primary founder of the SLMC, Ashraff, left the above-mentioned Muslim United Liberation Front (MULF), and in 1980/81, in the midst of the Tamil Tigers rebellion, he, together with others, formed the new party. This coincided with the beginning of the civil war and the arrival of the *da'wa* movements in Sri Lanka. Ashraff was a part of a *da'wa* movement, the Jamaat-e-Islami, in the 1970s, was educated in law, and came from a family with a political background.[125] Between the years 1989 and 1992, Ashraff and the SLMC were in opposition to the government.

The SLMC was not the first Muslim political party to emerge in the eastern part of Sri Lanka. In the early 1980s, the East Sri Lanka Muslim United Front (ESLMUF) tried to establish itself as the voice for the Muslims in the east but failed. The founders of the SLMC had no initial intention of forming a political party. The emergence of the SLMC challenged established leadership structures among Muslims in the country and also shifted the center of religion-based activism from Colombo and the south to the rural east.[126] When the leaders of the SLMC officially launched the party in 1986, the SLMC became a political platform that was, according to them, based on the traditions of Islam. This was not only a challenge to the established Tamil political parties (who saw themselves as representing all Tamils, including Muslims) but also to the Buddhist Sinhala activists.

The first years of the SLMC were turbulent. The party was accused by Tamil parties of being a hostile organization with an intention to take up arms against

---

[122] Hasbullah and Korf 2013: 38.

[123] Haniffa 2012: 58.

[124] For an article about Al Muslimaat, see Haniffa 2013.

[125] Spencer 2012: 728.

[126] Ameerdeen 2006: 234.

Table 1.1 Results of the 1989 parliamentary election

Name of party	Elected members of parliament
United National Party	125
United Socialist Alliance	3
Tamil United Liberation Front	10
Mahajana Eksath Peramuna	3
Sri Lanka Freedom Party	67
Sri Lanka Muslim Congress	4
Independent Group – Jaffna District	10
Independent Group – Vanni District	1
Independent Group – Trincomalee District	2

non-Muslim Tamils. In order to register the SLMC as a political party so it could run in elections, the founding members had to recruit 8000 other members. The process was not completed until February 11, 1988, and the SLMC was elected into parliament for the first time in 1989.[127]

In the election of 1989, one political party dominated the parliament: the United National Party (UNP). It had the majority of the votes (50.71%). However, a change in the electoral system since then has made it easier for smaller parties to get their representatives voted into parliament.[128] The UNP has been described as a liberal-conservative party, particularly in regard to economic issues. The main opposition party at the time was the Sri Lanka Freedom Party (SLFP), which held nearly 32% of the votes. The SLFP has a more center-left economic policy, and it is also described as leaning more towards Sinhala nationalism than the UNP. The Mahajana Eksath Peramuna (MEP) is a party that also can be described as left of center and as allied with the SLFP. The president at the time (1989–1993) was Ranasinghe Premadasa, a member of the UNP. He took over after Junius Richard Jayewardene (UNP) in 1989.

In addition, there was a socialist alliance that consisted of the Communist Party of Sri Lanka, the Lanka Sama Samaja Party, the Nava Sama Samaja Party, and the Sri Lanka Mahajana Pakshaya. Together, they won three seats in parliament. The Tamil United Liberation Front (TULF), in alliance with other Tamil parties campaigning under the TULF's flag, became the biggest Tamil coalition. On the TULF's agenda was a separate state for the Tamils. The independent parties (listed below in the figures) are actually Tamil parties that constituted the Eelam Revolutionary Organization of Students (EROS) (Table 1.1).[129]

---

[127] SLMC "Our History", retrieved 2014-12-03.

[128] Haniffa 2013: 174.

[129] See Centered Political Parties Parliamentary General Election – 1989, retrieved 2012-10-29. Members of parliament are elected by a proportional representation system. Votes are thus counted in proportion to the numbers received in each district, in total 196 seats. The remaining 29 seats are determined by how many votes a party received in proportion to the results from the entire country. For further information, see the Department of Election, retrieved 2012-10-29. To see the performance of the SLMC in the elections that took place between 1989 and 2000, see Ameerdeen 2006: 155.

With its members receiving constant death threats from the LTTE, the SLMC still participated in the parliamentary elections and won four seats out of 225. Most of the SLMC's votes came from the Batticaloa, Vani, and Ampara districts, but the SLMC also did well in the western province (Colombo area).[130] The SLMC was new in parliament and supported neither the government nor the opposition.

In the 1994 parliamentary election, Sri Lanka saw a shift in power when the People's Alliance (PA), with the SLFP as its front-runner, won the election. The SLMC joined this coalition but campaigned under its own banner in the eastern and northern parts of the country. It gained four of its seats from the eastern districts, Batticaloa, Digmadulla (Ampara), and Trincomalee but also from the Vanni and Jaffna districts in the north. The PA almost had a majority of the seats in parliament but became dependent upon the SLMC's seven seats (one on the national list) that the latter acquired when it ran under its own flag. The SLMC had a pivotal position and the independent candidates from the SLMC joined the PA with certain demands. Ashraff became the minister of rehabilitation and reconstruction and also served as the minister of shipping & ports and the minister ports & development between 1994 and 2000.[131] This was the first time in Sri Lankan history that a minority party became part of the government.[132] As minister of rehabilitation and reconstruction, Ashraff had some political success. He improved housing and the infrastructure in the east and established the South Eastern University of Sri Lanka.[133] The year 1994 also saw a presidential election, which was won by the SLFP candidate Chandrika Bandaranaike. The former president, Premadasa (UNP), had been assassinated in 1993.

The other period under investigation is 2006–2011, and leader during those years was Rauff Hakeem, who is also the current leader of the SLMC. Ashraff died in a helicopter crash in 2000, and after a power struggle with Ashraf's wife (which will be discussed in Chap. 4), Hakeem took over. Hakeem was born in 1960, and, like Ashraff had, he has background in law. He became the general secretary of the party in 1992, and after Ashraff's death in 2000 he took over the leadership position. In the period that lasted from 2006 to 2011, Hakeem and the SLMC went from being in opposition to government to being a part of it. Hakeem had two ministry posts during this period: the minister of post and telecommunication (2007–2008) and the minister of justice (2010–2014).

National elections were held again in 2004 and 2010. The SLMC was then part of a large coalition called the United National Front (UNF), a coalition that took the initiative for the peace process of 2002–2005.[134]

---

[130] Centered Political Parties Parliamentary General Election – 1989, retrieved 2012-10-29. In Ampara, Batticaloa, and Vani, the SLMC got one parliamentary seat each. The other seat came from the national list.

[131] Ameerdeen 2006: 176, 247.

[132] Lewer and Ismail 2011: 125.

[133] Ameerdeen 2006: 176.

[134] Haniffa 2013: 174.

Table 1.2 Results of the
2004 parliamentary election

Name of party	Elected members to parliament
United People's Freedom Alliance	105
United National Party	82
Illankai Tamil Arasu Kachchi	22
Jattika Hela Urumaya	9
Sri Lanka Muslim Congress	5
Up-Country People's Front	1
Eelam People's Democracy Party	1

The ruling party of Sri Lanka changed once again after the election of 2004. This time it was the SLFP and its coalition parties called the United People's Freedom Alliances (UPFA) that won the majority of the votes. The SLMC ran as an independent party in the eastern districts and with an alliance in the other districts.[135] This time the SLMC decided to run with the UNF and the biggest party, the UNP. This meant that the SLMC was in opposition for the first time in many years. The SLMC won five seats in parliament. In 2007 the SLMC joined the government but left the same year. Other political parties represented in parliament at the time in question included a Tamil alliance party called the Tamil National Alliance (TNA) (Table 1.2).

Due to the termination of the civil war, the president dissolved the parliament in 2009. In 2010, the United People's Freedom Alliance once again won the majority of parliamentary seats. The SLMC this time campaigned under the same flag as the UNP in all the districts in an alliance with the UNF, which also consisted of the Democratic People's Front.[136] The above-mentioned party the JHU, which consisted of Buddhist monks, won only two seats (in the United People's Freedom Alliance).[137] The SLMC won eight seats in the 2010 election, but it is difficult to establish the corresponding percentage of votes, since the party was running with the UNP. Later, the SLMC members crossed over to the UPFA, and the UNP tried to take legal action against the SLMC for doing so.[138] The government of the UPFA had, since the SLMC crossed over, a two-thirds majority in the parliament, and with the support of the SLMC, the government of Sri Lanka made constitutional changes, giving more power and advantages to Mahinda Rajapksa (SLFP), who had previously been prime minister and was the president at that time (Table 1.3).

[135] Besides the SLFP and the UPFA, in 2004 there was a coalition of the communist parties of Sri Lanka, the Desha Vimukthi Janatha Party, the Janatha Vimukthi Peramuna, the Lanka Sama Samaja Party, the Mahajana Eksath Peramuna, the National Unity Alliance, and the Sri Lanka Mahajana Pakshaya.

[136] After 2010 the alliance consisted of the following parties: All Ceylon Muslim Congress, Ceylon Workers' Congress, Communist Party of Sri Lanka, Eelam People's Democratic Party, Jathika Hela Urumaya, Lanka Sama Samaja Party, Mahajana Eksath Peramuna, National Congress, National Freedom Front, Sri Lanka Freedom Party, and Up-Country People's Front. The JVP had left the coalition and was running independently.

[137] Helbardt et al. 2013: 45.

[138] Weerarathne 2013.

Table 1.3 Results of the parliamentary election of 2010

Name of party	Elected members to parliament
United People's Freedom Alliance	144
United National Front	60
Tamil National Alliance	14
Janatha Vimukthi Peramuna	7

State, Nation, and Ethnicity

As briefly discussed in the introduction, Sri Lanka has a complex history including colonial rule and civil war. For this reason, the concepts "state", "nation", and "ethnicity", as well as the ways in which they are used in this book, need to be more fully explained.

"State" straightforwardly follows historian of religions Bruce Lincoln's definition: a "governmental apparatus that manages the political affairs of the nation or nations for which it takes responsibility and over which it exercises power".[139] According to sociologist Immanuel Wallerstein, a "nation" is commonly (but mistakenly) described as a socio-political category that is intimately connected to a certain state or a potential state with claims to a specific territory.[140]

Both Wallerstein and the philosopher Étienne Balibar contest this semantic practice. Following Wallerstein, Balibar claims that the history of a nation "is an illusion".[141] This illusion can build up the nation conceptualized as an old society with several hundred years of events linked to a common history.[142] In post-colonial societies, for example, the linear events of the illusory common history of the nation are utilized in the making of the state after decolonization.[143] Balibar asserts that no nation has a given, natural unity but that the people that make up a nation have to create national unity themselves.[144] Consequently, Balibar argues, an ideology of the nation is required; this ideology has to be both a "mass phenomenon and an individual phenomenon" at the same time.[145] Balibar claims that in this process the nation can indeed become more than an "illusion", for example, through the production of founding documents that members of the nation can relate to.[146] Nations are nevertheless socially constructed and can be referred to in various ways for different purposes.[147]

---

[139] See Lincoln 2003: 62f on why state should be separated from nation and ethnicity in an analysis.

[140] Wallerstein 2002: 107.

[141] Balibar and Wallerstein 2002.

[142] Balibar 2002: 118.

[143] Balibar 2002: 119–20.

[144] Balibar 2002: 127.

[145] Balibar refers to Althusser to explain his ideas, Balibar 2002: 128.

[146] Balibar 2002: 129.

[147] For an overview on the concept of nationalism, see Özkirimli 2010 and Delanty and Kumar 2006.

To overcome problems of nation-building in an area that contains people of different geographical origins, having diverse histories and speaking different languages, state actors in search of unity can use certain strategies. Political scientist Benedict Anderson discusses this matter in *Imagined Communities* (1983). The term "imagined" refers to the idea that a nation is a constructed entity because most of its members will never meet each other face to face.[148] The state can reproduce the notion of the nation via, for instance, monuments and museums to stress the idea of community. In countries with a history of colonization, a similar role is played by censuses and maps. Censuses involve a systematic quantification of the nation, which helps to create feelings of belonging and community. The introduction of the map had a huge impact on nationalism in post-colonial states, according to Anderson. It contributed to visualizing neighboring countries and rivers, as well as mountains and other physical boundaries of the imagined community. Another important part of post-colonial nation-building is the efficient state-apparatus inherited from the colonizers. The colonizers organized new systems of education and jurisdiction in the country, and this gave rise to a network of common habits among the inhabitants.[149] The problem of post-colonial nation-building, and the role of religion in this project, is a central aspect to keep in mind when approaching the discourse of the SLMC.

As the historical overview in this chapter implies, Sri Lanka is a country where the word "ethnicity" is used *emically* as a way to differentiate among communities. The way in which ethnicity is determined, that is, the basis for it, displays inherent contradictions and overlaps. In the Sri Lankan emic context, "Sinhala" refers to Sinhala-speaking people who are non-Muslims. In most cases, the term "Tamils" refers to Tamil-speaking people who are non-Muslims. In the official census, Tamils are further categorized into two subgroups: Sri Lankan Tamils and Indian Tamils. The Moorish identity in Sri Lanka is a claim to an Arab Muslim racial ancestry. Muslims are, as mentioned above, divided in terms of language, but most of them speak Tamil.[150] Nonetheless, the category does not cover all Muslim inhabitants of the country. There are additional groups such as the Sri Lankan Malay, who are exclusively Muslim. Hence, there are ambiguities in the emic construction of ethnicity used in the census, and this clearly illustrates, like a textbook example, how ethnicity is a matter of social construction.[151] In the ethnic categorizations used in the language of the census, stated religious affiliation and perhaps even place of birth *both* serve as markers of ethnicity, but in the case of certain segments of the population, formal religious affiliation also serves as a *differentia specifica*. It should be noted, however, that outside of the national census context there also circulate emic categories, such as "Tamil-speaking minorities", which refers to speakers of Tamil regardless of religious affiliation.

---

[148] Anderson 2006 (1983): 6.

[149] Anderson 2006 (1983): 163f.

[150] In the official census, the Malays are also identified as a separate group, and probably all of them identify themselves as Muslims.

[151] Census of Population and Housing 2012.

In the introduction to *Ethnic Groups and Boundaries* (1969), anthropologist Fredrik Barth stress the importance of boundary constructions in defining ethnic groups.[152] An analysis of ethnicity therefore has to focus on *which* boundaries matter in a specific case, *what discursive articulations are used* in their construction, and by *whom*. These are major themes of this book.

In her article "Behind the Ethnic Marker: Religion and Social Identification in Northern Ireland" (2005), political scientist Claire Mitchell criticizes previous research on religion and ethnicity for treating religion merely as an "ethnic marker" without considering the role of the content of religious discourse, beliefs, and practices in the process of ethnic boundary construction.[153] It is, she states, necessary to take a look at what hides "behind the ethnic marker". References to religious dogma, rituals, and symbols in the construction of ethnicity and nationhood are important, Mitchell maintains. Therefore it is important to analyze how religion is actually used in these contexts, what elements are utilized, and what elements are left out.[154] Mitchell argues that examining the relationships between religion and ethnic markers is important for reaching a deep level of understanding, since this can shed light on the interplay between religion and politics. Religious phenomena behind the ethnic marker can appear in the form of rituals, theology, and ideology, and these phenomena can in their turn can be substantial or subtle. Mitchell takes Northern Ireland as an example: the conflict between the Protestant and Catholic identities illustrates how the use of certain elements from Protestant and Catholic traditions can be particularly important in the creation of an ethnic identity while others are completely ignored.[155] Hence the question of ethnicity and nation can be intimately related to the understanding and use of a specific religious tradition. This is what the current book is all about.

Muslim Politics – Behind the Ethnic Marker

In this book, "Muslim politics" refers to the social use of discursive elements of an Islamic religious tradition, elements that "do not carry any inherent and stable meaning, but receive such meaning in the social contexts where they are employed and where their emotive charge may be utilized rhetorically", to use Islamic studies scholar Jonas Svensson's succinct phrasing.[156] According to anthropologist Dale Eickelman and political scientist James Piscatori, who coined the concept of Muslim politics in the book with the same name, this discursive practice is often intimately connected to the building of a community and the creation of a sense of identity.

---

[152] See Barth 1969.

[153] For a discussion on Islam as an ethnic marker, see Hjärpe 1987.

[154] Mitchell 2005: 3.

[155] Mitchell 2005: 18; see also Mitchell 2006 and Brass 1991: 18. He defines ethnic markers as "cultural markers".

[156] Svensson 2000: 17.

Eickelman and Piscatori do have a somewhat wider conceptualization of "Muslim politics" than the one used in this book, including in addition to the discursive aspect also how political activism relates to religious institutions. While the institutional aspects will be touched upon in the following, it is the discursive dimension of Muslim politics that is the focus of attention.

Muslim politics is a valuable analytical tool for penetrating behind the ethnic marker as it appears in the discourse of the SLMC. Eickelman and Piscatori criticize political scientists for taking a narrow "top-down" perspective of Islam and politics when they "have often focused on the state's role in setting down markers".[157] Religion has been treated in a simplistic fashion that assumes that elements of the religious tradition have fixed meanings. On the contrary, these elements do not in actuality carry any given meaning – they do, however, carry an emotional charge that can be utilized in politics. Political doings in the framework of Muslim politics relate to a "widely shared, although not doctrinally defined, [Islamic] tradition of ideas and practice".[158] This type of politics is neither fixed nor unchangeable but "lies rather in the specific, if evolving, values, symbols, ideas, and traditions that constitute 'Islam'".[159] The following instance can serve as an instructive example of Muslim politics: in France in 2004, the ban on wearing headscarves, or rather the ban on all religious symbols in schools, made a young Muslim girl shave her head. By doing so, she, in an innovative way, performed a political act in which she was at the same time loyal to both the religious tradition (in her understanding of it) and French state law.[160] The action of shaving one's head is not *in itself* a political act, but *in the context* of an ongoing debate it became one.[161]

It is a commonly held notion among Muslims that "there is an Islamically defined continuity to their ways of doing things", but despite this belief it is an undisputable fact that Islamic tradition is diverse and changing.[162] For example, there are diverse ways in which Muslims across the world approach the issue on what core Islamic ideals are and how they should be implemented. However:

> [A] constant across the Muslim world is the *invocation* [my emphasis] of ideas and symbols, which Muslims in different contexts identify as 'Islamic', in support of their organized claims and counterclaims.[163]

Muslim politics is an analytical concept that differs from other prevalent concepts in academic studies of Islam and politics, such as "political Islam", "Islamism", "post-Islamism", "Islamic revivalism", "fundamentalism", and "Islamic

---

[157] Eickelman and Piscatori 2004: 18.

[158] Eickelman and Piscatori 2004: 4.

[159] Eickelman and Piscatori 2004: 21.

[160] BBC 2004, retrieved 2013-10-03.

[161] Eickelman and Piscatori 2004: 4.

[162] Eickelman and Piscatori 2004: 28.

[163] Eickelman and Piscatori 2004: 4.

resurgence".[164] These concepts generally denote religio-political tendencies or movements. The context of this book is indeed a particular political organization and how its representatives utilize, and in the process transform, the "pool of resources" in terms of dogmas, terminology, practices, and sacred narratives that make up the Islamic discursive tradition.[165] "Muslim politics" may be part of the discourse found within such tendencies and movements, *but* it is by no means limited to these explicitly political contexts. The focus is instead on discursive acts, such as speeches, texts, and symbols, relating to a wide range of diverse cultural contexts.

A particularly important aspect of Muslim politics is what Eickelman and Piscatori refer to as the "objectification" of Muslim consciousness. This process is according to them a phenomenon peculiar to Muslim politics in the modern world:

> Objectification is the process by which basic questions come to the fore in the consciousness of large numbers of believers: "What is my religion?" "Why is it important to my life?" and "How do my beliefs guide my conduct?"[166]

This "objectification" is the result of various developments but in particular of the spread of literacy and the availability of inexpensive material on Islamic issues connected with the global *da'wa* movement from the 1970s and onwards. Mass communication and the activities of *da'wa* movements further the notion of "Islam" as an entity that may be separated from other entities (mainly other religions) and from everyday beliefs and activities. Through increased information and reflection, "religious beliefs and practices are increasingly *seen* as systems [...] to be distinguished from nonreligious ones".[167] But it also raises other important questions, such as who is (really) a Muslim and who (truly) speaks for Islam, that is, who is a (righteous) religious authority.[168] Both of these questions, as well as the question of what constitutes "Islam" in a Sri Lankan context, are important in the internal discourse of the SLMC.

Material

Aiming to avoid a too limited view of SLMC's politics, I have collected different kinds of sources between 2006–2013.[169] All of source material included in this study has, however, has one thing in common: the texts are written by the elite of SLMC,

[164]Hjärpe defines political Islam as: "Islam perceived as a social, political, and economic system, an ideology, and Islamic politics is when policies are motivated by Islam and Islamic solidarity". See Hjärpe 1983. See also Kepel 2002, Roy 2004, and Hjärpe 2010.

[165]Eickelman and Piscatori 2004: 29. For a similar discussion, see Hjärpe 1997.

[166]Eickelman and Piscatori 2004: 38.

[167]Eickelman and Piscatori 2004: 42.

[168]Eickelman and Piscatori 2004: 42–4.

[169]For a discussion regarding the advantages of using different kinds of material, see Burgess 1984: 143f.

and the interviews have been conducted with the party elite. They thus mirror the views of a small section of the party, namely, its leaders. The aim of this book is not to analyze the party as such but instead its official discourse and how this discourse relates to Islamic sacred terminology and symbols. My attention towards material produced by the party elite is thus motivated.

Parliamentary Speeches

The parliamentary speeches of the SLMC's first leader, M.H.M. Ashraff, who held office between 1989 and 1992, and the second leader, Rauff Hakeem, who held office between 2006 and 2011, are important parts of the material analyzed in this dissertation. The limitation in time of the parliamentary speeches is due to the availability of Hansard records (see below). However, the two periods covered are significant in Sri Lanka's history as well as in the history of the SLMC. The first period (1989–1992) represents the first years in parliament for the SLMC, and during the second period (2006–2011) the civil war ended.

The party published transcripts of Ashraff's parliamentary speeches in 2005 and 2006 in four volumes that were edited by the current party leader, Rauff Hakeem. These books are entitled *Ashraff in Parliament* and will be referred to in the notes in the following way: AP:year, page, type of speech, date. The transcripts have not, as I understand it, been changed in any way. During my 2011 stay in Sri Lanka, I visited the archive in central Colombo where transcripts of the parliamentary speeches are stored alongside various government documents. In these archives, I managed to obtain some of Ashraff's speeches from this period. In comparing these documents with the speeches in the Ashraff books, I could not find that anything had been changed.

The parliamentary speeches cover numerous topics and are of various sorts. Most of them are appropriation bills, but there are other recorded debates of different kinds. This collection only contains speeches held in parliament and as such provides valuable information on how the SLMC presents its politics in public debates. If someone in the parliament debates with Ashraff, his or her words are likewise included.

I collected the transcripts of Hakeem's parliamentary speeches myself from the Hansard online archives, and in the notes I will be referring to these documents in the following way: HA:date, page, and type of speech. On the official webpage of the Sri Lankan parliament, you can read that:

> Every word audibly uttered in Parliament is taken down by a Hansard Reporter, transcribed and then submitted to the Assistant Editor of the particular stream in which the speech is delivered. Upon reaching the Asst. Editor's desk, it is carefully edited and then passes through to the Deputy Editor and, finally, the Editor. At the end of the day, after the editing and dovetailing of the shifts have been done, a master copy is prepared. Once the Editor is satisfied with the master script and receives his imprimatur, it is transmitted to the Government Printer for printing. With the computerisation of the department, it is proposed

to transmit the entire Parliamentary proceedings to the Government Printer on a diskette.[170]

While there thus exists a difference in how the two sets of parliamentary speeches were collected, I have no reason to doubt that the books containing Ashraff's speeches published by the SLMC are anything other than correct renderings of the actual speeches. In both sets of speeches, there naturally occur minor misspellings. In quotations, I have corrected these when I deem the misspellings to be insignificant to the content. I have indicated my corrections by using brackets.

The SLMC's Official Documents

The official documents consist of material intended for the general public, mostly relating to the provincial election of 2012. The secretary general of the party, Hasen Ali, and the national organizer, Shafeek Rajabdeen, provided some of the material. Other material of this kind was purchased or collected at the SLMC's headquarters.

The Constitution of the Sri Lanka Muslim Congress is a 26-page document about the organization of the SLMC, from top to bottom. It also outlines how members are organized, the guidelines of the party, and different roles had by party members. It also contains some rules and presents affiliated bodies and their work. The *National Unity Alliance Constitution* is also discussed and analyzed in Chap. 4. The National Unity Alliance (NUA) was at first a part of the SLMC but developed into a separate party after the death of Ashraff in 2000. Another document related to the NUA that is also analyzed is *Signs and Greatness,* which discusses the SLMC's three symbols during the time when Ashraff created the NUA.

The *Sri Lanka Muslim Congress program to stabilize the party from village level* is a published document concerning the topic of how the party should be more effective on the village level. In addition to this, a letter of appointment for an area/ branch organizer in 2012 was also handed to me.

A particularly interesting document is *Code of Conduct.* It can be described as a collection of guidelines for how members of the SLMC are expected to behave. It consists of 11 pages and contains moral rules for both party leaders and ordinary members. Related to this particular document is the Affidavit, Agreement, Pledge document (*bay'a*), which will also be discussed in relation to *Code of Conduct.* Similarly moral-oriented is the document *Is Jihad the alternative?* (discussed in Chap. 4), which contains a speech Ashraff made in parliament in 1992 regarding a particular event that occurred in the north and the east. Some of Ashraff's convention speeches from the early 2000s have been published by the party in the volume *Ashraff's Convention Speeches.* A similar publication called *Sri Lanka Muslim Congress 15th Convention* is also analyzed. It contains convention speeches made

---

[170] Hansard Department, retrieved 2015-07-30.

by other high-ranking officials in the SLMC. The party publication *Signs and Greatness* deals with the tree symbol of the party, and *A.M. Rakeeb manifesto* is a pamphlet for the 2012 provincial election.

During my stays in Sri Lanka, I also acquired official documents from the negotiations between the SLMC, the LTTE, and the government. These are: *The proposal of the Sri Lanka Muslim Congress*; *Joint Communiqué of the Liberation Tigers of Tamil Eelam and the Sri Lanka Muslim Congress* and *Resolution to the conflict in the northern and eastern provinces: the Muslim dimension*.

In addition to the above, the SLMC's official website, www.slmc.lk, and its official Facebook pages also constitute part of the material to be analyzed. The authorship of the texts on the SLMC's official website is rather unclear, but the information should, according to General Secretary Hasen Ali, be considered as expressing the party's formal stance. Lastly, I use my photographs of the SLMC's election posters, other online resources, such as Facebook groups connected to the party, and diverse electoral material, including party leaflets.[171]

The majority of the texts analyzed are in English. The SLMC habitually publishes a large amount of English-language material. However, some of my source material was originally written in Tamil, and I have commissioned its translation into English. Among these translations are *Ashraff's Convention Speeches, Sri Lanka Muslim Congress program to stabilize the party from village level, A.M. Rakeeb manifesto* (2011), *Signs and Greatness*, and most of the material intended for the general public.[172]

Interviews

Before traveling to Sri Lanka for the first time, I contacted the SLMC's headquarters in order to introduce myself and state the purpose of my visit. My first contact upon arrival also became my first informant, namely General Secretary Hasen Ali, who invited me to his office and provided me with contact information for other potential informants as well as some of the party's published material.

I have since then interviewed 33 SLMC members. The majority have leading positions in the party, and most of these are members of the political decision-making body, the so-called "high command". The high command has at present 89 members, and I have interviewed 31 of them. My informants were selected from a list of the high command provided by the SLMC's national organizer, Shafeek Rajabdeen. I made calls to them in a random order when I attempted to set up interviews. In many cases, the people whose names were on the list were not available. Only one person directly declined the request to participate. Since the SLMC is highly hierarchical in its structure – and the focus of my study is on official poli-

---

[171] See References for further details on official documents and online sources.

[172] Two of the posters were in Arabic, and these were translated by Nilam Hameed, who also speaks Arabic.

tics – this choice of informants is apt. In general, it can be noted that most of my informants were men between the ages of 40 and 65 (there was only one woman in the high command). Their levels of income and education were high. For a brief introduction to the informants in the high command, see Appendix 1.

Besides the members of the high command, I interviewed two ordinary members of the party concerning its organizational structures. When visiting Colombo for the last time, in 2013, I tried to expand the material by interviewing members of the women's branch, the Ladies Congress. However, the individuals I contacted did not want to participate. No particular reason for this disinclination was given.

References

Abdullah, Rameez. 2004. Ethnic Harmony in Eastern Sri Lanka. In *Dealing with Diversity*, ed. Freks George and Bart Klem. Hague: Netherlands Institute of International Relations.
Ahmad, Zarin. 2012. Contours of Muslim Nationalism in Sri Lanka. *South Asian History and Culture* 3 (2): 269–287.
Ali, Ameer. 1986. Muslim Participation in the Export Sector of Sri Lanka 1800–1915. In *Muslims of Sri Lanka*, ed. A.M. Muhammed Shukri. Colombo: Aitken Spence Printing.
———. 2001. *Plural Identities and Political Choices of the Muslim Community*. Colombo: Marga Institute.
———. 2004. The Muslims of Sri Lanka: An Ethnic Minority Trapped in a Political Quagmire. *Inter-Asia Cultural Studies* 5 (3): 372–383.
———. 2009. Kattankudy in Eastern Sri Lanka: A Mullah-Merchant Urban Complex Caught Between Islamist Factionalism and Ethno-Nationalisms. *Journal of Muslim Minority Affairs* 29 (2): 183–194.
———. 2014. Muslims in Harmony and Conflict in Plural Sri Lanka: A Historical Summary from a Religio-economic and Political Perspective. *Journal of Muslim Minority Affairs* 34 (3): 227–242.
Alif, S.M.. 2012. Muslim Politics of Sri Lanka and Roles of Lanka Muslim Congress. A Research Journal of South Asian Studies.
Amarasingam, Amarnath, and Daniel Bass. 2015. Introduction. In *Sri Lanka: The Struggle for Peace in the Aftermath of War*, ed. Amarnath Amarasingam and Daniel Bass. London: Hurst.
Ameerdeen, Vellaithamby. 2006. *Ethnic Politics of Muslims in Sri Lanka*. Kandy: Center for Minority Studies, Kribs Printers.
Anderson, Benedict. 2006. *Imagined Communities*. London: Verso. First Edition 1983.
Arena, Michael P. 2006. *Terrorist Identity: Explaining the Terrorist Threat*. New York: New York University Press.
Balibar, Étienne. 2002. Nationsformen: Historia Och Ideology. In *Ras, Nation, Klass*, ed. Etienne Balibar and Immanuel Wallerstein. Uddevalla: Bokförlaget Daidalos AB.
Balibar, Étinne, and Immanuel Wallerstein. 2002. *Ras, Nation, Klass*. Uddevalla: Bokförlaget Daidalos AB.
Barth, Fredrik. 1969. *Ethnic Groups and Boundaries, The Social Organization of Culture Difference*. Oslo/Bergen/Tromsø: Universitetsforlaget.
Bartholomeusz, Tessa J. 2002. *In Defense of Dharma: Just-War Ideology in Buddhist Sri Lanka*. London: Routledge Curzon.
BBC. 2004. Muslim girl shaves head over ban. *BBC News Europe*. Retrieved October 3, 2013 from http://news.bbc.co.uk/2/hi/europe/3708444.stm.
Brass, P.R. 1991. *Ethnicity and Nationalism: Theory and Comparison*. New Delhi: Sage.

Brune, Cathrine. 2000. Spatial Practices of Integration and Segregation Among Internally Displace Persons and Their Hosts in Sri Lanka. *Norsk Geografisk Tidsskrift* 54 (3): 96–101.

———. 2003. *Finding a Place*. Trondheim: Department of Geographic Faculty of Social Science and Technology Management.

Burgess, Robert G. 1984. *In the Field: An Introduction to Field Research*. London: George Allan & Unwin (publishers) Ltd.

Census of Population and Housing 2012. n.d. Retrieved March 3, 2015, from http://www.statistics.gov.lk/PopHouSat/CPH2012Visualization/htdocs/index.php?usecase=indicator&action=Map&indId=10.

Centered Political Parties Parliamentary General Election – 1989. Retrieved October 29, 2012, from http://www.slelections.gov.lk/pdf/Results 1989%20GENERAL%20ELECTION.PDF.

De Munk, Victor C. 2005a. Sakhina: A Study of Female Masculinity in Sri Lankan Muslim Community. *South Asia Research* 25 (2): 141–163.

———. 2005b. Islamic Orthodoxy and Sufism in Sri Lanka. *Anthropos, Bd* 100 (H. 2): 401–414.

De Silva, C.R. 1986. Muslim Traders in the Indian Ocean in the Sixteenth Century and the Portuguese Impacts. In *Muslims of Sri Lanka*, ed. Shukri Muhammad. A.M. Colombo: Aitken Spence Printing.

De Silva Kingsley, M. 1986. Muslim Leaders and The Nationalist Movement. In *Muslims of Sri Lanka*, ed. Shukri Muhammad. A.M. Colombo: Aitken Spence Printing.

———. 1998. *Reaping the Whirlwind*. New Delhi: Penguin Books India.

———. 2005. *A History of Sri Lanka*. New Delhi: Penguin Books India.

Delanty, G., and K. Kumar. 2006. *The Sage Handbook of Nations and Nationalism*. London: Sage.

Department of Election Retrieved October 29, 2012, from http://www.slelections.gov.lk/ep.html.

Dewaraja, Lorna. 1994. *The Muslims of Sri Lanka: One Thousand Years of Ethnic Harmony 900–1915*. Colombo: The Lanka Islamic foundation.

Eickelman, Dale F., and James Piscatori. 2004. *Muslim Politics*. Princeton: Princeton University Press. First edition 1996.

Gaasbeek, Timmo. 2010. Bridging Troubled Waters: Everyday inter-ethnic interaction in a context of violent conflict in Kottiyar Pattu, Trincomalee, Sri Lanka. Ph.D. thesis, Wageningen University.

Goodhand, Jonathan, and Oliver Walton. 2009. The Limits of Liberal Peacebuilding? International Engagement in the Sri Lankan Peace Process. *Journal of Intervention and Statebuilding* 3 (3): 303–323.

Goodhand, Jonathan, Bart Klem, and Benedikt Korf. 2009. Religion, Conflict and Boundary Politics in Sri Lanka. *European Journal of Development Research* 21: 679–698.

Goonewardena, K.W. 1986. Muslims Under Dutch Rule up to the Mid-Eighteenth century. In *Muslims of Sri Lanka*, ed. Shukri Muhammad. Colombo: A.M. Aitken Spence Printing.

Gosh, Partha S. 2003. *Ethnicity versus Nationalism – The Devolution Discourse in Sri Lanka*. New Delhi: Sage Publications India.

Hallaq, Wael B. 1997. *A History of Islamic Legal Theories*. New York: Cambridge University Press.

Haniffa, Fara. 2005. P-Toms and Muslim Politics. *Polity* 2 (5 & 6): 12–14.

Haniffa, Farzana. 2013. Piety as Politics Amongst Muslim Women in Contemporary Sri Lanka. In *Islamic Reform in South Asia*, ed. C. Osella and F. Osella. New York: Cambridge University Press.

Hansard Department. Retrieved July 30, 2015, from http://www.parliament.lk/en/component/organisation/dept/departments?depart=4&id=4&Itemid=107.

Hasbullah, Shahul, and Benedikt Korf. 2009. Muslim Geographies and the Politics of Purification in Sri Lanka after the 2004 Tsunami. *Singapore Journal of Tropical Geography* 30: 248–264.

Helbardt, Sofia, Dagmar Hellmann-Rajanayagam, and Rüdiger Korf. 2013. Religionisation of Politics in Sri Lanka, Thailand and Myanmar. *Politics, Religion & Ideology* 14 (1): 36–58.

Hjärpe, Jan. 1983. *Politisk Islam*. Malmö: Gleerups Förlag.

———. 1987. *Islams värld*. Stockholm: Brevskolan.

————. 1997. What Will be Chosen from the Basket? *European Review* 5 (3): 267–274.

————. 2010. *Islamismer*. Malmö: Gleerups Utbildning AB.

Hussein, Asiff. 2011. *Sarandib: An Ethnological Study of the Muslims of Sri Lanka*. Pannipitya: Neptune Publications.

Höglund, Kristine, and Isak Svensson. 2009. Mediating Between Tigers and Lions: Norwegian Peace Diplomacy in Sri Lanka's Civil War. *Contemporary South Asia* 17 (2): 175–191.

Imtiyaz, A.R.M. 2005. Violent Muslim Mobilization in Sri Lanka: Some Questions. *Polity* 2 (5 & 6): 14–16.

————. 2009. The Eastern Muslims of Sri Lanka: Special Problems and Solutions. *Journal of Asian and African Studies* 44 (4): 407–427.

Imtiyaz, A.R.M., and M.C.M. Iqbal. 2011. The Displaced Northern Muslims of Sri Lanka: Special Problems and the Future. *Journal of Asian and African Studies* 46 (4): 375–389.

Ismail, Qadri. 1995. Unmooring Identity: The Antinomies of Elite Muslim Self-Representation in Modern Sri Lanka. In *Unmaking the Nation: The Politics of Identity and History in Modern Sri Lanka*, ed. Pradeep Jeganathan and Qadri Ismail. Colombo: Social Scientists' Association.

Ismail, Mohamed, Rameez Abdullah, and Mohamed Fazil. 2004. Muslim Perspective from the East. In *Dealing with Diversity*, ed. Freks George and Bart Klem. Hague: Netherlands Institute of International Relations.

Haniffa, Farzana. 2012. Three Attempts at Peace in Sri Lanka: A Critical Muslim Perspective. *Journal of Peacebuilding & Development* 6 (1): 49–62.

————. 2015. Who Gave These Fellows This Strength?: Muslims and the Bodu Bala Sena in Post-War Sri Lanka. In *Sri Lanka: The Struggle for Peace in the Aftermath of War*, ed. Daniel Bass and Amarnath Amarasingam. London: Hurst.

Hasbullah, Shahul, and Benedikt Korf. 2013. Muslim Geographies, Violence and the Antinomies of Community in Eastern Sri Lanka. *The Geographical Journal* 179 (1): 32–43.

Holt, C. John, ed. 2016. *Buddhist Extremists and Muslim Minorities Religious Conflict in Contemporary Sri Lanka*. Oxford: Oxford University Press.

Kapferer, Bruce. 2001. Ethnic Nationalism and the Discourses of Violence in Sri Lanka. *Communal/Plural* 9 (1): 33–67.

Kepel, Gilles. 2002. *Jihad, the Trail of Political Islam*. London: I. B Tauris & Co Ltd.

Klem, Bart. 2011. Islam, Politics and Violence in Eastern Sri Lanka. *The Journal of Asian Studies* 70 (3): 730–753.

————. 2014. The Political Geography of War's End: Territorialisation, Circulation, and Moral Anxiety in Trincomalee, Sri Lanka. *Political Geography* 38: 33–45.

Knoerzer, Shari. 1998. Transformation of Muslim Political Identity. In *Culture and Politics of Identity in Sri Lanka*, ed. Mithran Tiruchelcam and C.S. Dattathreya. Colombo: International Center for Ethnic Studies.

Lewer, Nick, and Mohammed Ismail. 2011. The Genealogy of Muslim Political Voices in Sri Lanka. In *Aid, Conflict and Peacebuilding in Sri Lanka*, ed. Jonathan Goodhand, Benedict Korf, and Jonathan Spencer. London: Routledge.

Lincoln, Bruce. 2003. *Holy Terrors: Thinking About Religion After September 11*. Chicago/London: University of Chicago Press.

Mahroof, M.M.M. 1990. Impact of European-Christian Rule on the Muslims of Sri Lanka: A Socio-Historical Analysis. *Islamic Studies* 29 (4): 353–373.

————. 1992. Malay language in Sri Lanka: Socio-Mechanics of a Minority Language in Its Historical Setting. *Islamic Studies* 31 (4): 463–478.

Marga Institute. 1988. *The Muslim Community of Sri Lanka*. Colombo: Marga Institute.

McGilvray, Dennis B. 1974. *Tamils and Moors: Caste and Matriclan Structure in Eastern Sri Lanka*. Chicago: Faculty of the Division of the Social Sciences, Department of Anthropology, Chicago University.

————. 1991. *Arabs, Moors and Muslims: The Mobilization of Muslim Identity in Sri Lanka*. Third Sri Lanka Conference, Center for Asian Studies, Amsterdam.

————. 1998. Arabs, Moors and Muslims: Sri Lankan Muslim Ethnicity in Regional Perspective. *Contributions to Indian Sociology* 32 (2): 433–483.

————. 2001. *Tamil and Muslim Identities in the East*. Colombo: Marga Institute.

————. 2004. Jailani: A Sufi Shrine in Sri Lanka. In *Lived Islam in South Asia: Adaptation, Accommodation & Conflict*, ed. Imtiaz Ahmad and Helmut Reifeld. Delhi: Social Science Press.

————. 2008. *Crucible of Conflict: Tamil and Muslim Society on the East Coast of Sri Lanka*. Durham: Duke University Press.

————. 2011a. Sri Lankan Muslims: Between Ethno-Nationalism and the Global Ummah. *Nations and Nationalism* 17 (1): 45–64.

————. 2011b. Celebrations of Maturity and Marriage. In *The Muslim Heritage of Eastern Sri Lanka*, ed. S.H.M. Jameel and Asiff Hussein. Colombo: Muslim Women's Research and Action Forum.

————. 2013. Sri Lankan Sufi Transnational Networks. In *The Encyclopedia of the Sri Lankan Diaspora*, ed. Peter Reeves. Singapore: ISAS and Editions Didier Millet.

————. 2014. A matrilineal Sufi Shaykh in Sri Lanka. *South Asian History and Culture* 5 (2): 246–261.

————. 2015. Sri Lanka. *The Encyclopaedia of Islam*, 3rd edn. Retrieved August 4, 2015, from http://referenceworks.brillonline.com/entries/encyclopaedia-of-islam-3/sri-lanka-COM_27597.

————. 2016. Rethinking Muslim Identity in Sri Lanka. In *Buddhist Extremists and Muslim Minorities: Religious Conflict in Contemporary Sri Lanka*, ed. John C. Holt. New York: Oxford University Press.

McGilvray, Dennis B., and Mirak Raheem. 2007. Muslim Perspective on the Sri Lankan Conflict. In *Policy Studies 41*. Washington, DC: East-West Center. Society of Environmental Economics and Policy Studies.

Meijer, Roel. 2009. *Global Salafism: Islam's New Religious Movement*. New York: Columbia University Press.

Meyer, Eric. 2001. *Sri Lanka: Biography of an Island*. Negombo: Viator Publications.

Mitchell, Claire. 2005. Behind the Ethnic Marker: Religion and Social Identification in Northern Ireland. *Sociology of Religion* 66: 3–21.

————. 2006. The Religious Content of Ethnic Identities. *Sociology* 40: 1135–1152.

Mohan, Vasundhara. 1987. *Identity Crisis of Sri Lankan Muslims*. Delhi: Mittal Publications.

More, J.B.P. 2004. *Muslim Identity, Print Culture and the Dravidian Factor in Tamil Nadu*. New Delhi: Orient Longman.

Mutalib, Hussin. 1990. Islamic Revivalism in ASEAN States: Political Implication. *Asian Survey* 30 (9): 877–891.

Natali, Cristiana. 2008. Building Cemeteries, Constructing Identities: Funerary Practices and Nationalist Discourse Among the Tamil Tigers of Sri Lanka. *Contemporary South Asia* 16 (3): 287–301.

Nuhman, M.A. 2002. *Understanding Sri Lankan Muslim Identity*. Colombo: International Center for Ethnic Studies. Ethnicity Course Series.

O'Sullivan. 1999a. *Identity and Institution in Ethnic Conflict: The Muslims of Sri Lanka*. Ph.D. thesis, Oxford: Oxford University.

O'Sullivan, Meghan. 1999b. Conflict as a Catalyst: The Changing Politics of the Sri Lankan Muslims. In *Conflict and Community in Contemporary Sri Lanka*, ed. Siri Gamas and I.B. Watson. New Delhi: Sage.

Osella, C., and F. Osella. 2013. Introduction. In *Islamic Reform in South Asia*, ed. C. Osella and F. Osella. New York: Cambridge University Press.

Roy, Olivier. 2004. *Globalised Islam: The Search for a New Ummah*. London: Hurst.

Saldin, B.D.K. 2003. *Portrait of a Sri Lankan Malay*. Kurunegala: Nihon Printers.

Samaratunge, Shilpa, and Sanjana Hattotuwa. 2014. *A Study of Hate Speech on Facebook in Sri Lanka*. Colombo: Centre for Policy Alternatives.

Schalk, Peter. 1997. Resistance and Martyrdom in the Process of State Formation of Tamililam. *Comparative Asian Studies* 18: 61–83.

Shukri, Muhammad A.M. 1986. *Muslims of Sri Lanka*. Colombo: Aitken Spence Printing.

SLMC "Our History". Retrieved April 2, 2013, from http://slmc.lk/about-us/sri-lanka-muslim-congress/.

Spencer, Jonathan. 2012. Performing Democracy and Violence, Agonism and Community, Politics and not Politics in Sri Lanka. *Geoforum, Special Issue, Space, Contestation and the Political* 43 (4): 725–731.

———. 2014. Anthropology, Politics, and Place in Sri Lanka: South Asian Reflections from an Island Adrift. South Asia Multidisciplinary Academic Journal [Online], 10.

Spencer, Jonathan, Jonathan Goodhand, Shahul Hasbullah, Bart Klem, Benedikt Korf, and Kalinga Tudor Silva. 2014. *Checkpoint, Temple, Church and Mosque, A Collaborative Ethnography of War and Peace*. London: Pluto Press.

Svensson, Jonas. 2000. *Women's Human Rights and Islam: A Study of Three Attempts at Accommodation*. Stockholm: Almqvist & Wiksell International.

Thiranagama, Sharika. 2011. *In My Mother's House: Civil War in Sri Lanka*. Philadelphia: University of Pennsylvania Press.

Uyangoda, Jayadeva. 2001. *Question of Sri Lankas's Minority Rights*. Colombo: International Center for Ethnic Studies.

Walker, Rebecca. 2013. *Enduring Violence: Everyday Life and Conflict in Eastern Sri Lanka*. Manchester: Manchester University Press.

Wallerstein, Immanuel. 2002. Konstruktionen av Folk: Rasism, Nationalism, etnicitet. In *Ras, Nation, Klass*, ed. Etienne Balibar and Immanuel Wallerstein. Uddevalla: Boförlaget Daidalos AB.

Warnapala, Wiswa W.A. 2001. *Politics in Sri Lanka*. Colombo: S. Godage & Brothers.

Weerarathne, Chitra. 2013. Ranil, Tissa restrained from acting against SLMC MPs. *The Island*. Retrieved October 27, 2013, from http://island.lk/index.php?page_cat=article-details&page=article details&code_title=73022.

Wickramasinghe, Nira. 2006. *Sri Lanka in the Modern Age: A History of Contested Identities*. London: Hurst.

Wilson, Jeyaratnam. 2000. *Sri Lankan Tamil: Its Origins and Development in the Nineteenth and Twentieth Centuries*. London: Hurst.

Wimalratne, K.D.G. 1986. Muslims Under British Rule in Ceylon. In *Muslims of Sri Lanka*, ed. A.M. Muhammed Shukri. Colombo: Aitken Spence Printing.

Zackariya, Faizoun, and Nadarajah Shanmugaratnam. 2003. Moving into the Extra Household Domain. In *In the Maze of Displacement Conflict: Migration and Change*, ed. N. Shanmugaratnam, Ragnhild Lundh, and Kristi Anne Stølen. Kristiansand: Hoyskoleforlaget AS-Norwegian Academic Press.

Chapter 2
Official Documents

Abstract The following chapter analyzes the ideology of the Sri Lanka Muslim Congress as expressed in the official documents of the party. I have divided the chapter depending upon who is the intended recipient of the document. The Constitution of the Sri Lanka Muslim Congress is the party's written political platform and is directed towards the general public, the government, other political organizations, and members of the party. The document *The proposal of the Sri Lanka Muslim Congress and Resolution to the conflict in the northern and eastern provinces: the Muslim dimension* can be seen as directed towards the government. Code of Conduct, on the other hand, is a document mainly for internal use. It outlines specific rules for the members of the party. Under the headline "Convention speeches", documents containing older party convention speeches, for example, Ashraff's convention speeches and Sri Lanka Muslim Congress 15th Convention are analyzed. These are documents for sale in the party's headquarters, with the members of the party as the intended audience. In "On the Internet and in public spaces," the approach by the SLMC elite to the Internet, and also some posters during election time, is examined. These can be seen as directed towards a general public, or potential voters. The last part in this chapter deals with the case of a certain public symbol in the text *Signs and Greatness*.

Keywords Muslim politics · Islam · Muslims · Sri Lanka · Sri Lanka Muslim Congress · Pragmatic politics · Religion and politics

The Constitution of the Sri Lanka Muslim Congress

The written political platform of the SLMC is *The Constitution of the Sri Lanka Muslim Congress.*[1] It was initially published in 1986. The very first chapter states that: "The Holy Quran and the Traditions of the Holy Prophet shall be the supreme

---

[1] The Constitution of the Sri Lanka Muslim Congress is a 26-page document on the SLMC's organization, from top to bottom. The document also outlines how members are organized, the guidelines of the party, and different roles of party members. It also contains some rules and presents affiliated bodies and their work. The National Unity Alliance Constitution is also discussed and

© Springer Nature Switzerland AG 2019   35
A. Johansson, *Pragmatic Muslim Politics*,
https://doi.org/10.1007/978-3-030-12789-3_2

Illustration 2.1 The party flag (*The Constitution of the Sri Lanka Muslim Congress, 2000* (1986) n.p.)

guidelines of the Party".[2] With the words "supreme guidelines", the leading members of the SLMC open up for the possibility of choosing whether or not to refer to these religious sources in their politics: even though the guidelines are said to be "supreme", they are still merely guidelines.

Moreover, the first chapter of the constitution contains religious symbols, for example, the green and yellow party flag which features the words "La-ilaha-illallaah Muhammadur-Rasoolullaah", that is, the Muslim profession of faith, written in Arabic, together with a crescent moon and a five-pointed star.[3] The references to Islamic terminology continue throughout the entire constitution. According to the text, the party anthem is "Bismillaah hir-Rahmanir-Raheem" (written in Latin script and translated as "In the name of Allah, the Beneficent, the Merciful" and sometimes shortened to *bismillah*).[4] In the constitution of the SLMC, we can furthermore learn that the party headquarters shall be referred to as Dharussalaam (Arabic, dar al-salam, house of peace) (Illustration 2.1).

The second chapter of the constitution outlines the ultimate aim of the party: it is the SLMC's duty to foster and safeguard the unity, sovereignty, and territorial integrity of Sri Lanka.[5] The text also cites other ethical standards that the party and its members should live up to, namely:

---

analyzed in Chap. 4. The National Unity Alliance (NUA) was initially a part of the SLMC but developed into a separate party after the death of Ashraff in 2000. Another document related to the NUA that also is analyzed is *Signs and Greatness* which discusses the SLMC's three symbols during the time when Ashraff created NUA.

[2] *The Constitution of the Sri Lanka Muslim Congress*, 2000 (1986), n.p. In the document entitled *Our Vision*, the SLMC encourages the use of religion in politics. Here it is stated that: "We are convinced of the reality that we cannot adopt an Islamic way of life for the community, if we discard the political aspects of Islam. We are also aware of the fact that Prophet Muhammad [...] did not separate Islam from the social, economic and political establishments [...] If his basic principle is accepted, it becomes crystal clear that if our political affairs are established on an Islamic foundation, our communal life too could be established according to the principle of Islam [...] We who are followers of that Prophet have now gone back to pre-Islamic times when politics was considered to be a separate entity from religion". Quoted in O'Sullivan 1999: 258–9.

[3] *The Constitution of the Sri Lanka Muslim Congress, 2000* (1986), n.p.

[4] See Graham 2013.

[5] *The Constitution of the Sri Lanka Muslim Congress*, 2000 (1986), n.p.

To uphold and honor the principles of democracy and the fundamental human rights of the people of Sri Lanka.

To strive to recognize and respect the distinct linguistic, cultural, ethnic, and religious identities of the communities of Sri Lanka, and promote friendship, peace and harmony amongst them.

To work towards the re-establishment and the preservation of the rule of Law.

To preserve and ensure the independence of the Judiciary.

To preserve and promote the sharia laws and to encourage the members of the Party and others to adopt the entire code of sharia laws in their private and community life.[6]

The second chapter of the constitution has a slightly different approach than the first. In this part, the nation gains a more prominent position. The SLMC does not make a plea for a separate state but instead accepts the continuance of the current state of Sri Lanka. The constitution emphasizes the importance of preserving the sovereignty of Sri Lankan law but at the same time declares that members of the party should adopt the entire code of Shari'a law. This latter aspect is interesting. Shari'a is referred to as a body of legal rules, that is, as the result of *fiqh* (Islamic jurisprudence) and not, as would have been likewise reasonable, an abstract "will of God".[7] Referring to Shari'a as the result of *fiqh* establishes an ambiguity within the document concerning the relationship between secular Sri Lankan law and Islamic law. There is no indication that these two might come into conflict.

Like the party's constitution, *The proposal of the Sri Lanka Muslim Congress* and *Resolution to the conflict in the northern and eastern provinces: the Muslim dimension* deal with questions regarding the nation and the state. In these two documents, the leading members of the SLMC express their wish to keep Sri Lanka as one undivided nation:

It is participation within a united Sri Lanka that the Muslim community is seeking, not separation. The community seeks to live within a united Sri Lanka, and prevent conflicts of the past dictating relationships of the future. Past discrimination and conflict need not be a guide to the future. Instead the challenge is to ensure that these are avoided and harmony established – an imperative for development.[8]

The leading members of the SLMC not only act as spokesmen for Muslims in general but moreover state that they canalize what Muslims want. It is nevertheless claimed that "Muslim nationalism has evolved itself on opposition to militant Tamil nationalism".[9] Furthermore, these documents continue to portray Muslims as peaceful inhabitants and highlight the language diversity among them. This diversity makes Muslims the perfect mediators in the negotiation process between the government and Tamil militants in Sri Lanka. The description of the peaceful Muslim population is followed by a suggestion for the creation of a Greater South East Autonomous Area. This is described as follows:

---

[6] *The Constitution of the Sri Lanka Muslim Congress*, 2000 (1986), n.p. These are also posted online. See the SLMC "Our Objective", retrieved 2013-09-30.

[7] For an overview of the laws in the Qur'an, see Hallaq 2014.

[8] *The Proposal of the Sri Lanka Muslim Congress*, 2004, n.p. This will also be discussed in the following chapters.

[9] *Resolution to the conflict in the northern and eastern provinces*: n.d., n.p.

SLMC proposes [...] the establishment of the Greater South East Autonomous Area (GSEAA), comprising Muslim majority areas within the East. [...] Within the proposed Autonomous Area, there would be members of other communities, and other Muslims will continue to live within other communities in the North East, outside the bounds of the GSEAA. Within the GSEAA there would be full democracy, genuine inclusiveness and respect for others.[10]

Hence, even though the SLMC wants the Sri Lankan nation to remain intact, it apparently still aspires for a Muslim-controlled autonomous region in the north and the east, areas claimed to be the "traditional homeland of the Muslim population".[11] The documents are very detailed regarding how this autonomy would function. For example, the leading members of the SLMC suggest that religious scholars from the major religions in Sri Lanka would "have the function of protecting and fostering the culture of the community in question".[12]

The third chapter and the following chapters of the constitution deal with the structural and hierarchical orders of the party. It is stated that: "All decisions of the party shall be made by the High Command by consensus (*mashoora*) and such decisions shall bind all the members of the Party".[13] The Islamic term usually used for (religious) consensus is *ijma'*.[14] *Mashoora*, or the Arabic term *shura,* means "consultation"; both of these terms have religious connotations (this concept will be discussed further in the following chapter).[15]

According to my reading of this sentence, the consultation among the high command members should *result in* consensus as the ultimate goal. This consultation praxis is linked to the hierarchical order of the party, which is as follows:

1. The Leader
2. The Chairman
3. The Senior Deputy Leader
4. The Deputy Leader I
5. The Deputy Leader II
6. The Deputy Leader III
7. The Secretary General
8. The General Treasurer
9. The President Majlis-e-Shoora
10. The National Co-ordinating Secretary
11. The National Propaganda Secretary
12. The Additional Propaganda Secretary
13. The National Organizer.
14. The National Co-ordinating Secretary

---

[10] *The Proposal of the Sri Lanka Muslim Congress,* 2004, n.p.

[11] *Resolution to the conflict in the northern and eastern provinces,* n.d., n.p.

[12] *The Proposal of the Sri Lanka Muslim Congress,* 2004, n.p.

[13] *The Constitution of the Sri Lanka Muslim Congress,* 2000 (1986), n.p.

[14] See Bernard 2006.

[15] See Lewis 2006.

15. The National Propaganda Secretary
16. The Additional Propaganda Secretary
17. The National Organizer
18. Director International Affairs
19. Director Constitutional Affairs
20. Representatives of the Ulema Congress.[16]

The leader consults with his members of the high command. This consultation is carried out whenever a decision needs to be made. The leader, according to his rank, makes the final decision. The "president Majlis-e-Shoora" (listed above as number 9) is a president of a council that also works according to the consultation principle in its meetings with the leader. The fact that religious scholars (*'ulama*) have a distinct position but are ranked fairly low in the hierarchy system (20 out of the total 32) is also significant. They may, however, as individuals also be included in other levels of the organization. The Majlis-e-Shoora consists of "past members of the Politbureau who continue to be actively involved in Party activities".[17] The Politbureau was previously a separate body that dealt with political questions – today these members are included in the high command. Besides old members, this council "may also grant membership to two persons to represent organizations such as All Ceylon Jaamiyathul Ulema".[18] There is also a list of affiliated bodies, such as the ladies congress, student congress, and workers congress. The role of these affiliated bodies will be discussed in the next chapter.

Code of Conduct

Code of Conduct is a document directed towards ordinary members of the SLMC. We do not know when it was first printed, but since the original constitution of the SLMC refers to *Code of Conduct*, it should probably be dated to sometime around the mid-1980s. It contains a separate chapter with rules and regulations for the party's Muslim members in particular (implying that the SLMC includes members from other religions). Members that have been appointed an assignment within the SLMC receive a letter (see Appendix 2) that tells them to "abide by an act in accordance with the provisions of the Constitution, Code of Conduct and the decisions made by the Sri Lankan Muslim Congress".[19] When describing how one should behave in regard to campaigning for the party, the text is full of references to Islamic beliefs and ethics:

---

[16] The list covers a total 32 posts. *The Constitution of the Sri Lanka Muslim Congress*, 2000 (1986), n.p.

[17] *The Constitution of the Sri Lanka Muslim Congress*, 2000 (1986), n.p.

[18] *The Constitution of the Sri Lanka Muslim Congress*, 2000 (1986), n.p.

[19] This document was provided to me by Shafeek Rajabdeen. See Appendix 2. This is also stated in *The Constitution of the Sri Lanka Muslim Congress*, 2000 (1986), n.p.

Every member must make a covenant with Allaah and with his own conscience that the S.L.M.C. is his only Political Party. [...]

When contesting for positions – within the Party, or for places outside the Party – the Members must be completely free from falsehood, treachery, deceit, circumventions, trick, hypocrisy, pretext, cunning or any form of expediency, whatsoever. The result of such contests should be accepted in the spirit that it is "Deo Volente" (The Will of Allaah), without exhibiting any form of resentment, hatred, vengeance, vindictiveness, scandal or attempt at bringing disrepute to the opponents. The Members of the Party should guard themselves against such misdemeanor of felony.[20]

Code of Conduct indeed repeats, but using other words, the above message, and it also contains additional directives; in addition to the five pillars of Islam, there are thirty-one directives for how Muslim members should live their lives. Since these are all related to Islam and constitute a clear example of Muslim politics, they are here quoted in full:

1. To have implicit faith that: "THERE IS NONE WORTHY OF BEING WORSHIPPED OTHER THAN ALLAH" and that "MUHAMMAD [...] IS HIS SERVANT AND MESSENGER" ... and to act accordingly.
2. To pray regularly – five times a day – under ALL circumstances.
3. To entrust all affairs to Allaah, with implicit faith in Him and His Mercy, Help and Guidance.
4. To increase the Remembrance (Zikr) of Allah and pray for forgiveness.
5. To recite the "Salawaath" on Prophet Muhammad [...] and pray for forgiveness.
6. While being grateful to Allaah for all His Mercies, and Bounties, we should also be thankful to people, who help us.
7. Whilst observing the obligatory fast during Ramadan, Members must also cultivate the habit of observing optional fasts.
8. To know the importance and merit of distribution "Zakaath" (Poor Rate) annually; Members must also induce others to do so, with the view of endeavoring to bridge the economic gap in our community.
9. To know the merits of distributing "Sadaqah" (Optional Alms) and not give it for the sake of self pride, or publicity, but for the Glory of Allaah.
10. As the prayers and the good deeds of those who acquire wealth by prohibited means, lose merit, we should learn to be content with what we receive by lawful (Halal) means.
11. To fashion our lives in conformity with ethics and conscience, and to choose between the just and the unjust, between good and evil, and to have an inclination towards the just and the good.
12. To obey parents, and to attend to their comfort and welfare, and to respect our elders, relatives, friends, neighbors, the learned and the like.
13. To refrain from falsehood, perjury, back-biting, inciting quarrels and fights, theft, false accusations, usury, consuming forbidden food and liquor, indulging in deeds prohibited by Islam, etc.

---

[20] *Code of Conduct*, n.d.: 1–3.

14. To respect human feelings and to avoid hurting the feelings of others by word or deed.
15. If any calamities befall people in any part of the world, in general, and Muslims in particular, it should be considered the duty of the Members to initiate economic aid and enlist moral support, in order to abate their losses and pains.
16. To practice leading a simple life as far as possible.
17. To practice the habit of being in a state of cleanliness and "Wuzoo" at all times.
18. To learn and practice the meritorious qualities, taught by Islam.
19. To converse with others, according to their capacity, to understand and comprehend.
20. Never to postpone for tomorrow what we can be done for today [sic].
21. To be patient in recovering a loan, give to another at a time of need, but it is meritorious to forego a loan, if one can afford to do so.
22. To consider serving others as being more meritorious than self-service.
23. To work for the advancement and upliftment of humanity.
24. To use kind words and good behavior to convert others.
25. To accept our faults without shame or hesitation and NOT put the blame on others to conceal our faults.
26. To avoid extravagance and not to become a slave of avarice and miserliness.
27. To remember with gratitude anyone who has helped you, or favored you with some kind deeds.
28. To remember that your duties are as important as your privileges and prerogatives.
29. To guard against jealousy, pride and superstitions.
30. To praise the good qualities and virtuous deeds of others, and to boost your own charitable disposition and good deeds.
31. To remain patient, and see Allaah's forgiveness, in times of sorrow and danger.[21]

The text lists several specific Islamic rules and regulations, all of which may be found in traditional Islamic teachings. Many of them can be directly related to Islamic laws traceable back to the Qur'an and the hadiths. For example, theft and false accusations are discussed in the Qur'an.[22] It is noteworthy that many of the regulations that are put forth, although easily connected to traditional Islamic ethical teachings, boil down to "being nice". One of the terms that is highlighted in *Code of Conduct* is gratitude (*shukr*). Gratitude here concerns a quality related to God and His presence in all living beings.[23] Although the rules explained in *Code of Conduct* are to a large extent general recommendations to be nice, there are some specific rules that do refer to exclusively Islamic rituals, such as the recitation of the *salawat* (Peace be upon him) when mentioning the Prophet Muhammad. These constitute examples where *Code of Conduct* promotes Muslim distinctiveness as part of the construction of the community.

[21] *Code of Conduct*, n.d.: 9–11.
[22] For examples, see Rowson 2014 and Hallaq 2014.
[23] Reinhart 2006.

Code of Conduct specifies that when members enter the party, they must sign a particular document that General Secretary Hasen Ali calls a *bay'a* and which is appended to *Code of Conduct* (see Appendix 4). The *bay'a* is an oath, an Arabic term having religious connotations. The term goes back to the time of Muhammad and the early caliphs, and it is mentioned in the Qur'an.[24] *Bay'a* has been (and usually is) explained as the pledging of allegiance to someone verbally or by signing a contract. It has also traditionally been interpreted as an oath not only between superiors and "clients" but also between God and man.[25] There are other documents with similar examples. In the text *The Sri Lanka Muslim Congress program to stabilize the party from village level*, members of the SLMC are urged to take classes on the Qur'an and hadiths, as well as to "[maintain] Islamic art, craft and cultural tradition and [...] Islamic tradition".[26]

The *bay'a* document is divided into three parts: "Affidavit", "Agreement", and "Pledge". All of them have to be signed by the nominee. The *bay'a* is exclusively for Muslim members, and one of the first things a member has to verify in the document is that they in fact are Muslim. Consequently, only Muslim members can run for election. The second part of the *bay'a*, "Agreement", concerns loyalty to the party and specifies that the members should respect the constitution and the rules of the party as they are outlined in *Code of Conduct*. "Pledge" is basically the same, with the exception of its focus on loyalty to the leader and the party, and "Pledge" can be related to the early history of Islam when loyalty was sworn to the early Islamic leaders by the principle of *bay'a*.[27]

Convention Speeches

The SLMC has a number of earlier convention speeches for sale at its headquarters. Most of these speeches were made by the late leader Ashraff. In these texts, the leaders of the SLMC stress the party's uniqueness as a consequence of the fact that it adopts an "Islamic separateness".[28] The following quote from Ashraff, which positions religious beliefs and practices as a legitimate basis for ethnicity, is quite typical:

> If the Quran and Allah's messenger Mohamed's (PBUH) way of life is the basis on which our community is identified as a separate ethnic group, the individuality of the Muslim community can never be defined on the basis of language.[29]

---

[24] See Hawting 2013.

[25] Hawting 2013.

[26] *The Sri Lanka Muslim Congress program to stabilize the party from village level.* n.d., n.p

[27] See Tyan 2012.

[28] See *Sri Lanka Muslim Congress 15th Convention.*

[29] *Ashraff's Convention Speeches*, n.d., n.p.

It is symptomatic that Ashraff in this speech refers to allegiance to normative texts as a basis for ethnicity. It would appear that such a definition of who is a Muslim could be hard for any believer to question, which might have been the case if any more detailed theological niceties had been cited. Divisions between Muslims on other grounds are downplayed. Indeed, Ashraff explicitly rejected the division of the Muslim community into Sinhala Muslims and Tamil Muslims. He even stated that different languages are something that had been forced upon the Muslims in Sri Lanka, who ought to be considered as one undividable community.[30] Ashraff also mentioned that other Muslim political organizations existing prior to the emergence of the SLMC had to be acknowledged in the creation of the party. Ashraff also maintained that voters did not accept the Muslim United Liberation Front (MULF), another party active at that time, as a true representative for the Muslim community.[31] Ashraff called Muslims that were represented in the majority Sinhala-speaking parties "puppets" with no real power to change anything in the government within which they had been acting.[32]

According to Ashraff, the *'ulama* in Sri Lanka had historically played an important role in protecting "the Islamic way of life", a life that was threatened especially under British rule, that witnessed, for example, conversions to Christianity.[33] The *'ulama* and, today, the SLMC are consequently portrayed as heroes. Despite his criticism of British rule, Ashraff stated clearly that he saw English as an important language in addition to Arabic-Tamil.[34] Arabic-Tamil, however, is special. In the pamphlet *Sri Lanka Muslim Congress 15th Convention*, its author, Maruthoor Ghandi, describes with a sense of pride the Arabic Islamic element in particular:

> Despite objections and disruptions from the Muslim factions, for the first time, through Sri Lanka Muslim Congress we are able to hear the Arabic verses of 'Bismillah ir-Rahman ir-Rahim and Allahu Akbar' in the parliament.[35]

We can detect a sense of satisfaction when Ghandi mentions the use of these religious formulas, uttered in Arabic in the parliament. Speech, particularly speech spiced with "religion", is one aspect of Muslim distinctiveness, but there are others as well.

In the following excerpt of one of his speeches, Ashraff makes it clear that Shari'a law were another element that distinguished Muslims from other communities:

> In other words, it can be said that the taproot of the identity of the Muslim community entirely depends on sharia laws. The Muslim community cannot exist without the sharia laws and the present Muslim personal law. We have to be clear that all the sharia laws are not included (in the Muslim personal law). Traditions against the sharia are continuing in

---

[30] *Ashraff's Convention Speeches*, n.d., n.p.

[31] Ashraff mentions the Islamic United Front, the Islamic Socialist Front, the Anti-Marxist Front, the Colombo Muslim United Front, the East-Ceylon Muslim United; see *Ashraff's Convention Speeches* n.d., n.p.

[32] *Ashraff's Convention Speeches*, n.d., n.p. HC member 2, 2013-02-17.

[33] *Ashraff's Convention Speeches*, n.d., n.p.

[34] *Ashraff's Convention Speeches*, n.d., n.p.

[35] *Sri Lanka Muslim Congress 15th Convention,* n.d., n.p.

the name of Muslim law. […] In such a background, for the tree called Muslim community to last strongly, its roots have to be strengthened. The present contemporary historical need, in addition to the present sharia aspects, attempts should be made for the Muslim community to be able to lead their life completely based on the sharia law. This huge attempt cannot be made by the United National Party, Sri Lankan Freedom Party or the atheistic left parties. […] whether it is possible, in the present political and social set up, to perform this task that has to be handled by Ulemas, law scholars, law […] and members of the law council jointly.[36]

This speech was delivered in response to criticism concerning the application of Muslim personal law in Sri Lanka, an issue that takes on a symbolic role in the claim for Muslim distinctiveness in the country. It should be noted, however, that Ashraff demands an expansion of Islamic law extending beyond laws pertaining to the family. Shari'a in this latter context becomes an equivalent to "Divine will" and is consequently not specified further. It has a symbolic role.

Even though the SLMC strives on a local level to raise Muslim awareness – and the civil war contributed to the creation of a Muslim identity – there is yet another crucial dimension that needs to be considered: the SLMC presents the Muslims in Sri Lanka as part of the world's Muslim community (*umma*). The focus on one united world Muslim community is visible in a series of statements made by the party.[37] According to a speech made by Ashraff, for example, the timing was right for the emergence of a Muslim party in Sri Lanka, not only due to local circumstances but also due to the situation of Muslims worldwide. Muslims in Sri Lanka are seen as a part of this "game":

Today, we have been enraged by seeing evidently the minority communities in every country being victimized by the waves that rise in this international arena. We shed tears of blood here for the Islamic world that is losing its power, trapped in the hands of mean international might. Iraq-Iran war, Palestine struggles for her right, the devil dance of the aggression of American imperialism against Libya and so on have caused bleeding wounds in our hearts. On the other hand, our Muslim community losing its rights in our motherland is an unbearable wound that has become gangrenous. Our doubt whether Sri Lankan Muslims are being used as dice for these inland and foreign atrocities is being strengthened in us.[38]

Muslims are thus facing injustice on a global scale, and injustices towards Sri Lankan Muslims are just one part of this situation. For the Muslims in Sri Lanka, there exists, according to this passage, both an external threat and internal discrimination.

---

[36] *Ashraff's Convention Speeches*, n.d., n.p.

[37] For more information on *umma,* see Denny 2012.

[38] *Ashraff's Convention Speeches* n.d., n.p. Ashraff is also harsh in his criticism of the government but points out that the SLMC does not want to divide the country, nor does it advocate terrorism; it wants to unify the country. He accuses the government of being chauvinistic and states that the creation of the SLMC is the only peaceful way to guarantee Muslim rights, and he continually asserts that the purpose is not to divide the country further.

In the material analyzed, God is presented as an active part. It is even claimed that God and His prophets, in giving their blessings, have played an active part in the creation of the party and its growth.[39] Thanks are due, and praying to God is hence something that is encouraged for people who want to join or leave the party.[40] God is also described as the protector of the party and is said to be actively working for its unity. The active God of party politics is, furthermore, a common character when Ashraff comments upon the party and its relation to the nation:

> This party is not for the Muslim community only. Allah has given this party the quality of guiding all the communities in this country. There are many matters that come in the parliament. We did not vote supporting the government in all those matters. We support the government in matters we deem correct. We oppose those that we think are not correct. We support them in the state of emergency. S. L. F. P. opposes it saying they do not want it. They ask us why we are supporting emergency.[41]

In this passage, God is presented as having given a particular task to the SLMC, that is, as being a guide for the country as a whole. In another printed document, we find a poem that likewise has the theme of the nation as a whole. With the help of Allah, and implicitly then the SLMC, all Sri Lankans will rise up together.[42]

The Party on the Internet and in "Public Spaces"

The official webpage of the SLMC contains the *bismillah*, written in both Arabic and Latin scripts.[43] The use of Arabic scripts can also be seen on the invitation to the 23 delegates' conference.[44] The webpage has also published the constitution of the party and describes the SLMC as "Islamic centric".[45] There is additional material concerning the civil war published on the webpage. This is how the SLMC explains its official view on the conflict, again stressing its own role as a potential mediator:

> Our proposals are forward looking, and grounded in the vision of [a Sri Lanka] that is sovereign, united, and democratic and that respects human rights, pluralism and the rule of law. We are a multi ethnic, multi religious and multi lingual country and the [challenges] to all of us is to balance identities that flow from this diversity within an overarching Sri Lankan identity.[46]

---

[39] See *Sri Lanka Muslim Congress 15th Convention* n.d., n.p.

[40] *Ashraff's Convention Speeches* n.d., n.p.

[41] *Ashraff's Convention Speeches* n.d., n.p.

[42] *Sri Lanka Muslim Congress 15th Convention*. n.d., n.p.

[43] SLMC "Home", retrieved 2014-12-02.

[44] *Invitation to the 23 delegates' conference* n.d., see appendix 5.

[45] SLMC "Our Party", retrieved 2013-09-30.

[46] SLMC "Our Policy", retrieved 2014-12-03.

Understanding and language-learning are explicitly mentioned as important means by which ethnic differences might be overcome.[47] In the same text from which the above quote has been taken, that is, a speech delivered by current leader Rauff Hakeem, English is specified as one of the keys to learning how to overcome ethnic barriers. "Knowledge" is stressed with reference to a hadith: "Those who seek knowledge are the inheritors of the Prophet".[48] The hadith is a general one. Traditionally, it has been interpreted as referring specifically to the 'ulama as "heirs of the Prophet".[49] The theme of Sri Lankan national identity, which is an important one, could also be observed in other texts on the webpage that refer to allegations of extremism:

> The observation that the Muslim communities may have some elements with extreme parochial prejudices is both possible and probable. Yet, we are extremely disturbed by the specific reference to the Muslim community of Sri Lanka as possible breeding grounds of extremism within the country.[50]

The quote is attributed to Hakeem, who in this statement clearly refutes allegations of Muslim extremism and rejects extremist elements, a necessary move for safeguarding the ideal of coexistence.

However, the nation is not always on the agenda:

> Muslims of the North and East now need autonomy in areas where they are a majority, to give them a sense of security that derives from being able to make or fully participate in decisions that most directly affect them. We have developed detailed proposals on autonomy which are now being discussed within the Muslim community. The rights of all communities living within the Muslim autonomous area will be fully protected. The SLMC wants to make clear that the autonomy will be designed to offer to the Muslim community in the North and East not a fortress, but a home within the broader homeland of Sri Lanka. It is intended to be a stepping stone for the greater involvement of the Muslim community within a united Sri Lanka, and not a drawbridge to keep the rest of the nation at bay.[51]

The SLMC's allegiance to the Sri Lankan nation comes with a formal request from the party that in the representatives' view will further peaceful coexistence: an autonomous, geographical region over which Muslims will have control. When it comes to this proposed autonomous region, it is clear that the focus on Muslim identity is more prominent than the Sri Lankan national identity spoken of earlier. This was formulated in the context of the Tamil separatist demand for an independent homeland called Tamil Eelam.

Furthermore, an interesting construction of Muslims as an ethnic/religious category appears in the section about the history of the party:

> When we achieved independence in 1948, all communities came together at that time. Muslims were serving the Majority Parties and building up their own image and [were] not

---

[47] SLMC "Dr A.M.A. Azeez Birth Centenary Oration", retrieved 2013-09-30.

[48] SLMC "Dr A.M.A. Azeez Birth Centenary Oration", retrieved 2013-09-30.

[49] Bearman, et al. 2006.

[50] SLMC "Statement by Minister of Justice and Leader of Sri Lanka Muslim Congress Rauff Hakeem", retrieved 2014-12-11.

[51] SLMC "Our Policy", retrieved 2014-12-03.

interested in Muslims coming together as a Muslim community. [...] in the General Elections that took place in 1956 we were able to witness an unfortunate turn in the country and the most affected community from the minority at that time were the Muslims – language wise. Tamils were waiting for an opportunity to be identified as a separate minority community. So were the Sinhalese people who wanted to be identified as the majority Sinhalese community and the Muslims who were in between were the most affected lot.[52]

In terms of not being Sinhala or Tamils, clearly language-based groups, Muslims are identified as a unique community. Based on a shared religion, and not language, they are described as a unified entity:

If the Muslims had joined the Tamils with an understanding a new chapter would have been opened for the separate identity of the Muslim community, which the leaders of that time for their selfish motives did not make use of the opportunity. At the same time the Muslims of that time were slaves to the majority community [...].[53]

The term Tamils on the official webpage, then, refers to Tamil-speaking non-Muslims. The historiography of the party and the outlines of ethnic groups exist mainly in order to legitimize the SLMC as a representative for the Muslim community. The "understanding" in the quote above is directed towards the Tamil militants who, according to the SLMC, did *not* recognize Muslims as having a separate ethnicity. Using terms such as "slaves", the authors further delimitate Muslims, and, what is more, underline the need for the SLMC as a political force. The final step towards proving that the SLMC is a legitimate representative for all Muslims in Sri Lanka can be found in a text about the party's first years in parliament:

In this country from time to time, the Muslims were giving their support to the UNP and SLFP. For the last 35 years their aspirations were not fulfilled. If the Muslim Congress was not established the grievances of the Muslim community would not have been looked into in the proper way.[54]

The SLMC is depicted as the (only) true savior of the Muslims, who are described as an adaptable, but distinct, community. The ability to adapt is what has previously hindered their recognition as such:

As a minority, we Muslims experience the same disadvantages as the Tamil minority. However, our community has historically adopted a policy of accommodation with the majority Sinhalese in the Sinhala majority areas and with the Tamils in the Tamil majority areas. The Eastern Province demography dictates that all three communities are equal stakeholders. [...] Today, Sri Lanka is a country where the war has ended. It has won the war. It now has to win the peace.[55]

According to the text, Muslims are, unlike other communities, ready to accept their neighbors regardless of language. The text on the SLMC's homepage is unconstrained in regard to what the SLMC presents itself as, namely, the true voice of all Muslims: "We are the voice of the community that can and does address issues in a

---

[52] SLMC "Our History", retrieved 2014-12-03.

[53] SLMC "Our History", retrieved 2014-12-03.

[54] SLMC "Our History", retrieved 2014-12-03.

[55] SLMC "Keynote Address at the World Muslim Forum", retrieved 2014-12-03.

multicultural, multiracial and multilingual society that makes up the nation state of Sri Lanka".[56] Additionally, it also portrays the SLMC as the heir of influential Muslim leaders in Sri Lanka by praising previous Muslim leaders who are not affiliated with the party.[57]

The SLMC is active on social media and has several Facebook pages and groups. The party leader has his own official page, which is dominated by pictures with short descriptions of the leader in different situations. There are some themes that appear frequently; the first category of picture concerns when Rauff Hakeem meets representatives of other countries.[58] The second has to do with when Hakeem spends time with his family. The third shows the leader when he meets his voters in town meetings, speaks to them or even visits them in person. Hakeem is also described as a person who could unite people in the spirit of the nation as "[h]e excels in his ability to bring different groups together for a shared purpose".[59] A fourth and final category shows Hakeem in religious contexts.[60] There are pictures of him performing prayers, wearing a *taqiyya* (a Muslim cap), performing the *'umra* (the lesser pilgrimage to Mecca), and meeting with different religious leaders (mostly Muslim and Buddhist).[61]

At election time, their presence on social media and in public places is characterized by a flood of various sorts of electoral material.[62] I have chosen to examine more closely the material that the SLMC disseminated in conjunction with the 2012 election, in particular the material handed out in the eastern provincial election. There is considerable diversity to be found in it.

In general, diverse references to Islam are scattered throughout the publicly distributed material analyzed, for example, calls on God to protect the people from evil: "Oh Allah [...] also we seek protection from you from their evil deeds".[63] God is called also upon to protect the Muslim community, and loyalty to God is sworn: "We are certainly (existing) for Allah. We are those who have certainly to return to him [sic]. Oh Allah! Save me from this trial. Change this into something good for

---

[56] SLMC "Our Achievements", retrieved 2014-12-03.

[57] SLMC "123rd Commemoration Oration of Alhaj Dr. T B Jayah", retrieved 2014-12-03.

[58] Rauff Hakeem Facebook page, retrieved 2014-12-11. The official webpage also offers some of the speeches that Hakeem has made at international conferences. For example, see SLMC "Responsibility to Protect: Asian-African Perspectives", retrieved 2014-12-11.

[59] SLMC "A Pen Portrait of Our National Leader – Abdul Rauff Hakeem", retrieved 2014-12-03. And SLMC "Inaugural Oration at the KC Kamalasabeyson Memorial Lecture", retrieved 2014-12-03. There is also a public speech published on the same site of a Tamil political leader. See SLMC "M. Sivasithamparam Commemorative Lecture", retrieved 2014-12-03.

[60] This could also be seen on the official webpage. See SLMC "Leaders Poetry", retrieved 2014-12-03.

[61] Rauff Hakeeem's Facebook page, retrieved 2014-12-11. Some of these themes could also be observed in the SLMC's official webpage, see SLMC "Gallery", retrieved 2014-12-03.

[62] For example, www.lankamuslims.com, which was active some years after the tsunami that struck the Indian Ocean in 2004. This webpage is no longer active. C. Tuan Nazzer 2006-11-20.

[63] SLMC "Colombo District Facebook page", retrieved 2013-10-02.

Illustration 2.2 "For tomorrow's dream to come true, our tree should live with a lot of roots like a banyan tree"

me".[64] At times, the material contains personal information about the individual running for election; sometimes their occupation is highlighted, specifying that the person running as an SLMC candidate is a lawyer or a policeman, for instance.

Like the online material, the posters and pamphlet that I found while in Sri Lanka have very diverse messages. Most of the posters are election-related. There are posters with poem-like messages directed in particular towards Muslims and where Tamil script is used (see Illustration 2.2). One example of such focus on Muslims focus is visible in the pamphlet entitled *A.M. Rakeeb manifesto* (2011). It states that:

By establishing Islamic preschools, Islamic scholars will get job opportunities and create an
atmosphere where they go to school according to their own system of teaching of the
Islamic way and teacher training.[65]

The script is almost always Tamil, but there are instances where Arabic script is
used. Tamil poetry on Islamic themes is a subject taught in Islamic schools in Sri
Lanka.[66] When Arabic is used, it is often in connection with short verses from the
Qur'an, such as *bism i-llahi r-raḥmani r-raḥim* (In the name of Allah, the most
gracious, the most merciful) or *Ma sha'Allah* (God has willed it, or what God wills)
(see Illustration 2.5). There are also *dua* (supplication) verses, for example, the *dua*
used when entering a house (see Illustration 2.6). One also finds pictures, just like
on social media, of the leaders bearing distinctly Muslim attributes, such as a
Muslim *taqiyah* (cap).

There are also prints produced by the SLMC other than electoral posters that are
of interest here as they illustrate the party's claim to be the sole representative for
Sri Lankan Muslims as a unified community. One example is a poster depicting
Muslims protesting the demolition of the Dambulla Mosque (see Illustration 2.8).
However, not all posters allude to religion; some are more dedicated to the nation,
written in English, and have no religious symbols (see Illustration 2.3).

The leaders of the party, Ashraff and Hakeem, are often portrayed on these
posters. The late leader is sometimes shown wearing Muslim apparel (see Illustration
2.4). Most of the flyers and messages (often painted on walls as graffiti) have the
same basic formula: the name of the party, the tree symbol, and the number to mark
in order to indicate support for an individual who is running in an election (see
Illustration 2.7). The tree symbol merits its own analysis since it is a clear example
of constructive Muslim politics (Illustrations 2.5, 2.6, 2.7, and 2.8).

Illustration 2.3 "We are Sri Lankan"

---

[65] *A.M. Rakeeb manifesto* (2011).
[66] Mahroof 1995: 33.

Illustration 2.4 "The freedom tree of the community, resisting, Ashraff let us pray for him"

Illustration 2.5 "Mashallha, M.T.A. Jabbaar Ali"

Illustration 2.6 "Nassar Hajji, in the name of God we enter and in the name of God we go out and we trust our trust in God our Lord

Illustration 2.7   "A.L. Abdul Majeed, 11"

Illustration 2.8   "A party for Muslims"

The Tree as a Public Symbol

The tree is a central symbol for the SLMC. In the SLMC's constitution, we can read that "The symbol of the Party shall be a 'Tree' as assigned by the Commissioner of Elections", and so we learn that this symbol was given to the organization in 1988 when the SLMC was recognized as a political party.[67] However, it has since gained a religious dimension in the discourse of the party. In one pamphlet produced by the SLMC, *Signs and Greatness*, the symbol is given a divine essence; when the tree is described, it is said that it was in "God's interest that the Sri Lanka Muslim Congress Party got the sign of the tree".[68] This text was published around the year 2000, a time when Ashraff, the former leader of the SLMC, established another party, the National Unity Alliance (this party will be discussed in Chap. 4). In the foreword to *Signs and Greatness*, Ashraff, narrates how, while visiting Mecca where he performed the *hajj*, he was inspired by God and Jesus to *choose* the symbol of a tree as a sign of peace and the struggle of Muslims, and, moreover, as a sign that all the communities of Sri Lanka would be united in peace. The text continues:

> Later, in the east of Sri Lanka when we decided to participate in the state elections we needed to search for an election sign. With this in the heart, the party chose "Tirasu" sign to represent equality, justice, law, righteousness in its election campaign. [...] the sign of a "tree" as our party's logo. [...] We thought that perhaps it is God's wish that the tree should symbolize Muslim people's struggles. And this is how we accepted the sign of the "tree". [...]Why not vote for us, our party that carries the tree symbol which God gave to us, no matter which party we are going to work with during elections [...].[69]

The author hence presents what could be seen as a contradictory narrative on how the tree came to be the party's symbol. It was decided by others and "accepted", but it was also "chosen" or, rather, it was a result of fate in which there could be divine guidance in line with the claim that God is indeed active in relation to the party. The next step is to find a solid religious basis. The author turns to Islamic tradition and whatever references to trees that can be found there:

> God has promised also upon a tree that produces olive oil known as "Saithoon". This tree sign that was given to our party is blessed by a special will of God, something we are now able to realize. [...] When the prophet Noah asked God to get rid of those who disobeyed, God instructed him to grow [a] particular form of tree. [...] Once the prophet Abraham asked God for wealth. God gave the prophet a land of garden of trees, as far his eyes could see. [...] The prophet Zechariah was seeking for a place to hide from his enemies. After running away from them a long while he finally found refuge in a tree. [...] The prophet Musa [...] had a stick that comes from a tree. In the Koran, there is the question, "Musa, what is in your right hand?" In response to God's question, Musa said, "This is my protection". Through this stick which comes from the tree, came 70 different miracles. [...] We have to think of this relationship between God and the tree. If the tree symbol was not originally what we wanted, it means that the symbol is meant for us by God. [...] By using the tree sign, God saves the party. Therefore, the party can never be destroyed by any other force [...] When mother Miriam was about to give birth to Isa our prophet, God sent a tree to them.[70]

---

[67] *The Constitution of the Sri Lanka Muslim Congress*, 2000 (1986), n.p.

[68] *Signs and Greatness*, n.d., n.p. This text is authored by Jamal Abdul Majid Alim, who is presented as a member of the Muslim Congress. The text also contains a foreword by former leader Ashraff in which he explains that he has instructed Jamal Abdul Majid Alim to write it. The foreword is dated to the year 2000; the text itself has no date, however.

[69] *Signs and* Greatness, n.d., n.p.

[70] *Signs and Greatness*, n.d., n.p.

Analysis

It is apparent that there is a selective use of the Islamic "pool of resources" in the Muslim politics of the SLMC and that its role is mainly to promote an image of the party as an inclusive party for all Muslims and of its leaders as pious believers.[71] It should be noted that there is very little elaboration to be found regarding the meaning of the particular elements selected. Vagueness is the key and is related to the fact that the audience, despite the image provided of Muslims as one community, is diverse. *A political organization needs to take different centers of power into consideration: the three obvious intended audiences of the SLMC's official documents are the voters, the members, and the state. The prime example of vagueness is the references to Shari'a.* Instead of specifying the meaning of this crucial term, it is used rhetorically in relation to a Muslim audience who would agree that "following Shari'a" is indeed mandatory but who also, most likely, have quite diverse views on what this entails in practice. Thus, when economic researcher Stanley W. Samarasinghe states that the SLMC "has even committed itself to the establishment of the Sharia Law" or, like when Zackariya and Shanmugaratnam assert that the "SLMC had also promised to institute 'Islamic rule' if elected to power", they misread such references to Shari'a.[72] The constitution of the SLMC has to be contextualized. It was written in the 1980s at a time during which there was an ongoing public discussion concerning limiting the role of separate family laws for Muslims in Sri Lanka.[73] Attempts were made by the authorities to abolish these laws, and this led to strong protests among Muslim activists in Sri Lanka. Ashraff's discussion regarding protecting and implementing Shari'a law in all aspects of life should be seen against this background. That the Shari'a is a symbol for the rights of Muslims as a minority in the country is evidenced by the fact that in addressing the Shari'a there is a simultaneous acknowledgement of the secular laws of the country.

The prime role of the use of religious terminology and symbols by the SLMC is as markers of distinctiveness. There is seldom any elaboration on meaning and content that mainly has to do with distinctiveness and the unity of an imagined, nationwide Muslim community. The SLMC's leadership balances on a thin line between being accepted as representatives for all Muslims and not alienating any prospective followers, since Muslims in Sri Lanka are in many ways a heterogenic group. The more specific the discourse on what constitutes Islam is, the larger the risk of losing votes becomes. Hence, the selection of general and uncontroversial elements from the "pool of resources" is natural.

Code of Conduct appears, then, to be an anomaly in the SLMC's official documents. It is quite specific in its demands on how members should practice their religion. In this text, members get detailed directions for how they should live as

---

[71] Cf. Sadam Hussein, in Eickelman and Piscatori 2004: 63.

[72] Samarasinghe 2009: 447 and Zackariya, and Shanmugaratnam 1997.

[73] O'Sullivan 1999: 109.

proper Muslims. The document outlines an ideal that could hardly be seen as achievable in practice, at least in detail. As far as I know, no one in the party polices its implementation. So, why is it handed out to members? Why are they obligated to sign it upon becoming members? It is likely that *Code of Conduct* is connected to the process that Eickelman and Piscatori call "the objectification of Islam". There are similarities with other mass-produced *da'wa* material that started to circulate in the 1970s throughout the Muslim world.[74] Many pamphlets from that time contain this kind of list of rules for how Muslims should behave and what Islam "is" in terms of it being a clearly delimited "object". It may well be that *Code of Conduct* is a copy-paste construction or product inspired by some text belonging to this genre of widely spread *da'wa* material. Still, even though the regulations expressed in *Code of Conduct* are detailed, they are also commonplace in general descriptions of what Islam "is" and are therefore uncontroversial, like the rest of the material analyzed above.

One note should be made regarding the use of Arabic script. In the constitution, the name of the SLMC's headquarters, Darussalaam (house of peace), is written in Latin letters.[75] The script used in the Internet-based material and on the posters directed towards the general public is Arabic. The use of Arabic, not Tamil, is a way to signal "Islamicness". The posters are visual media, and the use of Arabic script, although unreadable to most Sri Lankans, can be seen in this light. It is a parallel to what the Muslim elite in Sri Lanka did in the late 1800s when they started to wear fezzes as a manifest Islamic symbol.[76]

The example of the tree symbol shows how Muslim politics can be quite innovative and creative. A symbol need not be directly part of the "pool of resources" but may easily become so. A chain of events leads up to a situation where the tree *becomes* an Islamic symbol.[77] While "trees" in general figure in Islamic scriptures, the link forged in the SLMC text between the Islamic tradition and a plant that is distinctively South Asian is an example of innovative religious imagination.[78]

The organization of the SLMC shows some interesting similarities to the Pakistani Islamist organization the Jamaat-e-Islami. The founder of the Jamaat-e-Islami was Sayyid Abul-A'la Mawdudi (d.1979), and his thoughts and ideas were widespread within the Muslim world in the 1960s–1970s. Considering the fact that Mawdudi was from the Indian subcontinent, it is not unlikely that his and the Jamaat-e-Islami's ideas spread to Sri Lanka.[79] We know that the founding leader of the SLMC, Ashraff, was part of a 1970s *da'wa* movement which is said to be have been linked to the Jamaat-e-Islami. It is therefore highly possible that the SLMC's early documents were influenced by the *objectification of* Islam. The SLMC was

---

[74] There are a number of reasons why these books started to spread at this time. For example, mass education began to increase in the Middle East. See Eickelman and Piscatori 2004.

[75] Denny 2013.

[76] Ismail 1995: 73.

[77] Eickelman and Piscatori 2004: 58.

[78] See Waines 2013.

[79] Hjärpe 2010: 131.

perhaps not trying to copy the Jamaat-e-Islami but instead was copying the discursive elements from the *da'wa* movements. The first indication of a discursive genealogy between these two organizations is the very idea that Islam can constitute the foundation of a political party within a democratic system.[80] The second indication is the elite character of the SLMC, which is similar to that of the Jamaat-e-Islami: there is an *'amir* (leader) at the top who holds most of the power and there is a hierarchical structure. The third indication is that the SLMC and the Jamaat-e-Islami both put emphasis on an active membership entailing submission to a set of pre-specified rules (*Code of Conduct*) and loyalty towards the leadership (*bay'a*).[81] The fourth indication is the affiliated bodies, such as the students' and women's organizations, which are similar to those of the SLMC's Pakistani counterpart. The last indication is the majlis-e-shoora in the SLMC, which in both cases works as a consulting assembly in the party.

While similarities thus exist, there are also important differences. Foremost among these differences is the fact that there is no aspiration within the SLMC, at least not explicitly, for political domination of Sri Lanka as a whole. There is no notion of a theocratic Islamic state. Instead, the party upholds the value of the integrity of the post-colonial state of Sri Lanka. The SLMC's choice to promote a harmonious nation is furthermore connected to the acceptance of the nation's multi-ethnic basis (the Sri Lankan nation). In the texts examined, "Muslims" are described as co-existing on the same premises as other members of the nation.

It can be noted that the category of "Sri Lankan Moors" in the national census is rarely, if ever, used by the SLMC to refer to those they claim to represent. This can be interpreted as a conscious strategy to create a more inclusive category of "Muslims" but even more importantly to connect this category of Sri Lankans to a larger worldwide Muslim nation (*umma*). Hence, the use of the term "Muslims" is part of a strengthening of an "umma-consciousness" in Sri Lanka in line with the reference to "Muslim issues" worldwide, for example, the situation in Palestine, which has become a "major element" in the symbolism of the "politics of Islam".[82] Ashraff refers to Islam and Muslims on a global level and not in relation to a specific territory (such as Sri Lanka). This focus on global issues corresponds to what political scientist Oliver Roy has referred to as the "deterritorialization of Islam", a particular feature of contemporary Islam worldwide.[83]

[80] Hjärpe 2010: 132.
[81] Hjärpe 2010: 137.
[82] Eickelman and Piscatori 2004: 146.
[83] Roy 2004: 19.

References

Primary Sources

Official Documents

A.M. Rakeeb manifesto (2011). [unspecified publisher].
Ashraff's Convention Speeches, (n.d.). Colombo: Dahrussalam Publication.
Code of Conduct. (n.d.). Colombo: Dahrussalam Publication.
The Constitution of the Sri Lanka Muslim Congress 2010 (1986). Colombo: Dahrussalam Publication.
Invitation to the 23 delegates' conference (n.d.). [unspecified publisher].
Is Jihad the Alternative? (n.d.). Colombo: Dahrussalam Publication.
Letter of appointment as area/branch organizer 2012 (n.d.) [unspecified publisher].
National United Alliance (n.d.). Colombo: Dahrussalam Publication.
Pledges, agreements, affidavits (n.d.). [unspecified publisher].
The proposal of the Sri Lanka Muslim Congress (2004). [unspecified publisher].
Signs and Greatness (n.d.). Colombo: Dahrussalam Publication.
Resolution to the conflict in the northern and eastern provinces the Muslim dimension (n.d.). [unspecified publisher].
Sri Lanka Muslim Congress 15th national convention (n.d.). [unspecified publisher].
Sri Lanka Muslim Congress program to stabilize the party from village level (n.d.) Colombo: Dahrussalam Publication.

Online Sources

Rauff Hakeem Facebook page. Retrieved December 11, 2014, from https://www.facebook.com/RauffHakeemOfficial?fref=ts.
SLMC "123rd Commemoration Oration of Alhaj Dr T B Jayah". Retrieved December 3, 2014, from http://slmc.lk/123rd-commemoration-oration-of-alhaj-dr-t-b-jayah/.
——— "A Pen Portrait of Our National Leader – Abdul Rauff Hakeem". Retrieved December 3, 2014, from http://slmc.lk/leader/leader/.
——— "Colombo district, Facebook page". Retrieved October 2, 2013, from https://www.facebook.com/groups/251493301572339/?fref=ts.
——— "Dr A.M.A. Azeez birth centenary oration". Retrieved September 30, 2013, from http://slmc.lk/leader/leaders-orations-2/dr-a-m-a-azeez-birth-centenary-oration/.
——— "Gallery" Retrieved December 3, 2014, from http://slmc.lk/gallary/.
——— "Home". Retrieved December 2, 2014, from http://slmc.lk/home/.
——— "Inaugural oration at the KC Kamalasabeyson Memorial Lecture". Retrieved December 3, 2014, from http://slmc.lk/leader/leaders-orations-2/inaugural-oration-at-the-kc-kamalasabeyson-memorial-lecture/.
——— "Keynote Address at the World Muslim Forum". Retrieved December 3, 2014, from http://slmc.lk/leader/leaders-orations-2/leading-a-minority-muslim-community-a-sri-lankan-experience/.
——— "Leaders poetry". Retrieved December 3, 2014, from http://slmc.lk/home/leaders-poetry/.
——— "M. Sivasithamparam Commemorative lecture". Retrieved December 3, 2014, from http://slmc.lk/home/leaders-poetry/.
——— "Our Achievements". Retrieved December 3, 2014, from http://slmc.lk/about-us/our-achievements/.

——— "Our History". Retrieved April 2, 2013, from http://slmc.lk/about-us/ sri-lanka-muslim-congress/.

——— "Our Objective". Retrieved September 30, 2013, from http://slmc.lk/about-us/ sri-lanka-muslim-congress-2/.

——— "Our Party". Retrieved September 30, 2013, from http://slmc.lk/about-us/our-objective/.

——— "Our Policy". Retrieved December 3, 2014, from http://slmc.lk/about-us/our-policy/.

——— "Responsibility to Protect: Asian-African Perspectives". Retrieved December 11, 2014, from http://slmc.lk/leader/leaders-orations-2/leaders-orations/.

——— "Statement by Minister of Justice and Leader of Sri Lanka Muslim Congress Rauff Hakeem". Retrieved December 11, 2014, from http://slmc.lk/media/article/ statement-by-minister-of-justice-and-leader-of-slmc-rauff-hakeem/.

——— "T B Jayah Commemoration Lecture". Retrieved December 3, 2014, from http://slmc.lk/ news/more-news/t-b-jayah-commemoration-lecture/.

Literature

Bearman, P. Th. Bianquis, C.E. Bosworth, E. van Donzel, and W.P. Heinrichs. 2006. ʿIlm. *Encyclopaedia of Islam, Second Edition*. Retrieved March 24, 2016. 2015http://reference-works.brillonline.com/entries/encyclopaedia-of-islam-2/ilm-SIM_3537. First appeared online: 2012.

Bernard, M. 2006. Idjmāʿ. *Encyclopaedia of Islam, Second Edition*. Brill Online. Retrieved January 14, 2015, from http://referenceworks.brillonline.com/entries/encyclopaedia-of-islam-2/ id-j-ma-COM_0350.

Denny, Frederick Mathewson. 2012. Umma. *Encyclopaedia of Islam, Second Edition*. Edited by: P. Bearman, Th. Bianquis, C.E. Bosworth, E. van Donzel, W.P. Heinrichs. Brill Online, 2016. Retrieved November 28, 2013, from http://referenceworks.brillonline.com/entries/ encyclopaedia-of-islam-2/umma-COM_1291. First appeared online: 2012.

———. 2013. Community and Society in the Qur'ān. *Encyclopaedia of the Qur'ān*. Brill Online. Retrieved November 28, 2013, from http://referenceworks.brillonline.com/entries/ encyclopaedia-of-the-quran/community-and-society-in-the-quran-COM_00037.

Eickelman, Dale F., and James Piscatori. 2004. *Muslim Politics*. Princeton: Princeton University Press. First edition 1996.

Graham, William A. 2013. Basmala. *Encyclopaedia of Islam, THREE*. Brill Online. Retrieved December 19, 2013, from http://referenceworks.brillonline.com/entries/ encyclopaedia-of-islam-3/basmala-COM_23497.

Hallaq, Wael. 2014. Law and the Qur'ān. *Encyclopaedia of the Qur'ān*. Brill Online. Retrieved December 2, 2014, from http://referenceworks.brillonline.com/entries/ encyclopaedia-of-the-quran/law-and-the-qur-a-n-EQCOM_00106.

Hawting, G.R.. 2013. Oaths. *Encyclopaedia of the Qur'ān*. Brill Online. Retrieved November 20, 2013, from http://referenceworks.brillonline.com/entries/encyclopaedia-of-the-quran/ oaths-COM_00138.

Hjärpe, Jan. 2010. *Islamismer*. Malmö: Gleerups Utbildning AB.

Ismail, Qadri. 1995. Unmooring Identity: The Antinomies of Elite Muslim Self-Representation in Modern Sri Lanka. In *Unmaking the Nation: The Politics of Identity and History in Modern Sri Lanka*, ed. Pradeep Jeganathan and Qadri Ismail. Social Scientists' Association: Colombo.

Lewis, B. 2006. Mashwara (a.) or Mashūra. *Encyclopaedia of Islam, Second Edition*. Brill Online. Retrieved March 2, 2012, from http://referenceworks.brillonline.com/entries/ encyclopaedia-of-islam-2/mashwara-SIM_5010.

Mahroof, M.M.M. 1995. The ʿUlamāʾ in Sri Lanka 1800–1990: Form and Function. *Journal of Islamic Studies* 6 (1): 25–50.

O'Sullivan. 1999. *Identity and Institution in Ethnic Conflict: The Muslims of Sri Lanka*. Ph.D. thesis, Oxford: Oxford University.

Reinhart A.K.. 2006. Shukr. *Encyclopaedia of Islam, Second Edition*. Brill Online. Retrieved January 16, 2015, from http://referenceworks.brillonline.com/entries/ encyclopaedia-of-islam-2/s-h-ukr-COM_1061.

Rowson, Everett K. 2014. Gossip. *Encyclopaedia of the Qurʾān*. Brill Online. Retrieved December 2, 2014, from http://referenceworks.brillonline.com/entries/encyclopaedia-of-the-quran/ gossip-EQCOM_00077.

Roy, Olivier. 2004. *Globalised Islam: The Search for a New Ummah*. London: Hurst.

Samarasinghe, S.W.R.de A. 2009. Sri Lanka: The Challenge of Postwar Peace Building, State Building, and Nation Building. *Nationalism and Ethnic Politics* 15: 436–461.

Tyan, E. 2012. Bayʿa. *Encyclopaedia of Islam, Second Edition*. (eds.) Brill Online. Retrieved 24 March 2016 http://referenceworks.brillonline.com/entries/encyclopaedia-of-islam-2/ baya-COM_0107.

Waines, David. 2013. Tree(s). *Encyclopaedia of the Qurʾān*. Brill Online. Retrieved November 19, 2013, from http://referenceworks.brillonline.com/entries/encyclopaedia-of-the-quran/ tree-s-SIM_00425.

Zackariya, Faizoun, and Nadarajah Shanmugaratnam. 1997. Communalism of Muslims in Sri Lanka: An Historical Perspective. In *Alternative Perspectives: A Collection of Essays on Contemporary Muslim Society*, ed. Muslim Women's Research and Action Forum. Colombo: Muslim Women's Research and Action Forum.

Chapter 3
Narratives of the Party

Abstract This chapter is based on interviews conducted with members of the SLMC leadership. The interviews are categorized and analyzed according to different themes. Firstly, informants' views of the earlier history of the SLMC are presented. Thereafter follow their views on: the organization itself, on women, on the present political situation, and on the role of Islam in the party.

Keywords Muslim politics · Islam · Muslims · Sri Lanka · Sri Lanka Muslim Congress · Pragmatic politics · Religion and politics

The Genesis of the Party

The civil war is the reason most of the interviewed leaders cite for the genesis of the SLMC. General Secretary Hasen Ali, for example, stated that:

> The eastern provinces were infested with terrorist activities and [...] about 16 Tamil outfits were operating in those areas and most [...] Muslim youths joined the Tamil groups. They took to arms [...] without knowing their identity, because they were also talking Tamil, and they were also categorized under the Tamil-speaking people, and generally the Tamil-speaking people were portrayed as a discord in this country. [...] So, in 1984. the armed Tamil groups, they were gradually infiltrating the Muslim areas.[1]

Ali, as well as the majority of other members interviewed, claimed that the main reason for starting the SLMC was to stop Muslim youths, youths who did not know their (true) "identity", from getting involved in Tamil guerilla activities According to Ali, then, Muslims, although they may themselves be unaware of it, are unique in their identity and are distinct from non-Muslim Tamil-speaking citizens. The SLMC would hence create awareness of this as a political party. Ali stated that "We had to

---

[1] Hasen Ali, 2013-02-11. I also received similar responses from, for example, HC member 1, 2013-02-17; HC member 3, 2013-02-09; HC member 5, 2013-02-18; HC member 7, 2013-02-18; HC member 8, 2013-02-19; HC member 9, 2013-02-17; HC member 10, 2013-02-19; HC member 13, 2013-02-22; HC member 15, 2013-02-15; and HC member 16, 2013-02-16.

© Springer Nature Switzerland AG 2019
A. Johansson, *Pragmatic Muslim Politics*,
https://doi.org/10.1007/978-3-030-12789-3_3

put a stop to this, and we had to give a political leadership for the Muslim youths".[2]
What was at stake was the integrity of the nation of Sri Lanka:

> This is a democratic country. If this has been a country ruled by military or some other
> dictatorship of course we have to fight by taking arms. [...] We are minorities, and we are
> not asking for a separate country. [...] We only want to live peacefully in our areas, preserv-
> ing our own identity, culturally, politically, ethnically. We want to live peacefully on our
> traditional land. That was the reason why it started.[3]

Ali's starting point in talking about Muslims concerns certain geographical areas
and events occurring there. These areas, located in southeastern Sri Lanka, were
described by him as "Muslim".

One aspect mentioned by several of my informants concerning the genesis of the
party was the role played by the *'ulama*. A.L.M. Kaleel, a formally trained religious
scholar and a member of the high command, was part of the SLMC from the start,
and according to him the religious scholars had to be careful when they spoke about
SLMC politics:

> We stood near the Mosque. There were stones, and we stood on top on them and spoke. All
> the people were attracted to this, [...] and people thought that there was nobody to put our
> things forward, and since the 'ulama's did it, people liked it.[4]

The reason they had to stand on stones to preach was because loudspeakers had
been banned by the LTTE – if the members of the SLMC had used them, they would
have been shot.[5] Kaleel as well as others described the first members of the SLMC
as martyrs, stressing the dangerous situations they put themselves in as they strove
to form a political party: "Muslims were killed, abducted, shot dead. Among the
Muslims, there was a feeling that we were unsafe".[6]

Religious scholars, according to my informants, gave their blessings to Ashraff
in forming the party.[7] Ali stated that as a symbolic gesture the founding members
signed the document of agreement in blood, a gesture that appears odd given the fact
that blood in Islamic contexts is generally considered ritually impure. Many of the
members of the SLMC received threats afterwards, which Ali claimed came from
Tamil organizations. According to him, SLMC members soon found themselves
under attack by the armed Tamil groups, perhaps because they were successful.
Some of the Muslims who were involved in the Tamil groups changed sides and
joined the SLMC.[8]

---

[2] Hasen Ali, 2013-02-11.

[3] Hasen Ali, 2013-02-11.

[4] A.L.M. Kaleel, 2013-02-08.

[5] A.L.M. Kaleel, 2013-02-08.

[6] A.L.M. Kaleel, 2013-02-08. I also got similar responses from, for example, HC member 9, 2013-02-17 and HC member 5, 2013-02-18.

[7] Hasen Ali, 2013-02-11.

[8] Hasen Ali, 2013-02-11. Here, Ali gave an example of a Muslim leader (Rafi) who changed sides when he and Ashraff convinced him to do so. That person was later killed by armed Tamil groups.

The narratives of the party's earlier years are filled with stories about the sacrifices made by SLMC members:

> [W]e had [...] enormous problems in those areas, [...]. Ashraff was threatened, and, once, the EPRLF tried to kill him while he was driving his car [...] They visited my house several times. They wanted us to do away with these political activities. But with all that we came to this level running in the election and there they sent the letter, the threatening letter demanding withdrawal, and at that time our leader Mr. Ashraff was forced to leave from Kalmunai, taking refuge in Colombo. He couldn't come back because a lot of threats were made against him. The main threat was from the government at that time.[9]

I found this way of narrating the early history of the SLMC, with the trials and tribulations faced by the founding persons, to be common among other members with whom I spoke as well.[10]

In 1986, the SLMC became in fact a political party. At a meeting in Colombo that was only attended by a few members, Ali recalled that Ashraff held a great lecture inspired by the history of Islam, which he used as a parallel to the current situation:

> [H]e was quoting examples from the holy wars during the early Islamic period, how the Muslims overcame the enemy's plots and all that and that they won the hearts of the enemy, you know. These kinds of things, you know. He gave a lot of examples from Islamic history, and he said that we are not going to withdraw. If we withdraw now, that will be the end of the Sri Lanka Muslim Congress, and we will never be able to establish our identity, our separate identity in our area, in our traditional areas.[11]

In the internal party narratives, the notion that the time was ripe for a "Muslim" party abounds. According to A.L.M. Kaleel, the need for a Muslim voice in Sri Lanka was required, and it had to come through a new voice. Even though a recent census aided in strengthening the notion of a common Muslim identity, the need for a specific Muslim voice seemed to have grown even stronger after 1983 when the civil war started, and creating a Muslim voice in politics was one of the main reasons for forming the SLMC:

> [S]o in the majority community, the Buddhists have their own party. The problems were discussed by them. The Tamil had parties [...] They spoke on the behalf of Tamils. Even we, the Muslims, had representation. Those people were there. They were very silent. They didn't speak on the behalf of the Muslims. Since they went with majority parties, they were not able to speak on the behalf of our community [...].[12]

"If the others have parties, so should we" is a recurrent theme among the leading members of the SLMC with whom I spoke.

---

[9] Hasen Ali, 2013-02-11.

[10] For example, HC member 1, 2013-02-17; HC member 2, 2013-02-17; and HC member 5, 2013-02-18.

[11] Hasen Ali, 2013-02-11.

[12] A.L.M. Kaleel, 2013-02-08.

Organization

The national organizer, Shafeek Rajabdeen, asserted that most of the approximately 60,000 SLMC members are Muslim.[13] According to him, there are non-Muslim supporters, but they are few.[14] That the party is generally viewed as one exclusively for Muslims can be exemplified by the words of one member who expressed the reason why he personally wanted to join the SLMC: "I realized that the Muslims need a common identity".[15] Throughout the country, the party is organized on different levels. Every village and district is encouraged to have a chief organizer, and basic party units are advised on the village level.[16] There are also affiliated bodies within the district and village organizations. The national organizer, Shafeek Rajabdeen, described the activities that take place on a grassroots level:

> We have lot of poverty programs and programs for underprivileged people. As soon as a mother is pregnant, we start a milk program that provides this mother with food and so on. When the child grows up to a certain age, they are given free education, free books, free uniforms, free school, and when the child reaches their teens, they earn free scholarships from the government. These programs also look after streetlights and waterlines and so on. Also, when you're dead, we take care of the burial ground free of charge, and [...] all these services are given to the poor Muslims.[17]

These social activities, directed towards "poor" and "underprivileged" Muslims, are important in the party's construction of a common Muslim identity and itself as the champion of Muslims.[18] Rajabdeen continued by saying:

> The SLMC was formed for a cause, and today we have achieved some of this cause. On the road, we see that we want to lead our people to freedom, education and above the limits of poverty. We are sent into this world to guide people on the correct path. [...] What is the benefit of being an SLMC member? So, if you became a member and serve under me, I will take care for you. I will give you all the benefits, like machines and the whole thing. We give you footballs. We give you cricket material and educational programs.[19]

This statement provides an important insight into how the party officials view the SLMC as the sole representative of Sri Lankan Muslims. To receive the benefits as a Muslim, you have to be a member of the SLMC, and to be a member you have to subscribe to the party guidelines. Rajabdeen refered to a metaphor from the Qur'an – *al-sirat al-mustaqim*, which can be understood as meaning "to guide people on the truthful path" – when he talks about the role of the SLMC. This metaphor is to be found in the first surah of the Qur'an, and it is generally considered to be a central

---

[13] Shafeek Rajabdeen, 2013-02-07.

[14] This is also confirmed by M.G.M. Rizvie, 2013-02-07, and HC member 6, 2013-02-12.

[15] HC member 14, 2013-02-18.

[16] Shafeek Rajabdeen, 2013-02-07.

[17] Shafeek Rajabdeen, 2006-11-20.

[18] Cf. Osella and Osella 2009.

[19] Shafeek Rajabdeen, 2006-11-20.

idea in the Islamic tradition.[20] In response to my question about why the benefits are restricted to members of the party, the answer I received was evasive:

[W]e are not in the position to guide ourselves. We are dependent on the majority, and we are unemployed. We are poor. We are not in the army. We are not in the navy. We are the community that has no tomorrow. We have to be loud because we are not sure about tomorrow, so we live for today.[21]

Rajabdeen stressed that the way of organizing and helping people is the reason why the SLMC has become a successful party:

[W]e have won over Muslim voters from the UNP. Today, we are proud to say that we have political grassroots-level backing of about 40,000 SLMC supporters within the district of Colombo. Also, because we come from the grassroots level's families, and we have a social program that from the time that you are in your mother's womb to the time that you are dead looks after you, and we are very humorous when we talk about this program. We say from the time you have a need to the time you resurrect, we look after you.[22]

Rajabdeen stated that the SLMC has won over many Muslim voters because of these programs. There are also affiliated bodies, such as the Ulema Congress, that are a part of the SLMC and work all over the country:

These affiliated bodies are:

The Ulema Congress
The Undergraduates Congress
The Youth Congress
The Ladies Congress
The Teachers Congress
The Farmers Congress
The Liberation Workers Congress
The Port Workers Congress
The Traders Congress
The Professionals Congress[23]

The goal of these organizations is, according to Rajabdeen, to correct the "shortcomings of the community", meaning Muslims, but what these needs are is not something always specified by the SLMC.[24]

An important part of the SLMC's claim to represent Muslims is to incorporate religious scholars into the party's ranks. Rajabdeen stated that main role of the Ulema Congress is to inform the party of the grievances of Muslims in Sri Lanka:

[W]e got the Youth Congress, the Ladies Congress, and we have different sub-bodies in the high command. The main role of the Ulema Congress is to meet every month [...] to express the view of the Muslim community. Because they are the people who know the shortcomings on the grassroots level, they are the people who are connected to the mosque in the Muslim-populated areas [...] They are the people who choose who are the rightful people,

---

[20] See Monnot: 2015.

[21] Shafeek Rajabdeen, 2006-11-20.

[22] Shafeek Rajabdeen, 2006-11-20.

[23] *The Constitution of the Sri Lanka Muslim Congress*, 2000 (1986) n.p.

[24] Shafeek Rajabdeen, 2013-02-06.

the trustees of the mosques. They are the local leaders of the people. They are not political; the 'ulama are the bodies that guide the people in their religious lives.[25]

The affiliated bodies are, according Rajabdeen, most active during election times. In my interview with him, he asserted that, "we at times of election […] go and meet the 'ulama […]. The 'ulama communities have connections all over the country […]".[26] As the leader of the Ulema Congress, the task of H.M.M. Ilyas is to unite the country's 'ulama under the SLMC, so that they, in turn, may mobilize the Muslim population to vote for the party.[27]

There is also a tendency to focus on the SLMC as a *national* party. The only connection with Muslim parties elsewhere in the world that my informants mention is one with the Muslim League in India. According to Rajabdeen, this limitation is a party policy:

We have no foreign affiliations of any kind […] Politics is in our motherland […] We just have a "hello, hello" connection, and we go there to discuss their problems, and they discuss our problems. We discuss especially in India the Muslim League. The Sri Lanka Muslim Congress has nothing to do with the Muslim League […] We meet and when we go there, their leaders invite us for a discussion and they want to know what is happening here. Then we ask them if they have a problem there and how do you resolve that problem in India? […] Our party is a very independent party. We don't want to [support] Muslim parties, for example, the Brotherhood of Islam or something.[28]

The mention of the "Brotherhood of Islam" is in fact a reference to the established party the Muslim Brotherhood, which is mainly active in Egypt. At the time of the interviews, there was an ongoing public discussion on Muslim terror organizations such as al-Qaʻida and the Taliban.[29] This may be the reason why Rajabdeen emphasized the lack of connections the SLMC has with Muslim organizations outside of Sri Lanka.

Women in the Party Organization

Ashraff's death in a helicopter crash in 2000 set in motion an internal political power struggle within the SLMC. Ashraff's widow, Ferial Ashraff, aspired for the leadership position, but one branch favored the general secretary, Rauff Hakeem. In the end, it was Hakeem who would lead the party into the new millennium. Ferial Ashraff became the leader of the National Unity Alliance (NUA), a party (discussed in the next chapter) that her late husband had created. The power struggle is still part of the internal discourse of the party, affecting, for example, the issue of female leadership. According to one of my informants, a woman cannot lead the SLMC:

---

[25] Shafeek Rajabdeen, 2013-02-06.
[26] Shafeek Rajabdeen, 2013-02-06.
[27] H.M.M. Ilyas, 2013-02-11.
[28] Shafeek Rajabdeen, 2013-02-06.
[29] Bandara 2013.

> [I]n our religion, the rising up of women was not accepted, not accepted by everybody, especially, you might say, Pakistan, Benazir [Bhutto], but it is totally different there than here. In Sri Lanka, the religious component is very strong so when Ferial came, no one was welcoming her, that's why we went separate ways.[30]

However, there were also other leading members I talked to who supported the notion of Ferial Ashraff being in a leadership position.[31]

Generally, the role of women within the SLMC is limited to their own organization within the overall party structure. Very rarely do women run for parliament under the SLMC banner although I was informed that there were a couple of women who were running for the SLMC in a different election.[32] Only one woman serves the high command.

I interviewed the female representative in the high command, Sithy Rifaya. She is also the leader of the Ladies Congress. Rifaya claimed that the Ladies Congress is mostly active during election time and noted that the SLMC had strong support among poor women.[33] I visited one of the Ladies Congress meetings, which was held at the SLMC headquarters; it was an event for impoverished Muslim women who were given sewing machines. On that occasion, Rifaya said:

> From time to time, I summon women for meetings, and I do a little bit of counseling, and we try to show them the benefit of this. To reach the poor, you sometimes have to hand them something, and they will come. At the end of our meeting, it is like an open forum for questions. It could be a personal issue. Sometimes, it could be that someone wants their child admitted to a school, or another woman says that I want a job for my family. There are basic requirement in lives that push them to take a step into politics.[34]

Charity bestowed by the SLMC is for Muslims only, and in the party's internal discourse those who benefit are furthermore described as "poor Muslims". Rifaya told me that she used to work with all communities but has come to devote herself entirely to the SLMC. By limiting charity in this manner, one could claim that the SLMC is true to its delimitation of "Muslims" as a particular group.

Being Muslim

As has been noted above, the SLMC, claims to represent Sri Lankan Muslims as a distinct group, a third and separate ethnicity on the Sri Lankan island alongside Tamils and Sinhalese. This is also evident from the interviews, albeit these do display some confusion as to which exactly are the distinguishing traits. A quote that sums this up pretty well comes from the general secretary:

---

[30] HC member 12, 2013-02-07.

[31] For example, HC member 17, 2013-02-12, and HC member 3, 2013-02-09.

[32] The information was written in shorthand, and the member could not give any names. HC member 23, 2013-02-13.

[33] Sithy Rifaya, 2006-11-24.

[34] Sithy Rifaya, 2006-11-24.

I mean, we are Moors, [...], not by religion, but by race we are Moors, like the Tamils are another race and Sinhalese another race. I said don't confuse the language we are speaking. We belong to a different race [...] and Tamil, of course, they are fighting for their rights [...].[35]

The essentialist notion underlying this statement is interesting, with its reference to the concept of "race" to characterize Muslims. It implies that Muslims are born Muslims and will stay Muslims. Muslim is furthermore an inclusive category, transcending other differences, which is the reason why the SLMC focuses on it.

[T]here were two Muslim groups here. One was Moors and the other Malays [...]. I mean in a sizable amount, you know. So, when we go with the Moors' banner, then we couldn't accommodate the Malays into that [...]. That is why they change to Muslim. It is not religion, actually, so the Sri Lanka Muslim Congress is really the Sri Lanka Muslim ethnic community congress.[36]

Moors and Malays are different, but they become one under the banner of the SLMC and its Muslim politics. Ali does admit that "Muslim" is not a matter of specific religious ideas or a particular stand regarding dogma. Being "Muslim" is a matter of formal religious affiliation, not theology.[37]

There are certain markers that do play an important role in defining Sri Lankan Muslims as a group. One such marker is linguistic. One informant claimed that even though most of the Muslims speak Tamil, it is a different form of Tamil that is exclusively Muslim and thus serves as a signal for separation: "we use Arabic words. When we are talking to Tamil people, they will understand that we are Muslim".[38] He refers to this form of Tamil as "Arabic Tamil", and it includes not only religious terminology but also the use of special words (different from Hindu Tamil), for example, for family members.

One part of the public image of the SLMC as a party for Muslims in general is the way in which its highest leaders are portrayed, both the previous one and the current one. Ashraff is often described as a person deeply involved in both politics and Islam. According to one of his associates, he strongly opposed the "Muslim" alternative party, the Socialist Islamic Front, on the grounds of socialism being incompatible with Islam.[39] He organized a demonstration in 1969 against the burning of the al-'Aqsa mosque in Jerusalem.[40] Ashraff is described as having been committed to Muslim welfare and Islam locally and globally. His knowledge of religion is said to have been extensive, and he served as president of the Sri Lankan Islamic Student Federation.[41] Ashraff is also said to have been influenced by both Sufism

---

[35] Hasen Ali, 2013-02-11.

[36] Hasen Ali, 2013-02-11.

[37] Hasen Ali, 2013-02-11.

[38] HC member 5, 2013-02-18.

[39] Athambawa, 2013-02-14.

[40] Athambawa, 2013-02-14.

[41] O'Sullivan 1999: 252.

and reformist ideas.[42] These narratives about Ashraff are very much alive in the party, and even though he is gone, the memory of Ashraff as a devout Muslim still provides legitimacy for the SLMC.[43] The current leader, Hakeem, does not have the same credentials in the internal discourse as the memory of Ashraff does. However, Hakeem is portrayed as a pious Muslim having extensive knowledge of Islamic theology.[44]

The Current Situation in Sri Lanka

When I asked members of the high command what they considered to be the most important question for the SLMC, their answers were surprisingly diverse. However, the answers had one thing in common: they all framed them as "Muslim". Hence, one topic was the status and performance of Muslim schools, another was the development of Muslim-dominated areas, for example, in terms of infrastructure, and still others were Muslims as internally displaced persons, and a need for a separate Muslim administrative "unit".[45] In all of those issues, the Sri Lankan government was cast as the main adversary, and it was characterized as being partisan in relation to Sinhala-speaking Buddhists:

> After the war, there is kind of a religious hegemony that is being built up now supported by the powers [the government]. It is an overdrive of trying to enforce it on everybody to now, look here, this is a Sinhala Buddhist land, and the rest have to be subservient to the Sinhala Buddhist, and if you are subservient you will be looked after and you will be comfortable. We know what rights you need, and we know what is good for you [...]. That seems to be the motto of the current government, and there are a lot of tensions working now after the war. There are a lot of anti-Muslim activities as well going on totally unchecked and in a country that is totally, I mean, government has total control over every inch of the territory of Sri Lanka right now [...].[46]

The partisan nature of the government becomes the reason why the SLMC demands a separate Muslim administrative unit (as discussed in the previous chapter). During the last election in the eastern province, the SLMC signed a Memorandum of Understanding with the government:

> [W]e can't be thinking of winning those things in the opposition at the time when the government needs our help. For instance, we formed the eastern province government. We signed some agreements with this government, a Memorandum of Understanding, where all these things are mentioned, you know, so when the ethnic problem is solved, when they come to that level, they have to accept our request. One of the items is that they have to

---

[42] Athambawa, 2013-02-14.

[43] HC member 2, 2013-02-17.

[44] For example, in an interview with HC member 1, 2013-02-17; HC member 4, 2013-02-18; and HC member 8, 2013-02-19.

[45] HC member 21, 2013-02-19; HC member 7, 2013-02-18; HC member 12, 2013-02-07; HC member 16, 2013-02-15; HC member 3, 2013-02-09.

[46] HC member 17, 2013-02-12.

carve out a separate southeastern province for the Muslim community in the eastern province. It may be a non-contiguous one, but there will be [...] nine provinces in this country. So we have seven provinces dominated by the Sinhala community, one by the Tamils, right, that's the northern province, and the eastern province is neither Tamil, Muslim nor Sinhala. All three communities live there in almost equal proportion, but the latest census shows that the Muslims are a majority in the eastern province, [...] Ampara is a Sinhalese-dominated area and [...] the government agent will always be a Sinhalese, [...] Similarly, in Trincomale Muslims are also a majority, but a Sinhala man will be in control. This is why we want some form of autonomy, not that we want a division in this country, no, we are not for that. We want to live peacefully, managing our own affairs, with our own people, maintaining our separate cultural things, identity and all. That is the reason why we are fighting politically.[47]

According to my interpretation, the claim for a separate Muslim administration unit essentially has its foundation in land issues; at least this was one of the most common answers I got from the members when I asked about it. According to the SLMC members I interviewed, the government of Sri Lanka gives land to the Sinhalese-speaking population, and the land taken is perceived as being "Muslim": "The government is forcefully taking our lands, and they are not resettling any Muslims or Tamils, only Sinhalese".[48] This is a common understanding of the government's land policy: land that has been owned by families for generations now becomes occupied by foreigners. State-sponsored land colonization has been going on since the early 1900s, and it has increased since independence was achieved. Between 1911 and 1981, the Sinhala population in the Ampara District, for example, increased from 7% to 37.7%.[49] The matter of land distribution was mentioned by many of my informants as the most important post-war issue for the SLMC:

Policy is, you see, the first issue of reconciliation with the understanding that in a multi-ethnic country identity politics has to be taken forward with the understanding of proper give and take, where we will be able to pursue our goal of achieving the redress of the grievances we have suffered over the time of conflict, even starting from the time of independence. [...] In the new scenario, it is important for the Muslim community to devise and rethink strategies to achieve national unity and in the meantime also fight for our community existence problems where we have to collectively mobilize the strength of the Muslims, [...] National political parties have failed the Muslims over a period of time, and there is a lot of common ground with other minorities on achieving and being marginalized from mainstream politics. That is land and land distribution – every sector, we have to fight for our cause, and then still there are many areas which have not been addressed properly. There are certain projects being implemented [...] They make it out as if it is for the common good, stating that it is not for the common good, instead Sinhalese are getting land. [...] so in [...] a multiplicity of ways, we are addressing the existential issues of the community.[50]

---

[47] Hasen Ali, 2013-02-11.

[48] HC member 1, 2013-02-17. I also got similar responses from, for example, HC member 10, 2013-02-19; HC member 12, 2013-02-07; and HC member 20, 2013-02-16. Regarding land colonization, see Korf 2006.

[49] See O'Sullivan 1999.

[50] Rauff Hakeem, 2013-02-23.

Another important part in my informants' construction of Sri Lankan Muslims as a group is the external threats perceived as being directed against it, particularly in the guise of the Bodu Bala Sena. This Buddhist Sinhala nationalistic organization is mentioned as one of the reasons why the SLMC is needed to protect Muslims.[51] The Bodu Bala Sena (BBS) is supposedly attacking Muslim interests in particular, including Muslim economic interests, such as the No Limit clothing chain and halal certification.[52] The anti-Muslim propaganda that the BBS spreads serves to strengthen the SLMC's *raison d'être*, that is, it constitutes a parallel to the situation that existed during the civil war. Moreover, some of my informants accused the government of secretly supporting the BBS:

> [R]ight now, the Buddhist monks are threatening the stability or existence of the Muslims. After Rajapaksa defeated the terrorists, the president is following the principle of one nation, one people [...]. The minority peoples could not accept this theory [...] There are three minorities in this country, Tamils, Muslims and Christians. They have different cultures [...] He brought this theory [...] because he doesn't want to keep the rights of the minority. [...] It is said that the government is behind these protests, against the mosque and halal [...] As far as the minority is concerned, the rules and regulations of the land are not being observed [...] The monks that destroyed the Dambulla mosque, why were they not arrested?[53]

Not all of the people with whom I spoke, however, blame the government for the Bodu Bala Sena's actions. Some say that there are external forces behind this Buddhist group, naming, for instance, the American state or Norway, the latter being mentioned due to its vital role in peace negotiations in Sri Lanka.[54] One informant said: "We are getting controlled by another set of uniforms", hence claiming that the government had replaced Tamil militants.[55] The role of Tamil militants in providing the Muslim ethnicity with a boundary has thus now been taken over by a new enemy – a nationalistic Buddhist organization. New enemies seem to create "new" friends: one member said in an interview that it is important to look after all the minorities in the country and consequently transform the SLMC into a party that safeguards the rights of all the communities in Sri Lanka, including Sinhala- speaking Buddhists.[56] In several of the interviews, the SLMC's relationship to the government is presented as being a troubled one. The then-powerful government (with two-thirds of the seats in parliament) that the SLMC was a part of has an advantage over the opposition. The SLFP government was regularly accused of trying to divide the SLMC by offering ministerial posts to members of parliament in order to gain their support:

---

[51] HC member 9, 2013-02-17.

[52] HC member 17, 2013-02-12; HC member 9, 2013-02-17; HC member 13, 2013-02-22; HC member 18, 2013-02-20; and HC member 15, 2013-02-25.

[53] HC member 2, 2013-02-17.

[54] For example, in interviews with HC member 22, 2013-02-14; and HC member 12, 2013-02-07.

[55] HC member 11, 2013-02-13.

[56] HC member 3, 2013-02-09.

[T]hrough the eighteenth amendment, the government wanted the Muslim Congress to join them. Rauff Hakeem and the High Command then made the decision to join forces with the government. The leader, Rauff Hakeem, he made a speech in the high command and said "I am not prepared, and I don't like to join the government, but considering the present situation in this country, and the Muslim community especially in the party, we have no way otherwise of joining with the government".[57]

Informants describe themselves as puppets in a political "game" that they cannot win.

Islam

Scripture and Law

The actual ideological role of the Islamic scriptures, that is, the Qur'an and the hadiths, within the party's ideology is not altogether clear from the interviews, apart from their serving as a sort of "general inspiration". In the words of one of my informants:

> The SLMC's guidelines [...] are based on the Qur'an. Some people don't believe it, but we go by the principles of Islam. For example, in decision-making, it is not done by showing hands. It is done by discussion at length with people, the 'amir, the leader making the decision [...].[58]

Certain key concepts taken from the "pool of resources", however, have a firm grounding. The decision-making principle that Rajabdeen is referring to is commonly known as *mahsoora* (*shura*), and this principle is something that most of my interviewees addressed (as will be discussed further below). Ali, the general secretary, explained that the *shura* practice is unique in Sri Lankan politics:

> Islam has a lot of politics within it. Without politics, there is no Islam [...] because we believe that the Prophet Muhammad was one of the noble politicians [...]. That is our belief [...]. Now, in our constitution, it says [...] that we are guided by the Qur'an and hadiths [...], so our constitution begins with that. No other Muslim political party has this in their constitution.[59]

Ali is quite explicit in claiming that the SLMC is not one-hundred percent religion- based, but nevertheless one-hundred percent ethnically-based.[60] The fact that the SLMC does refer to the Qur'an and the hadiths in its constitution seems to be more important than dwelling further upon what these scriptural sources actually contain in terms of beliefs, practices, rules, and regulations. Some of the members

---

[57] HC member 5, 2013-02-18. I also got similar responses from, for example, HC member 12, 2013-02-07; and HC member 17, 2013-02-12.

[58] Shafeek Rajabdeen, 2013-02-07.

[59] Hasen Ali, 2013-02-11.

[60] Hasen Ali, 2013-02-11.

argued that following Islam is basically a private matter and not a political one relevant for the SLMC apart from some general guidelines:

> [W]ith an Islamic concept this party is established by the law. We have to follow the Qur'an
> and hadiths. That does not mean fundamentalism. You know what Islam says, Islam says
> that it is politics also, so you have to follow Islam in politics […] It is to do work for the
> poor people and work for the voters. […] Some people get into politics. They use the
> SLMC's platform. They don't know what Islamic politics [are]. We have to, as I told you,
> reset SLMC policy. We have to change the current policy.[61]

In fact, it appears that the informants were rather reluctant to view the policy of the SLMC as one of furthering a specifically Islamic religious agenda, and this reluctance was connected to the fact that Sri Lanka is a multi-ethnic, multi-religious nation:

> The basic policy is based on the Qur'an and hadiths. In this country, it is very difficult to
> follow this fully […] You can't adopt all these things, you know. This is a Buddhist country
> […] All the problems' solutions can be found in the Qur'an […].[62]

Among my informants, there is an apparent separation made between religion and politics and a limiting of the influence of religion to the private sphere, which could be seen as being rather noteworthy for a religious party.

> OK, religion is something, politics is something, […] So when we join the government with
> the majority Sinhala parties, and when we work with non-Muslim governments, we apply
> the study of laws for ourselves. If the government says you can drink, you can eat pork, we
> do not do that. We have our laws and norms, and we use them. We apply our system to our
> community, the Christians apply theirs, the Tamils apply theirs, the Buddhists apply theirs.
> So there is no interference. No one is not asking us to not practice it […].[63]

The "study of law" that is mentioned refers to the above-mentioned Muslim family law that plays an important symbolic role in terms of the acceptance of Muslims as a distinct group in Sri Lanka. One member of the high command asserted that the reference to Islam in the constitution actually is a tactical move with the sole purpose of getting more votes and in this way it really is political.[64]

From the interviews, it becomes clear that the downplaying of Islam is a matter of pragmatic expedience. Islam cannot be put forward as a general solution to society's problems in Sri Lanka. Arguing for non-interference in the internal affairs of Muslims is as far as one could go, according to my informants.

When it comes to referring to Islam, the Qur'an or the Prophet in rhetoric, some of the individuals with whom I spoke were fairly open in claiming that using religious terms and symbols was a tactical choice:

---

[61] HC member 4, 2013-02-18. Sometimes, it is only recognized in the interviews and not developed further as it was in the interviews with HC member 20, 2013-02-16; and HC member 22, 2013-02-14.

[62] HC member 21, 2013-02-19.

[63] Shafeek Rajabdeen, 2013-02-07.

[64] HC member 21, 2013-02-19.

[W]hen they started the Muslim Congress, most of the Muslims supported the Sinhalese parties [...], so that was introduced as a tactic of our leader in the name of Muslims. [...] only Muslims are supporting us. If I am Muslim, I must accept the Qur'an and hadiths [...], so if we want to do politics among the Muslims and attract the Muslim community [...], that is it. [...] We can't not do Qur'anic politics.[65]

Another member stated that the role of religion in the party, when it comes to body politics, is basically nil. It is all about religion as an ethnic marker:

[O]ur party is [a] community-based party. This is a community-based party, not a religion-based party. This party in Sri Lanka is the voice of the Muslims, so we are not religious. The religion is Islam, Muslims, but we are not religious, we look at the community.[66]

Some of my informants regarded this view on references to Islam as merely a surface feature of the party as problematic and criticized the leadership for it. According to them, the lack of Islam constituted a change in party policies. Islam had had a more vital role during the late leader Ashraff's time: "We are not allowed to do Shari'a politics here. In Ashraff's, time we used to do communal politics the Islamic way. Under Hakeem, it is practical politics with an Islamic label".[67] Shari'a politics is in this sense equal to what historian of religions Bruce Lincoln labels "a maximalistic view" on the role of religion in society.[68] Hanifa, one of the religious scholars in the party, said to me:

The Sri Lanka Muslim Congress was established by the late leader Ashraff. When he established it, he said that this party will be on the basis of the Qur'an and hadiths. This is written in the constitution when the multi-ethnic people live in a country where there is ethnic difference. At these times, these ethnic differences are becoming very sharp. [...] Now, the Muslim Congress is having difficulties because of this. The president of the party and the important people in the high command [...], the people that are following this party, most of them are not doing anything that is against Islam. They act in a way that is suitable for Islam. However, with the passage of time, things have to be renewed, because people are slacking off. They become weak. Compared to the time of the founding president of the Sri Lanka Muslim Congress, we now find people are slackening off or weakening in regard to certain things, like the religious matters. It has to be renewed and reintroduced. I think that the current president and the people with him have the duty of renewing these things.[69]

Hanifa views his own role as that of a party guardian, ensuring an authentic influence from Islamic tradition. Islam should be reinforced in the party, which, according to his understanding, means bringing back religious considerations when making political decisions.

In regard to my question of what Shari'a means when members use expressions such as "Shari'a politics", Shafeek Rajabdeen was clear in expressing his opinion that the concept extends beyond the already existing legislation in Sri Lanka, with

[65] HC member 5, 2013-02-18.

[66] HC member 12, 2013-02-17. I also got similar responses from, for example, HC member 15, 2013-10-08.

[67] HC member 8, 2013-02-19.

[68] See Lincoln 2003.

[69] Hanifa, 2013-02-24.

Muslims being allowed to follow Islamic legal tradition in matters of family law. He claimed that Shariʿa designated a total code of laws on all levels of society. He did not, however, further explain the details of this assertion, which leaves the matters of what the SLMC's overall views of Shariʿa and its role in national legislation ideally should be unclear.

Some informants did claim that the notion of introducing Islamic ideals into politics has become weaker over time. In the words of one of them:

> We are the party of Muslims, but we are not doing any Islamic things. They are not doing any work for […] Islam […] There was a boy that went abroad and won the hadith competition. They gave that little boy a donation or something. That was the only thing that the Muslim Congress has done for Islam. […].[70]

More than once during my interviews, the lack of a policy on how to implement Islamic ideals in practice was the focus of criticism directed at the party leadership or at Hakeem, the leader. Hakeem himself had the following to say on the issue:

> You know the Muslim Congress is a party that believes in the positive features of political Islam, but, being a minority, we have no agenda to impose Islamic solutions onto every part of life. It [Islam] ideologically remains the core of our policy platform, but we are cautious and careful not to be promoting that as general policy for everything […], but we don't miss out on offering it as a vital alternative […] Even on the economy side […], interest-free banking has its own growth […] in the non-Muslim countries with a large Muslim population, and it has had a very satisfying effect as an alternative banking system. […] and various mainstream banks have also adopted their own window for Islamic banking […] You see, the Islamic principle has its own system […] which has its salutary effect, so we have never failed to advance or to offer it as an alternative, you know, if things don't work out well in other systems. […] We have a long history of personal laws which are based on Shariʿa principles, and we have our own system for marriages, heritages, and other things, which has been recognized by our legal system as well […] We have our courts and so on.[71]

In this quote, it becomes clear that the discourse on the role of Islam is more about what *is* than about what *could be,* in terms of any political vision. Indeed, Hakeem claims that there is no need to provide specifically "Islamic" solutions to social or political problems that Sri Lanka as a nation is facing. This is of course a reasonable position, given that only a small minority of the country's inhabitants are Muslims, and perhaps only a minority among them would care for any large-scale Islamization policies. The context makes any theocratic ambitions rather unfeasible, and none of the informants actually openly embrace such ambitions. They all support the notion of a secular state and a multi-cultural, multi-religious Sri Lanka.

---

[70] HC member 9, 2013-02-17.

[71] Rauff Hakeem, 2013-02-23.

Majlis-e-shoora and Shura

While Islamic tradition appears to be rather marginal when it comes to my informants' views on the SLMC's involvement in national day-to-day politics, Muslim
politics is particularly important in internal discourses on organization, authority,
and power. Some central practices in the organization are the council of Majlis-e-
shoora, *shura*, and the ideal of consensus (*'ijma*).[72]

General Secretary Ali emphasized to me the importance of Islamic values (via
Code of Conduct) and Islamic traditions in the internal structure of the party. He
stated that the Ulema Congress has a special position within the Majlis-e-shoora.
The party's decisions regarding various issues are made by the high command,
which is a council formed of the party leadership and the Majlis-e-shoora.[73] The
latter body also includes other members from the All Ceylon Jaamiyathul Ulema,
one of the councils of Muslim religious scholars in Sri Lanka.[74] It furthermore contains retired members of the decision-making body of the party who then continue
to be actively involved in party activities. The current president of Majlis-e-shoora
is Moulavi A.L.M. Kaleel.

When the leader of the party has issues that he wants to discuss with the Majlis-
e-shoora, the members assemble and discuss a common response. One such issue
that came up recently concerned the occurrence of burning effigies at demonstrations. Kaleel told me that:

> When we make a decision, we look if it is compatible with Islam, […] This is what I am
> going to do. Is it right or wrong? […] They wanted to organize a strike, do some picketing,
> […], then they make a figure of the president, and finally they burn the figure of the presi-
> dent […] He [leader] will come to ask me if it is acceptable to do something like that
> according to Islam. And we can't accept that, because Islam doesn't allow [it] […]. We have
> stopped a lot of demonstrations like this, after jummah prayers. And in some villages, they
> put stones or wood on the road. Islam does not allow people to block the road with these
> things; Islam says to clear them.[75]

One of the tasks of the Majlis-e-shoora would then appear to be safeguarding the
internal order of the party, with the help of interpretations of Islam. Exactly what
interpretation was used to reach the conclusion that spontaneous roadblocks are un-
Islamic was not explained further to me. The role of the Ulema Congress as a safeguard for the "Islamicness" of the SLMC was stressed by the informants, as it also
is in this utterance by the general secretary of the party, Hasen Ali:

> In our high command meetings, we do not make decisions by raising hands; we follow the
> mashoora concept. We also have the code of conduct that every member needs to follow. It
> is based only on Islamic values, so every meeting is followed by Islamic traditions. […],

---

[72] See al-Baghdadi, and Wheeler 2013, Bosworth et al. 2006, Bernard 2006, and Findely 2006.

[73] According to Hasen Ali, 2013-02-11. The high command list, updated 2012-12-30. Since 2012,
it has expanded to include the Politbureau, the number of members increasing from 20 to 89. This
was done in order to get a wider diversity of opinions in the decision-making section of the party.

[74] A.L.M. Kaleel, 2013-02-08.

[75] A.L.M. Kaleel, 2013-02-08.

and almost everything in the party is based on Islam [...], and we have a permanent member of the Ulema Congress, and the president and the secretary will always be members of the high command. "[W]e [....] discuss it with the Ulema Congress and they will advise us and guide us to the right answer.[76]

Shura was the concept most frequently referred to in the discourses on the role of Islam in the internal politics of the party. One of my informants stated that: "We are following Islamic politics, mostly on consensus, then discussion (consultation)".[77] The *shura* principle means that every decision is made by the principle of consultation and that 89 members (of which three are formally educated religious scholars) can give guidelines for certain questions; however, it is the function of the party leader to make the final decision. The religious scholars' role in this process is to make sure that the high command members do not forget to consider Islamic tradition when making decisions:

[W]hen it is an attempt to do something that is against Islam, or when there is some important duty set in Islam that is going to be stopped in that meeting, I have to remind them of these laws. For example, today there is a [...] problem in this country. An organization called Bodu Bala Sena is interfering with things regarding halal. They are creating a lot of problems for the Muslims. There was a meeting in Darussalam in regards to this. I expressed an opinion there. I said when there is a tense situation ethnically, we have to be patient. If we [...] put out our feelings, then riots may occur. We have to be careful in dealing with these things [...] The Muslim Congress has to express its message [...] We have to say it in a tactical way. We have to say it in a very nice way to the extent that it is possible to do so. We have to tell the people from our community to be patient, [...] and they should understand that being patient is good. We have to send the right messages to the government as well. We have to express opinions to BBS also. [...] I said this in the meeting [...] as a scholar in Islam.[78]

I asked Hakeem how he would like to describe the function of the religious scholars within the party, and he replied that:

[T]hey are called upon to look at issues and problems from an Islamic perspective, based on the Qur'an and the Sunna, how problems should be approached, [...] when we are discussing problems they become useful because they are learned [...] more than [...] secular educated, those people are able to give us that dimension [...] it helps the leadership [...] to come to a decision [...] but at the end of the day, you see, it should not be seen as a position of Islamic values into the society which is multi-ethnic [...] but try to see it as an alternative that also has its values, own values that would be useful.[79]

The statement is indicative of the role of Islam in the party. The role of the religious scholars is that of one voice among many within its leadership. They do not influence the general direction in which it goes. Hakeem stressed that the current conditions existing on the island make Islamic solutions a possible alternative but not necessarily the first choice. The party's internal policies serve as a good example

---

[76] Hasen Ali, 2006-11-14.

[77] HC member 22, 2013-02-14. I received similar responses from HC member 23, 2013-02-13; and HC member 19, 2013-02-19.

[78] Hanifa, 2013-02-24.

[79] Rauff Hakeem, 2013-02-24.

of how the political problems come first and how the Islamic solutions, if there are any, come second.

Shafeek Rajabdeen stated that:

> In the high command, we have a few members that are connected religiously. When the party takes the wrong track, there are few members that tell us that you are wrong, you are going the wrong way, you must correct it, Islam doesn't like you […], so they are the policemen inside the party that tell what is right, what is wrong, they guide us, they tell you are doing the wrong thing and that is not the way you should go.[80]

Rajabdeen thus presents the *'ulama* in the party mainly as guardians, a religious conscience, whose role it is to steer the party in the right general direction. At the same time, he also claims that the *'ulama* played a bigger role in the party during Ashraff's time.[81] Ali confirms this role of *'ulama* as primarily serving as guides:

> [H]e [the *'alim*] will quote something from the Qur'an and the hadiths and the life of the Prophet and the history of Islam and then say something, and finally that will guide us to make a decision.[82]

The paradox of this is, as far as I can tell, that a practice (*shura*) established with reference to Islamic tradition works to limit the influence of Islam as a religious tradition within the party. *'Ulama* might advise but will not have the final say on what constitutes the Islamic way of conducting party politics. Even though there are a few scholars present in the high command, this command is made up of 89 members in total, and each one can give his or her opinion. Ultimately, it is the leader who makes the final decision even if no one else agrees with him.

In the internal discourse on *shura* and the Majlis-e-shoora, I did encounter quite diverse views among informants. There were differences concerning what kinds of issues it was thought that the Majlis-e-shoora should address, and, moreover, about how active it should be. Some would nostalgically claim that things were much better during the time of Ashraff, the former leader, when the Majlis-e-shoora was more active and the role of the *'ulama* as religious advisors was more thorough.[83] Some of my informants claimed that the practice of *shura* and the Majlis-e-shoora were not active at all today.[84] It is not uncommon for these individuals to paint the late leader as a very pious Muslim who (unlike the current leadership) truly followed the concept of *shura*:

> He [Ashraff] used to pray […] Then he came back and made a decision, and he was convinced that the decision was based on God almighty, and I know that he believed in it. There

---

[80] Shafeek Rajabdeen, 2013-02-06.

[81] Shafeek Rajabdeen, 2013-02-06.

[82] Hasen Ali, 2013-02-11. I also got similar responses from, for example, HC member 15, 2013-02-25; HC member 20, 2013-02-16; and HC member 21, 2013-02-19.

[83] HC member 1, 2013-02-17.

[84] HC member 4, 2013-02-18. I also got similar responses from, for example, HC member 8, 2013-02-19; and HC member 17, 2013-02-12.

is no question about it. He didn't act it or put it up there for others to think. He believed in it.[85]

The lack of a clear foundation for politics in Islamic tradition is again used internally as a means to criticize the current leadership. Pointing out that the former leader was pious often seems to imply that the current leader is not. One member even stated that the *shura*, as it was practiced in the party, actually gave all the power to the leader:

> [T]he constitution provides for the high command to make all the decisions. Decisions are to be made even in case of emergency. If the leader makes the decision, he has to verify with the high command. But basically, as I said, the high command will in most cases likely [...] follow the leader.[86]

There exists among some of the members of the high command an observable distrust for the current leader. The constitution and the structure of the party prompt a notion of authority that is, in a way, religiously based, but it is based rather on a selection from the "pool of resources" and interpretations of elements found there in a manner that is innovative and context specific, that is, Muslim politics in a Sri Lankan political environment.

Analysis

This chapter, based on interviews with persons within the SLMC's leading positions, has clearly shown that Islam in the politics of the party is rarely a matter of theological elaborations of Islamic tradition for the purpose of creating an Islamic political agenda with concrete suggestions for particular policies. In the center stands instead the use of religion to carve out and mobilize a particular group of Muslims among Sri Lankan voters. References to Islamic tradition are part of a boundary construction using different symbolic demarcations. When the party leadership talks about "Muslims", they consciously distance themselves from established categorizations, such as the ones used in the official census, distinguishing, for example, between "Sri Lankan Moors" and "Malays".[87] The SLMC constructs a concept of Muslim ethnicity that transcends internal diversity and positions Muslims alongside other recognized groups: that is, the linguistically-based division of Sinhalese and Tamil. Muslims are, according to the leading members of the SLMC, a unique ethnicity in Sri Lanka, and much of the public discourse of the party aims at safeguarding this image of a separate community. The existence of this imagined community is in fact the *raison d'être* of the SLMC, and much effort is put into identifying it, although not necessarily with reference to religious beliefs and practices. For instance, Muslims are said to be "the people of no tomorrow". They are

---

[85] HC member 17, 2013-02-12.
[86] HC member 3, 2013-02-09.
[87] Ismail 1995: 78.

"without power in the army", moreover, they are "poor". These phrases are recurrent in the leading members' demarcations of the Muslim community. They blame the state apparatus for the miserable situation and thereby they justify their own existence. Muslims are furthermore described as having a "unique language" and a "specific land in the country". In sum, there is very little religion "behind the ethnic marker" when it comes to the SLMC's construction of Muslims as a separate group in these interviews.

Some of my informants explained to me that the SLMC became a political party because "the others" already had political representatives and therefore it was legitimate for them to form the SLMC.[88] This is only partly true. Muslims were represented in other political parties and still are, both in Sinhala and Tamil parties and in other Muslim political parties as well; however, it is true that there was no Muslim political party before the SLMC that had managed to enter parliament. That the SLMC was the first Muslim political party goes hand in hand with portraying the founding members of the SLMC as heroes and martyrs. The SLMC's appearance was perceived as an attempt by Muslim political leaders to assert what they thought of as being a common Muslim identity, although the claim that Muslim politicians in the Sinhala parties did not stand up for Muslim interests is somewhat excessive, as Muslim political leaders in the opposition *did* protest against decisions that they felt was to the disadvantaged of Muslim communities.[89]

Some of the more problematic aspects of the SLMC's construction of Muslims as a particular group, and the party itself as this group's political representative, can be mentioned here. One problem is language. Most Muslims in Sri Lanka speak Tamil as their native language and could hence easily be categorized as Tamils. The need to stress that the Tamil of Muslims is a *different* Tamil because it contains loan words from Arabic is then understandable.[90] These loan words, often with a meaning connected to religion, become ethnic markers, regardless of whether there is any consensus on their basic meanings.

It is clear from the data I collected that the main objective of the SLMC's leadership is to be a "Muslim voice" in the new post-war era, one that safeguards "Muslim interests" within the nation-state of Sri Lanka. The particular issues addressed point in this direction, hence the focus on such symbolic markers of Muslim distinctiveness as *halal* certification, veiling, and the system of separate family laws. The right for Muslims to practice their faith is today a major subject for the SLMC.

As mentioned above, the SLMC's rhetoric on Muslims is an example of what Eickelman and Piscatori call the objectification of Muslim consciousness and probably has connections with the Muslim *da'wa* movements that came to Sri Lanka, mainly from the Indian sub-continent, in the 1970s. But there are also local resources to be tapped in the process, such as the notion of a common Muslim history on the

---

[88] Eickelman and Piscatori refer to Hobsbawm's discussion about the invention of tradition.

[89] For example, see O'Sullivan 1999: 120.

[90] This argument is seen among other Muslim elite prior to the formation of that SLMC. See Ismail 1995: 78–9.

island of Sri Lanka, which members of the party's leadership highlight, claiming a common heritage stemming from Arabic "forefathers" involved in trade.

The SLMC's construction of Muslims as a group is done within the framework of a Sri Lankan, post-colonial society that is characterized by diversity.[91] The focus put on the nation has not received much attention in previous research, which focuses more on the internal discourse of the party, as, for example, in Nuhamn's book *Understanding Sri Lanka Muslim Identity* (2002). Many of the leading members stressed in the interviews that as much as they are Muslims, they are Sri Lankans, and the call is for being recognized as a separate group, particularly as a way to receive state protection when under attack.

The image of a Muslim unity of interests that the SLMC puts forward is somewhat compromised by the fact that, as my interviews have shown, there is internal disagreement in the party, mainly, but not exclusively, concerning what exactly the role of Islam as a religious tradition is in this context. This is to be expected. Muslim politics is a matter of selecting from a "pool of resources" that is diverse and contradictory in itself. This sets the stage for competition and conflict when it comes to defining in detail what the elements selected entail. Eickelman and Piscatori discuss this potential for conflict in Muslim politics with reference to how religious scholars and non-traditionally educated Islamic experts often come into conflict over the correct interpretation of key concepts and dogma. My data suggest that this is also taking place on an internal level within the organization of the SLMC, where it appears as if a once important role for the *'ulama* in the party has been sidestepped.[92]

As discussed in the previous chapter, the central texts of the party indicate in some crucial ways a maximalistic view regarding the role of religion in society. This impression is much challenged in the interviews. In the interviews, it becomes clear that there are few, if any, aspirations to a political implementation of Islamic norms on society as a whole. By and large, the role of Islam in the SLMC is mainly to mobilize voters.[93] It could be argued that the downplaying of Islam as a basis for a body politic is strategic, given contemporary worldwide suspicion regarding political Islam (Islamism). I maintain that this is not the case for the SLMC. Their political agenda primarily concerns honoring "the legitimacy of the nation-state to which they belong" and respecting "state's governing institutions, the principle of equality among all citizens, and the pluralistic, competitive nature of political life".[94]

---

[91] See Balibar 2002: 117f.

[92] Cf. Eickelman and Piscatori 2004: 44.

[93] Brown and Hamzawy 2010: 2.

[94] Brown and Hamzawy 2010: 3.

References

Interviews with Named Informants

A.L.M. Kaleel 2013-02-08.
C. Tuan Nazeer 2006-11-20, 2006-02-22.
H.M.M. Illyas 2013-02-11.
Hasen Ali 2006-11-14, 2013-02-11.
M.G.M. Rizvie 2013-02-07.
Rauff Hakeem, 2013-02-23, 2013-02-24.
Shity Refiya 2006-11-24.
S.H. Athambawa 2013-02-14.
S.L.M. Hanifa 2013-02-24.
Shafeek Rahaabdeen 2006-11-20, 2013-02-06, 2013-02-07.

Other Interviews

HC Member 1 2013-02-17.
HC Member 2 2013-02-17.
HC member 3 2013-02-09.
HC member 4 2013-02-18.
HC member 5 2013-02-18.
HC member 6 2013-02-12.
HC member 7 2013-02-18.
HC member 8 2013-02-19.
HC member 9 2013-02-17.
HC member 10 2013-02-19.
HC member 11 2013-02-13, 2013-02-14.
HC member 12 2013-02-07.
HC member 13 2013-02-22.
HC member 14 2013-02-18.
HC member 15 2013-02-25.
HC member 16 2013-02-15.
HC member 17 2013-02-12.
HC member 18 2013-02-20.
HC member 19 2013-02-19.
HC member 20 2013-02-16.
HC member 21 2013-02-19.
HC member 22 2013-02-14.
HC member 23 2013-02-13.

Literature

al-Baghdādī, Aḥmad Mubārak, and Brannon M. Wheeler. 2013. Consultation. *Encyclopaedia of the Qurʾān*. Brill Online. Retrieved November 19, 2013, from http://referenceworks.brillonline. com/entries/encyclopaedia-of-the-quran/consultation-COM_00041.

Balibar, Étienne. 2002. Nationsformen: Historia och Ideology. In *Ras, Nation, Klass*, ed. Etienne Balibar and Immanuel Wallerstein. Uddevalla: Bokförlaget Daidalos AB.

Bandara, Kelum. 2013. SL to ratify ban on Al-Qaeda, Taliban. *Daily Mirror*. Retrieved April 5, 2014 from http://www.dailymirror.lk/25401/sl-to-ratify-ban-on-al-qaeda-taliban.

Bernard, M. 2006. Idjmāʿ. *Encyclopaedia of Islam, Second Edition*. Brill Online. Retrieved January 14, 2015, from http://referenceworks.brillonline.com/entries/encyclopaedia-of-islam-2/id-j-ma-COM_0350.

Bosworth, C.E., Manuela Marín, and A. Ayalon. 2006. Shūrā. *Encyclopaedia of Islam, Second Edition*. Brill Online. Retrieved March 3, 2012, from http://www.paulyonline.brill.nl/subscriber/entry?entry=islam_COM-1063.

Brown, Nathan J., and Amr Hamzawy. 2010. *Between Religion and Politics*. Washington, DC: Carnegie Endowment for International Peace.

Eickelman, Dale F., and James Piscatori. 2004. *Muslim Politics*. Princeton: Princeton University Press. First edition 1996.

Findely, C.V. 2006. Madjlisal-Shūrā. *Encyclopaedia of Islam, Second Edition*. Brill Online. Retrieved March 3, 2012, from http://www.paulyonline.brill.nl/subscriber/entry?entry=islam_SIM-4745.

Ismail, Qadri. 1995. Unmooring Identity: The Antinomies of Elite Muslim Self-Representation in Modern Sri Lanka. In *Unmaking the Nation: The Politics of Identity and History in Modern Sri Lanka*, ed. Pradeep Jeganathan and Qadri Ismail. Colombo: Social Scientists' Association.

Korf, Benedikt. 2006. Who Is the Rogue? Discourse, Power and Spatial Politics in Post-War Sri Lanka. *Political Geography* 25: 279–297.

Lincoln, Bruce. 2003. *Holy Terrors: Thinking About Religion after September 11*. Chicago/London: University of Chicago Press.

Monnot, G. 2015. Ṣirāṭ. *Encyclopaedia of Islam, Second Edition*. Retrieved 11 February 2016 from http://referenceworks.brillonline.com/entries/encyclopaedia-of-islam-2/sirat-SIM_7065 First appeared online: 2012First Print Edition: isbn: 9789004161214, 1960–2007.

Osella, C., and F. Osella. 2009. Muslim Entrepreneurs in Public Life Between India and the Gulf: Making Good and Doing Good. *Journal of the Royal Anthropological Institute* 15: 202–221.

O'Sullivan. 1999. *Identity and Institution in Ethnic Conflict: The Muslims of Sri Lanka*. Ph.D. thesis, Oxford: Oxford University.

Chapter 4
Ashraff in Parliament 1989–1992

Abstract This chapter focuses on the former leader M.H.M. Ashraff's speeches in parliament and how Muslim politics are presented in these speeches. As described above, the political conditions during the period of 1989–1992 were to a large extent dominated by the civil war. This chapter will therefore be divided into parts that correspond to different phases in the civil war and to when Islamic references are notable.

Keywords Muslim politics · Islam · Muslims · Sri Lanka · Sri Lanka Muslim Congress · M.H.M Ashraff · Pragmatic politics · Religion and politics

The Civil War

The Indo-Lankan Accord

One of the first themes connected to the civil war relates to the Indo-Sri Lankan Peace Accord (1987–1990). In this context, it becomes clear how the Indo-Sri Lankan Peace Accord was important in the construction of Muslims as a particular group represented by the SLMC. In general, Ashraff condemned the agreement for several reasons: he considered the Indo-Sri Lankan Peace Accord to be a threat to the nation's unity, mainly because Muslims as a separate category were completely excluded. According to him, this accord was orchestrated by the former president J.R. Jayewardene. Ashraff stated on one occasion that Muslims had become a "helpless, pathetic community [...]".[1] As we can see in the following, Ashraff moreover rejected the merger of the eastern and northern provinces into one and claimed on one occasion that:

> We still continue to have the grievance that the aspirations of the Muslims were not accommodated while drafting and signing the Indo-Lankan Accord. The Muslims who were

---

[1] AP: 1989: 142 Provincial Councils (Consequential Provisions) Bill. 11/5 1989.

© Springer Nature Switzerland AG 2019
A. Johansson, *Pragmatic Muslim Politics*,
https://doi.org/10.1007/978-3-030-12789-3_4

33 percent in the Eastern Province, the only province where Muslims were in a considerable
majority – 33 percent – were reduced overnight to 17 percent.[2]

In the above quote, Muslims are discursively presented by Ashraff as a unified
group, one which it is possible to delimitate and quantify. They are, according to the
quote, in need of political representation, which the SLMC could provide. Ashraff
also casts Muslims in the same speech as a possible target for militant Tamil activism; they are therefore in need of protection. On another occasion, Ashraff even
went so far as to call the accord a conspiracy against Muslims:

They want to do away with the political leadership of the Muslims, they want to do away
with the Muslim intelligentsia, they want to intimidate the Muslim youth and they want to
destroy totally the Muslim economy.[3]

This quote clearly shows how the notion "Muslim" was constructed by using the
term Muslim as an adjective, giving rise to expressions such as a "Muslim intelligentsia", "Muslim youth", and "Muslim economy". This discursive practice was
later further strengthened when Ashraff stressed the importance of considering *religious affiliation* as an important boundary marker between the various communities
in Sri Lanka.[4]

In Ashraff's construction of Muslims as a unified category, and the SLMC as the
legitimate representative of this Muslim community, violent clashes played an
important role. Despite the fact that such clashes frequently took place between different groups, Ashraff tended to focus on the violence directed towards local Muslim
communities.[5] In one particular speech, Ashraff listed a variety of issues that he
argued, following the signing of the accord, affected Muslims in particular. Among
the issues listed was that of Muslims who had been killed, kidnapped, or who had
become refugees. The restricted mobility was also something that, according to
him, disturbed Muslim workers in the east, especially the fishermen, who had to
stay home instead of being able to work.[6]

Ashraff opposed the Indian and Sri Lankan negotiations with Tamil-speaking
militant groups because these did not include Muslims. He called such negotiations
a "betrayal of the Muslim community".[7] In general, he resented that the accord did
not at all acknowledge the existence of a Muslim community but merely included
Muslims in the category of Tamils.[8] In a statement to the Ministry of Defence in
1989, Ashraff gave the government and the Sri Lanka Freedom Party (SLFP) suggestions on how to maintain peace in the eastern part of the country:

---

[2] AP: 1989: 235, Provincial Council Election Petition Rules. 8/11 1989.

[3] AP: 1989: 319, Police Commission Bill. 9/12 1989.

[4] AP: 1989: 140, Provincial (Consequential Provisions) Councils. 11/5 1989.

[5] AP: 1989: 118, Appropriation Bill 1989 Ministry of Finance. 11/4 198, see also AP: 1989: 148,
151, 177, 265.

[6] AP: 1989: 118, Appropriation Bill 1989 Ministry of Finance. 11/4 1989.

[7] AP: 1989: 324, Police Commission Bill. 9/12 1989. See also AP: 1989: 235, 278, 314, and AP:
1990: 9, 174.

[8] AP: 1989: 46, Appropriation Bill to the Ministry of Foreign Affairs. 3/4 1989.

> The Government should consider, in conjunction with the Indian Government, the concept
> of community-oriented devolution of power. As far as the Muslims are concerned – we have
> already made a number of representations.[9]

Hence, community-oriented devolution of power meant, according to Ashraff's understanding, a recognition of Muslims as a unified ethnic group. Ashraff's suggestion was to renegotiate the accord, including Muslims as a separate group represented by Ashraff and his party:

> As far as the view of the SLMC is concerned, the solution to the problems faced by the
> Eastern Province Muslims is nothing but the creation of a Muslim-majority Provincial
> Council. I said that the conference should pass a resolution supporting the creation of a
> Muslim majority Provincial Council.[10]

Part of the construction of Muslims as a group is thus related to the construction of particular political structures that would delimitate them as such. The Indo-Sri Lankan Peace Accord functioned, in Ashraff's rhetoric, as a springboard for claims for more political influence. But there were other aspects in this accord. Ashraff stressed the eastern part of the country, the SLMC's stronghold, as the original home of the Muslims of Sri Lanka; one-third of all Muslims live in fact on the east coast and the remaining two-thirds are spread throughout the country. The SLMC asserted that it at this particular point in time was working to make the Muslim voice in the east heard.[11] But in advocating the devolution of power, Ashraff did not focus on geography but on community instead.[12] According to Ashraff, this would also be reflected in his suggestion for the Muslim provincial council:

> [W]e identify that unit as a Muslim Provincial Council or a Muslim Majority Provincial
> Council, let this House not understand that unit to be a 100 percent Muslim unit [...]. When
> we talk about Sri Lanka although 74 percent of the people are of the Sinhala majority we do
> not call it a Sinhala nation.[13]

Once again, the term "Muslim" is limited to the east-coast "Muslims" in the sense that the Muslim majority council should be located there. Ashraff's notion of Muslim self-rule would, according to this proclamation, not exclude other groups. Ashraff accepted the nation's borders but also pointed to its limitations. A few years later, in 1995, Ashraff presented concrete proposals for Muslim political self-rule in the east in the form of an autonomous Pradesheeya Sabhas (local government) in the southeastern region.[14] These proposals were offered as an alternative to the merger

---

[9] AP: 1989: 46, Appropriation Bill to the Ministry of Foreign Affairs. 3/4 1989. See also AP: 1989: 318–9, Police Commission Bill 9/12 1989.

[10] AP: 1989: 236, Provincial Council Election Petition rules. 8/11 1989. The districts that Ashraff wanted to form this council in were Ampara, Pottuvill, and Batticaloa.

[11] See Knoerzer 1998.

[12] Ameerdeen 2006: 200.

[13] AP: 1990: 225, Public Security Proclamation. 20/9 1990. These demands were made several times. For more examples, see: AP: 1989: 107–9, 139, 162, 218, 236, AP: 1990: 177, 192–3, 225, 255, and AP: 1991: 217.

[14] This is a summary of the SLMC's constitutional reform suggestions made in the Parliamentary Select Committee in 1995. Quoted in Ameerdeen 2006: 203–4.

of the northern and eastern provinces. However, the separation of the provinces did
not occur until 2006.

Jihad and the Aftermath of the Indo-Sri Lankan Peace Accord

After the IPKF and India withdrew as peacekeepers, Ashraff viewed the situation in
Sri Lanka as changing for the worse. Ashraff's concerns became evident in a parliamentary speech in which he expressed concerns about the withdrawal and called it
a threat to democracy.[15] This threat was mainly due, according to him, to Tamil rebel
activity. On the battlefield, the Liberation Tigers of Tamil Elam (LTTE) and its
leader Velupillai Prabhakaran were quite successful in their struggle against the Sri
Lankan government. During the IPKF period (1987–1990), the LTTE had formed
alliances with Muslim activist groups, such as the previously mentioned MULF, but
these alliances changed. In his parliamentary speeches, Ashraff now criticized those
responsible for national security, that is, the Sri Lankan government, the police, and
the army, claiming that several Muslim-dominated villages had been attacked by
Tamil militant groups after the IPKF had left. Even though he saw the situation as
deteriorating, Ashraff endorsed the withdrawal of the IPKF in principle, saying that
no foreign forces should be present in the country.[16] He argued that the withdrawal
had been too hasty. The IPKF should not have been removed before the safety of the
civilian population could be guaranteed.

Ashraff stated that the civilian population had been completely left on their own
and had become vulnerable to bands of the Tamil Tigers and the Tamil National
Alliance (TNA).[17] According to Ashraff, the LTTE was openly collecting taxes in
the north and east and therefore the people had to pay double taxes.[18] When Ashraff
spoke of militant Tamil factions, it was usually the LTTE that he was referring to,
and the civilians referred to were implicitly Muslims. He stated that Muslims "have
suffered at the hands of every Tamil group that was armed".[19] This suffering was,
according to him, not an accident. Calling the LTTE "fascist barbaric murderers",
he claimed that a great conspiracy and master plan that specifically targeted Muslims
existed.[20] In the same speech from 1990, Ashraff declared that the LTTE had placed
a death sentence on him.[21]

---

[15] AP: 1989: 39, Question by Private Notice Security Situation in Ampara District. 31/3 1989.
Translated from Tamil.

[16] AP: 1990: 250, Supplementary Supply: Contribution to Provincial Councils for Integrated Rural
Development Project. 13/11 1990.

[17] AP: 1990: 155, Local Authorities (Special Provision) Bill.14/6 1990.

[18] AP: 1990: 100, Unilateral Declaration of Independence by EPRLF. 6/3 1990. See also AP: 1990:
113.

[19] AP: 1991: 185, Public Security Proclamation. 25/9 1991.

[20] AP: 1990: 158, Security Situation in Eastern Province and AP: 1990: 166.

[21] Previously, Ashraff also mentioned that the LTTE had banned the SLMC as a political party. See
AP: 1990: 102.

As demonstrated in his parliamentary speeches, Ashraff saw indications of a grand conspiracy also among representatives of the Tamil political parties in parliament, for example, when Eelam People's Revolutionary Liberation Front (EPRLF) changed its views on the suggestion for a Muslim majority council, as the EPRLF were at first positive to the suggestion but later did not support it.[22]

In 1989 and the beginning of 1990, Ashraff had at first taken a neutral position towards the LTTE. He welcomed them into the democratic process.[23] His view of the LTTE changed, however, when, according to Ashraff, after the withdrawal of the IPKF, the LTTE started targeting Muslims in the east and the government did nothing about it.[24]

When the Tamil Tigers expelled Muslims from the northern part of the country in 1990 – due to the fact that they were Muslims – the resulting refugee situation became another opportunity for Ashraff and the SLMC to reinforce their claim to represent Muslims as a unified group:

> We know what happened to the Muslims; we know that more than 90,000 Muslim refugees […] were driven out from their homes. They are suffering in more than 100 refugee camps; their conditions are worse than the conditions of animals.[25]

In 1991, Ashraff also made a suggestion about how Muslim refugees could help the government's resettlement plans in the north, namely, by taking up arms and fighting against the militant Tamils.[26] He even suggested that the government should consider arming Muslim refugees.[27] When describing the conflict as part of an anti-Muslim, mainly Hindu, conspiracy, he mentioned mosques turned into Hindu temples and churches, and he claimed that the LTTE had said that these changes were what they were aiming for.[28] In one speech from 1990, Ashraff explained that the Tamil Tigers treated Muslims like slaves.[29] In another speech, he also pointed out that Muslim names on road signs had been altered by the LTTE, that is, Muslim road names such as Hijra (Arabic, "emigration") Road had been changed to non-Muslim names.[30]

---

[22] AP: 1990: 100, Unilateral Declaration of Independence by EPRLF. 6/3 1990.

[23] AP: 1990: 117, Public Security Proclamation. 26/4 1990. See also AP: 1990: 101. In this speech, Ashraff referred to the LTTE as murderous but also said that it was welcome in the democratic process.

[24] AP: 1990: 41, Question by Private Notice Security Situation in Ampara District. 30/1 1990.

[25] The exact number of people that were actually evicted is rather unclear; Ashraff refers to 90,000 in his speech AP: 1992: 108, Defence Levy Amendment Bill 7/7 1992. In the speech AP: 1990: 250 Supplementary Supply: Contribution to Provincial for Integrated Rural Development Project, he talks about 22,000 people. AP: 1992: 109, Defence Levy Amendment Bill 7/7 1992. For another example, see AP: 1990: 263, Public Security Proclamation 22/11 1990.

[26] AP: 1991: 63, Public Security Proclamation. 23/4 1991.

[27] AP: 1991: 234, Appropriation Bill 1992. 15/11 1991.

[28] AP: 1990: 240, Plight of Muslims in North & East. 9/11 1990.

[29] AP: 1990: 141, Public Security Proclamation. 25/4 1990. Translated from Tamil.

[30] AP: 1990: 148, Public Security Proclamation. 24/5 1990.

After an attack on Kattankudy's Grand Mosque in August 3, 1990 that resulted in over 100 deaths, Ashraff made a speech in the parliament in which he talked about the rules of war in the Qur'an, thus condemning the attack:

[E]ven in a war the Holy Quran does not permit or condone a Muslim killing women, invalids and innocent [people] [...] Our Prophet Muhammad [...] has thought that under no circumstances shall you enter a place of worship, because a place of worship is considered to be a place of refuge.[31]

In the above quotation, Ashraff criticizes the attackers by posing their actions against what is presented as an Islamic religious ideal of just warfare waged in accordance with well-defined and honorable rules. The Islamic reference thus functions as a way of stressing boundaries based on religious dogma between Muslims and non-Muslims.[32] But he also – still referring to religious dogma – goes on to claim the right to self-defense. He explains to the parliament that being a Muslim does not only imply that you pray five times a day but "that you have faith in Allah, faith in the prophet, faith in the Day of Judgment and commitment to jihad is also a part of our faith".[33] In this speech, in regard to Jihad, or "struggle in path of Allah", Ashraff refers specifically to defensive action traditionally construed as an individual's religious duty, *fard al-'ayn,* in the event of an attack. Such individual jihad is a religiously justified option for Muslims under attack:

After the Kattankudy massacre the blood of every Muslim is boiling today. We should be thankful to the Muslim community for their patience. [...] Muslims are no longer interested in development at the moment. The only issue is our right to defend our lives. [...] The Prophet [...] said that patience is the greatest form of Jihad or Holy War. But the Holy Koran enjoins on every Muslim the right to fight against the oppressors, against the oppression, it is the duty of every Muslim to fight. [...] Is LTTE giving a message to the Muslim Community that we cannot freely practice our faith? Is it a message from the LTTE that the Muslims cannot have their mosques and cannot pray? [...] The circumstances are sufficient, the circumstances justify a situation in which a Jihad can be declared today in this country. Our ulamas will accept it. But nevertheless we follow the Prophet, who taught us that patience is the greatest form of Jihad and we will remain patient.[34]

As mentioned in the introduction, even though Ashraff spoke of Muslims as a unified group, the real state of affairs looks different. As was previously stated, Sri Lankan Muslims are in reality divided by many concerns, one of which is the division between Sufis and reformist Muslims. Ashraff himself was torn between these groups throughout his political career. Although this might explain details in the quotation above in which he acknowledges that jihad in terms of an armed struggle is justified, he nevertheless also put forward the ideal of patience, *sabr,* which is also

[31] AP: 1990: 170, Security Situation in the Eastern Province. 10/8 1990.

[32] The rules of war in the Qur'an are, however, often contradictory. Regarding the law of war, see Landau-Tasseron 2013.

[33] AP: 1990: 170, Security Situation in the Eastern Province. 10/8 1990.

[34] AP: 1990: 169–171, Security Situation in the Eastern Province. 10/8 1990.

a form of "struggle" (thus a form of jihad) in the writings of traditional Sufi teachers.[35]

In the same speech about the security situation in the east, Ashraff furthermore emphasized that communities need to co-exist:

Once the Prophet of Islam, [...] Muhammad [...] told his companion that if you find injustice it is your duty to prevent it by your hand, if you cannot by word of mouth; and if [you] cannot do the first two, then you keep away, reject by your mind. But he said rejection mentally is the weakest form of one's Iman.[36]

Two years later, in a speech delivered on July 23, 1992, Ashraff once again mentioned jihad, and implicitly martyrdom, in a debate regarding Muslim deserters from the Sri Lankan army. Interestingly enough, this plea for sympathy also opened up for comparisons with Buddhist ethics:

If we are being killed because of the simple reason that we are Muslims it is the commandment of the Holy Koran that we should declare Jihad against them and kill every LTTE. [...] I will be the happiest if I can die in battle at the time of slitting the neck of this bloody Prabhakaran. These are our feelings [...] If our faith is that we must die by declaring Jihad and by fighting the LTTE the Government has a duty to encourage us. But do not make us defenseless. We do not believe in living in this world only. This is a temporary world [...] You Buddhists agree with the concept of the Anithya, which Lord Buddha preached. The same Anithya we Muslims believe.[37]

The comparison between Muslim religious notions of the just war and Buddhist teachings (*anithya* or impermanence) was of course directed towards Buddhist members of the parliament. This openness towards Buddhism was a recurring theme in Ashraff's parliamentary speeches. This particular speech was later (not dated) released in a separate pamphlet by the SLMC under the title *Is Jihad the Alternative?* In the foreword of this pamphlet, the SLMC elaborates upon how Buddhism should be understood: the teachings of the Buddha should be seen as philosophy and not religion; consequently, other religions might embrace his teaching without renouncing their own.[38] In another speech, Ashraff suggested that other members of the parliament should follow the Buddha in the way that he himself does, and he claimed that the nation's fundamental principles are closely tied to Buddhism:

But we who follow the teachings of Buddha, the teachings which this country has accepted and adopted, we who have accepted the teachings of Buddha at the political level, we who follow his teachings as a commitment, and we who follow the teachings of Buddha who said that we cannot even kill a living organism as small as an insect, yet it is we who create conditions to kill human beings.[39]

[35] Alexander 2015.

[36] AP: 1990: 171, Security Situation in the Eastern Province. 10/8 1990.

[37] AP: 1992: 129, Public Security Proclamation. 23/7 1992. The question of jihad had come up in a debate 2 years earlier in which Ashraff was vague in his description; however, he stated that the question of jihad had arisen. See AP: 1990: 65.

[38] AP: 1992: 220–7, Appropriation Bill 1993 Minister of Post and Telecommunications (cont'd). 11/12 1992. Translated from Tamil.

[39] AP: 1989: 341, Public Security Proclamation. 22/12 1989. Translated from Tamil.

Also, outside the parliament, Ashraff's referred to the Buddha. On another occasion, this time in 1999, he paid homage to the Buddha in one of his poems. His poem did stir up some controversy since he asserted that the Buddha only spoke Tamil. Since the Buddha in the Sri Lankan context is affiliated with the Sinhalese language, Ashraff's statement that he only spoke Tamil led to protests among Buddhist organizations.[40] While Buddhism thus was a favorite theme for Ashraff, he also mentioned Hinduism as a religion of peace in at least one parliamentary speech.[41]

Ashraff continuously described Muslims as victims of Tamil violence, and he stated that over 1700 Muslims had been killed between 1987 and 1990, not only by the LTTE but also by other militant Tamil factions.[42] When Ashraff talked about refugees, he spoke about refugees in general terms without specifying ethnicity; however, when he gave examples of the situation faced by refugees, he referred most of the time to Muslim villages being affected.[43] When addressing the issue of internal refugees and a generally chaotic situation that had arisen as a result of the conflict, Muslims were then his main concern, either as displaced from their homes or as being unable to pursue their livelihood.[44]

In an appropriation bill from 1992, Ashraff suggested the creation of a Civil Volunteer Force (CVF) that would give protection especially to Muslims. In this speech, he cited a hadith justifying Muslims having the right to receive training in the armed forces: "[T]he Hon. Muslim Members will agree with me – this is a part of our faith. The Prophet Muhammad [...] has said that getting military training is part of one's personality".[45]

This use of reference to the scriptures should be seen in the context of Ashraff, in his call for military training for Muslims in the east, asking for support from other Muslim members of the parliament, more specifically, those in the government. According to his view, the military forces in the east should use Muslim soldiers exclusively.[46] Ashraff developed these thoughts in terms of a Home Guard force with Muslim soldiers protecting Muslim villages.[47] The solution to the LTTE problem, according to Ashraff, was to give the Muslims arms or to incorporate more Muslims into the CVF. Ashraff claimed that Muslims, portrayed as an extraordinarily vulnerable group, are defenseless and therefore ought to arm themselves. He believed that the lawless society in the eastern side of the country – with kidnappings, rapes, and the colonization of farmlands belonging to Muslims – had left them with no other choice.[48]

---

[40] See De Silva and Farook 1999, retrieved 2015-07-31.

[41] AP: 1992: 191, Appropriation Bill 1993 Minister of Power and Energy. 7/12 1992.

[42] AP: 1990: 165, Security Situation in the Eastern Province. 10/8 1990.

[43] For example, see AP: 1991: 130, AP: 1991: 170, and AP: 1991: 188.

[44] AP: 1991: 65, Public Security Proclamation. 23/4 1991.

[45] AP: 1990: 163, General Sir John Kotalawela Defence Academy (Amendment) Bill. 7/8 1990.

[46] AP: 1990: 163, General Sir John Kotalawela Defence Academy (Amendment) Bill. 7/8 1990.

[47] AP: 1990: 220, Public Security Proclamation. 20/9 1990. See also AP: 1990: 317.

[48] AP: 1989: 183, Security of Muslims in the Eastern Province: Statement by MR. M.H.M Ashraff. 25/8 1989 and AP: 1989: 220 Public Security Proclamation 19/10 1989.

The parliamentary speeches advocating the right of Muslims to arm themselves were recurring. In 1989, Ashraff was at one time accused of turning to Libya's leader, Muammar al-Gaddafi, to ask for weapons. Even though the links between the SLMC and Muslim organizations and states outside of the country are somewhat clouded, it was at this time common knowledge that Ashraff had links to Libya and that Libya sponsored the Muslim separatist group in the Philippines. The suspicion was therefore not that far-fetched.[49] Ashraff responded to these allegations by questioning why he should not turn elsewhere for help. If the government did not provide Muslims with weapons, he argued, why should he not try other options?

> If my country is not prepared to listen to me I am prepared to go out of my country for what I want. That is my position. If my country, the country in which I was born, my Sri Lanka, is not prepared to listen to my voice I will go outside my country and raise my voice […] but I am first a Sri Lankan, second a Sri Lankan and third a Sri Lankan.[50]

Again, as we can see from the above, Ashraff declared to his audience his loyalty to the nation and spoke of turning "outside" only when all other options had failed. He continued to put "inside" alternatives first, for example, by referring to the fact that there existed "home guards", armed legally by the government, in other places in the country.[51]

In reality, there already existed Muslim "home guard" militias, and when a member of the parliament stated that "Muslim home guards were harassing innocent Tamils", Ashraff responded by declaring that the unhappy incident alluded to should not prevent Muslims from being allowed to defend themselves. On another occasion, Ashraff explained that "home guards" did in fact function well, and he gave an example from the Muslim-dominated town of Kattankudy, where the "home guards" had effectively driven out the LTTE. Ashraff in this context used a nationalist, rather than religious, rhetoric: armed Muslim groups are, in reality, serving the nation. They seek to defend Sri Lanka's borders against separatist Tamil rebels.[52]

The Nation

As already noted, the Sri Lankan nation serves as an important reference point in Ashraff's speeches. This aspect of his discourse relates to several important areas.

---

[49] O'Sullivan 1999: 278–9 and Eickelman and Piscatori 2004: 105.

[50] AP: 1989: 214–21, Public Security Proclamation. 19/10 1989. See also AP: 1990: 111–129, P and AP: 1990: 161–3.

[51] AP: 1989: 217–223, Public Security Proclamation. 19/10 1989. The request for Muslims to acquire guns and receive weapons training can also be found in AP: 1990: 163 Security Situation in Easter Province.

[52] AP: 1990: 221, Public Security Proclamation. 20/9 1990. See also AP: 1990: 48 for similar arguments.

Democracy

In regard to the institutions of the Sri Lankan state, not least the parliament, some of
the first matters Ashraff touched upon as a new member of parliament were his
intention to implement Islamic ideals in society and how these religious ideals could
contribute to solving some of Sri Lanka's main problems:

> The Holy Koran [...] and the supreme life of the Holy Prophet are the guidelines of our
> party. We are not compelling anyone who does not accept the policies of our party to join
> our party. [...] No one can stop the Muslim community from accepting the Sri Lanka
> Muslim Congress as its sole spokesman in the near future. [...] We believe that Islam is a
> complete way of life [...] The difference between Islam and with respect to other religions
> is that Islam shows to us how an orderly and a disciplined society can be built up.[53]

The approach to religion in this quote was instrumental and is similar to the way
in which Islam is presented in the constitution of the party (see above). In the above,
Ashraff conflates the Qur'an, the Sunna and the documents of the SLMC, and he
reinforces the notion of Muslims as a homogenous group and the party as its political representative. However, since there were Muslims working within other parties
as well, this way of putting it could potentially be a problem. Ashraff sometimes
approached other Muslim members of the parliament. For example, in 1989, Ashraff
welcomed the new Muslim speaker of the parliament, M. H. Mohamed, who represented the UNP, stating that the SLMC was guided by the Qur'an and the Sunna and
that he, and the party, were glad that a Muslim had become the speaker of the parliament. In addition, in the same speech, Ashraff declared that Islam, being a universal
religion, is for everyone. In another speech made in 1991, Ashraff remarked that
while Islam has more than 124,000 prophets, he chose to talk about the Buddha:

> Islam promises a way out which is the middle path, a path which is advocated by the most
> respected Buddha himself. Buddha himself had advocated the middle path. He advocated
> the concept of Nirvana as opposed to the various sufferings of human beings. As to how the
> human soul can liberate itself has been the doctrine of Buddha himself. [...] Capitalism and
> communism are the two extremes. Both of these are wrong, Islam advocates the middle
> path. [...] The middle path is that you allow, give the human being all encouragement so
> that he can develop himself morally, materially and spiritually.[54]

Ashraff's reference to the "middle path" is intriguing. Here, he seems to refer to
the Buddha in order to legitimize Islam. In the above quotation, Ashraff criticizes
what he describes as a Western way of thinking. Ashraff also makes reference to the
Qur'an and the concept of *wasatiyya* (middle path), which was commonplace within
modernist, political Islam, particularly during the Cold War era. Religiously
informed politics was often presented as a middle path between communism and
capitalism at this time.[55]

---

[53] AP: 1989: 20, Appropriation Bill. 23/3 1989.

[54] AP: 1991: 163, Government Policy of Privatization Peoplization State Establishment and
Corporation. 9/8 1991. See also AP: 1992: 115–121.

[55] Glynn 2012: 11.

Ashraff's attempt at reconciling Sri Lankan politics with Islam includes the country's constitution that he deemed to be in line with the basic view of Islam and to be a better alternative than Marxism for Muslims.[56] Possibly, this reference to Marxism, still a real option at the time in question, was directed at Tamil militant organizations (like the LTTE). It could, however, also be seen as criticism of the Islamic Socialist Party, which had competed with the SLMC for Muslim votes. The notion that Islam can be of general importance within Sri Lankan politics, through the SLMC, is also clearly detected when Ashraff claimed that the SLMC is "trying to bring in some new dimensions, new thinking into the body politic of this country".[57]

Ashraff claimed in an appropriation bill from 1989 that the SLMC had been misunderstood. He stressed that the Qur'an and the life of the Prophet served the party guidelines. He also touched upon in the same speech the importance of national unity:

> Sri Lanka is a multi-ethnic, multi-religious and multi-lingual plural society in which the Sinhalese, Tamil, Muslims, Burghers and others live side by side, yet they are lacking in understanding of one another. Fear of domination, prejudice, discrimination and suspicion bedevils communal harmony. The way that the 40 years of political independence has been managed has compounded the issue rather than promote peace and harmony among the communities. It seems to have driven certain sections of our people to demand separation.[58]

In the above, Ashraff hence points out that different religions, languages, and ethnicities divide Sri Lanka, but that he (and his party) has a multi-cultural agenda. His goal, he assures his listeners, is achieving a state of peace and harmony among the communities.[59] This multi-ethnic, multi-religious, multi-lingual, and multi-cultural agenda, resulting in support for democratization and peace, is then explicitly connected in the speech to the Qur'an, with an implicit reference to verse 49:13:

> As Muslims we believe in the Holy Koran, almighty Allah enjoins the unity of not only the Muslim community, but the unity of the whole human race.[60]

It is noteworthy that Ashraff's statements only refer in a general way to Islamic scriptures and dogma. While he clearly makes a selection from an Islamic "pool of resources", the element chosen (the Qur'an) is not the object of further explorations. The audience is expected to accept his view of a fundamental compatibility between Islam and the core values of the nation at face value. Indeed, the nation of Sri Lanka appears to be as equally important as the (religious) supreme guidelines of the party.

---

[56] AP: 1990: 289–90, Appropriation Bill 1991 Order read for Resuming Adjournment Debate on Question. 28/11 1990. See also AP: 1990: 101.

[57] AP: 1991: 163, Government Policy of Privatization Peoplization State Establishment and Corporation. 9/8 1991.

[58] AP: 1989: 21, Appropriation Bill. 23/3 1989.

[59] In this talk, he includes the Burghers, who are a small Eurasian group in Sri Lanka. See McGilvray 1982.

[60] AP: 1991: 119, Supplementary Supply: Agriculture Productivity Villages. 11/7 1991.

The focus on Sri Lankan identity becomes evident in the following excerpt from the same speech:

> The Sri Lanka Muslim Congress, however, is pledged to preserve the unity, sovereignty and territorial integrity of Sri Lanka and committed to build a Sri Lankan identity. Above all, the moral and spiritual development of our people is a sine qua non for peace and development to which the Sri Lanka Muslim Congress stands firmly committed.[61]

Ashraff thus asserted that he was committed to the building of a Sri Lankan identity and that the SLMC stands in this context for peace and for the development of the people of Sri Lanka as a whole. Also in regard to this topic, but in different speech, he invokes Islam, in this case through a reference to the Prophet Muhammad demanding that people should smile at one another and through this action foster a common national identity on the island of Sri Lanka.[62] In an amendment bill from 1991, he asserted that Sri Lankan identity cannot be built as long as there are dangers in the country.[63] These dangers, which Ashraff referred to as cancerous for the country, are the activities of certain groups engaged in the civil war, that is, the LTTE and the government.

Even though Ashraff was clear in his rejection of the LTTE, some representatives from the southwestern Muslim communities did accuse him and the SLMC of being linked to the Tamil Tigers. These allegations reached the media. Ashraff was publicly accused by one newspaper for wanting to cooperate with the rebels. The accusation was later retracted, and the newspaper had to publicly apologize to both Ashraff and the SLMC.[64]

In an amendment bill from 1989, Islamic dogma and scripture became directly relevant in the discussion on lowering the age of majority from 18 to 15. The SLMC supported this as a way to include frustrated youths in the *democratization* process.[65] In the following excerpt from a parliamentary speech, Ashraff refers to the different schools of Islamic law that have existed in Sri Lanka, and special attention is paid to the views within the Shafi'i school of thought:

> On the other hand the Muslim personal law is part and parcel of the divine laws as explained to the world by the Holy Prophet Mohamed, Sallallhu Aluhi Wasallam Peace be upon him […] The incapacity of a minor ceases at puberty only if his intelligence is sufficiently developed to allow […] his being entrusted with the administration of his property. The age of puberty is fixed by law for both sexes at 15 years completed […].[66]

---

[61] AP: 1989: 21, Appropriation Bill. 23/3 1989. See also AP: 1989: 279.

[62] AP: 1989: 65, No Confidence in Government. 19/3 1992.

[63] AP: 1991: 161, Tea Small Holding Development Amendment Bill. 8/8 1991. See also AP: 1989: 134–147, and AP: 1992: 61–8.

[64] O'Sullivan 1999: 313–6.

[65] AP: 1989: 249, Age of Majority Amendment Bill. 9/11 1989.

[66] AP: 1989: 249–253, Age of Majority Amendment Bill. 9/11 1989. Ashraff refers to a book written by Imam Navavi in Minah Ajjutalibeen, who is described as a scholar of the Shafi'i School.

According to traditional Shafiʻi interpretation, the age when a (male) person reaches religious maturity is 15 if it has not manifested itself earlier.[67] Hence, although the main argument had to do with the inclusion of youths in the democratic process, additional justification for the precise age of inclusion was a matter of choosing from the "pool of resources" — an example of Muslim politics.[68] Using Islamic values in politics is, according to Ashraff, not only in line with the SLMC politics but is also something that was happening in society as a whole:

> There again it shows the influence of the Muslim personal law on this subject. The Muslim personal law influencing the other systems of law in our country is not a new phenomenon.[69]

For Ashraff, Muslim family law could in this vein contribute in a positive way to solving the general problems of the country.

Ashraff denied that he or the SLMC had any aspirations to run the country on their own. His explicit ambition was solely to try to help build up the nation: the SLMC was thus not merely a party for Muslims but rather a party for the nation of Sri Lanka as a whole. In 1991, when the civil war was at an intense stage, he stated that "a national consensus must emerge at the [then planned] All Party Conference to resolve the present crisis that we are having [...]".[70] It was important that all democratic parties were present, including the LTTE, Ashraff argued.[71] Ashraff also questioned the democratic basis for the parliament:

> As far as we are concerned, we have always taken up the position that this Parliament does not represent the majority will of the nation. This has been our consistent position. [...] We, as responsible political parties, all of us, have a duty to examine whether there is a cancer that has set into the democratic framework of our country. [...] At the presidential elections only 55 percent of the people went to the polls. Therefore, one does not know what is the majority will of the nation.[72]

Ashraff's hypothesis was that the low level of voting was caused by fear of the militant groups in Sri Lanka.[73] In his opinion, the democratic solution was a coalition government with representatives of the major ethnic groups, for example, Tamils, Sinhalese, and, of course, the Muslims.[74]

In general, we find only slightly explicit references to Islam in Ashraff's publicly expressed views on how to solve the conflict. Following a series of states of emergencies during the 1990s, Ashraff argued for the restoration of democracy by referring not to Islam but instead to the constitution and the rule of law:

---

[67] Bearman, et al. 2006. See also Adams 2015.

[68] AP: 1989: 247–254, Age of Majority Amendment Bill 9/11. 1989. See also AP: 1990: 12 for similar arguments.

[69] AP: 1989: 247–254, Age of Majority Amendment Bill. 9/11 1989.

[70] AP: 1989: 201, Public Security Proclamation. 21/9 1989.

[71] AP: 1989: 201, Public Security Proclamation. 21/9 1989.

[72] AP: 1990: 3, No Confidence in Government. 1/12 1990. See also AP: 1989: 135.

[73] AP: 1990: 5, No Confidence in Government. 1/12.

[74] AP: 1989: 213, Public Security Proclamation. 19/10 1989. See also AP: 1992: 1–9.

[W]e will be faithful and loyal to the Constitution and it is our duty to uphold and protect the Constitution. The Constitution does not provide for a political vacuum in the North and the East. The Constitution says that if there is no Provincial Council there must be another election.[75]

In a later speech, he said:

Thereby we will be able to restore the ordinary law, we will be able to restore dignity and respect the fundamental provisions, the fundamental chapters, the fundamental rights enshrined in the Constitution. I believe that is the greatest service that we can do to this nation.[76]

Muslim politics, in terms of discourse, is, however, not totally absent. In a speech directed towards the minister of justice, Abdul Cader Shahul Hameed (UNP), also a Muslim, Ashraff quoted six verses from the Qur'an in order to substantiate the claim that the ideal of justice is always different in regard to laws (verses 4:58, 4:65, 4:105, 4:135, 7:29, and 16:90, all from Yusuf Ali's translation).[77] The point was to show that even the Qur'an acknowledged the gap between an ideal system and the law plus to convince the minister of justice to try to bring the law closer to the ideal, that is, to carry out the devolution of power among the communities, not only on regional levels but in parliament as well.[78] In this particular case, Ashraff also mentioned Aristotle and Cicero.

Education

If references to Islam as a religious tradition in the political discourse, that is, Muslim politics as defined in this book, were rather absent when Ashraff addressed politics in relation to the civil war, they were more frequent when other topics were on the agenda, for example, education. In reference the subject of education, Ashraff, when making speeches, consistently returned to two main issues. The first was the claim that he and the party were looking out for "Muslim issues" in the school system and in schools. One of the main problems was that Muslims were forced to go to non-Muslim schools. He stated in an appropriation bill to the minister of education that more Muslim schools and teachers for Muslim children were needed.[79] A particular religious aspect of this was the demand that the schools be gender segregated:

---

[75] AP: 1991: 56, Public Security Proclamation. 20/3 1991.

[76] AP: 1992: 90, Public Security Proclamation. 23/4 1992.

[77] It is unclear which translation of the Qur'an Ashraff used. AP: 1990: 320, Appropriation Bill 1991 to the Ministry of Justice. 4/12 1989.

[78] AP: 1989: 105, Appropriation Bill 1989 Ministry of Public Administration, Provincial Councils and Home Affairs. 10/4 1989. For similar arguments, see AP: 1989: 136 and AP: 1990: 321.

[79] AP: 1989: 71, Appropriation Bill to the Ministry of Education, Cultural Affairs and Information. 6/4 1989.

[H]e [the minister of education] has to select one school for the male Muslim students and one for the female Muslim students and he must concentrate on them. The Government must take it upon itself as its duty to provide everything possible, all assistance possible, to these schools […].[80]

In a similar vein, the issue of implementing a school dress code became political. According to Ashraff, Muslim girls were having problems in schools that catered to pupils belonging to different communities because they were not allowed to wear their traditional "Punjabi" uniform, which includes, as I understand it, the veil, or *hijab*. Female students wanted to dress decently, but were not allowed to do so.[81] Providing for the educational needs of Muslim pupils, including their need to express their religious identity with clothing, was, according to Ashraff, a duty of the state. He also stressed that more teachers were required at the Muslims schools, particularly emphasizing the need for Muslims to have Islamically educated teachers. What this recruiting of Islamic teachers meant in practice is unclear. At one time, Ashraff blamed the government for being too Sinhala-centric in its politics. He accused them of appointing teachers only for Sinhala victims of attacks by Tamil militants. He emphasized that there was also a need for these teachers in Muslim and Tamil families, which in fact had been even more gravely affected by the war.[82]

Ashraff was at times very specific when it came to dealing with different problem.[83] In one debate, while talking about Muslim schools in Colombo, he said that these schools were in very bad condition. They lacked furniture, for example, and teachers would often not even show up to class. He urged the government to take action.[84] Another example of Ashraff's focus on Muslim issues in schools was when he talked about the situation of the Muslim Ladies College in Colombo. According to him, it was without a principal for several months and this subsequently had a negative effect on the education of Muslim women.[85]

On a more general level, in regard to higher education, there was less emphasis put on religion. Ashraff said that he wanted more Tamil-language education at the university level, and he accused the government of promoting Sinhala colleges over their Tamil counterparts.[86] For example, Ashraff accused the Sri Pada College of Education for not accepting Muslims and Tamil-speaking non-Muslims.[87] At times,

---

[80] AP: 1990: 138, Supplementary Supply: Mid-Day Meal to School Children. 23/5 1990.

[81] AP: 1989: 74, Appropriation Bill to the Ministry of Education, Cultural Affairs and Information. 6/4 1989.

[82] AP: 1991: 138, Teaching Appointments to Digamadulla Districts. 24/7 1991.

[83] See AP: 1991: 282, Appropriation Bill 1992 Minster of Education & Higher Education. 2/12 1991.

[84] AP: 1990: 138–9, Supplementary Supply: Mid-day Meal to School Children. 23/5 1990.

[85] AP: 1990: 257, Question by M.H.M. Ashraff. 21/11 1990.

[86] AP: 1991: 124, Adjournment Motion: Situation in North Colombo Medical College, Colombo University and Ayurveda College. 12/7 1991. AP: 1989: 73, Appropriation Bill to the Ministry of Education, Cultural Affairs and Information. 6/4 1989.

[87] AP: 1992: 53, Question by Private Notice Selection of Muslims and Tamils to Sri Pada College of Education, Kotagala. 6/3 1992.

these two groups merge in the discourse and become Tamils, regardless of religious affiliation.[88] However, there also were cases when Islam was indirectly referred to in connection with higher education. Ashraff spoke on the importance of the Department of Arabic and said that the government should look into the development of this department at the University of Peradeniya. He said that the Arabic language is vital for many Sri Lankans, as many work in Middle Eastern countries, and he also argued that it was important for Muslims to learn Arabic since it is the language of the Qur'an.[89] Arabic had previously only been connected to the traditional teaching occurring in *madrasas*, and knowledge of Arabic among Muslims in Sri Lanka was generally low.[90] The SLMC's emphasis on education should be seen as part of a larger notion of the need to strengthen a common identity for the country's Muslims, such as promoting the creation of a Muslim newspaper and building a cultural library for Muslims.[91]

While religion and religious tradition thus have a given place in Ashraff's discussions on education, the main theme, for Ashraff, was the creation of a common Sri Lankan identity that would transcend community boundaries.

Ashraff saw education as the key to national unity. He stressed that education must have as its main objective the establishment of national unity.[92] The key was language. Ashraff complained in a debate with the minister of higher education that so few university graduates find employment, a situation he blamed on linguistic segregation.[93] Ashraff thought that if the people of Sri Lanka would learn its three languages (Sinhalese, Tamil, and English), this would further national unity.[94] He drew parallels to the pre-independence era, saying:

> [W]e were subjugated by the Portuguese and other European powers from 1508 to 1948 and we struggled for our freedom. When we fought we never thought of ourselves as Sinhalese, Tamil and Muslim. We fought as Ceylonese because there was no language barrier at that time.[95]

This fairly nostalgic reference to linguistic unity during the pre-independence era is an example of Ashraff's nationalist inclinations, which point to a common Sri

---

[88] There are other examples where Ashraff talks about Tamil-speaking people; however, he distinguishes between Tamils and Muslims in the cases that I have seen. See, for example, AP: 1991: 53.

[89] AP: 1990: 341, Appropriation Bill 1991 Ministry of Cultural Affairs and Information. 13/12 1990. AP: 1989: 68, Appropriation Bill 1989 Minster of Higher Education, Science and Technology. 5/4 1989. One year later, he repeated these arguments to the Minster of Higher Education. See AP: 1990: 328, Appropriation Bill 1991 Ministry of Education & Higher Education. 6/12 1990, and AP: 1991: 280, Appropriation Bill 1992 Minster of Education & Higher Education. 2/12 1991.

[90] Ameerdeen 2006: 42.

[91] Ameerdeen 2006: 113.

[92] AP: 1989: 63, Appropriation Bill 1989 Minster of Higher Education, Science and Technology. 5/4 1989.

[93] AP: 1989: 63–4, Appropriation Bill 1989 Minster of Higher Education, Science and Technology. 5/4 1989. See also AP: 1989: 129f, University (Amendment) Bill 27/4 1989.

[94] For similar arguments, see AP: 1989: 109.

[95] AP: 1989: 64, Appropriation Bill 1989 Minster of Higher Education, Science and Technology. 5/4 1989.

Lankan history. In another speech, Ashraff returned to the topic of languages when he spoke about jurisprudence in the country:

> After all, the Tamil language has become one of the official languages today. Therefore it is time that the Ministry of Justice concentrates on the question that the judges become trilingual. [...] Our constitution talks about the independence of the judiciary, about the judicial functions, judicial power of the people which is exercised by this Parliament through the established courts of law [...] therefore it is important that judges learn the languages of this country.[96]

Education in the country's languages is thus seen as the key to national unity. Ashraff wanted not only to change the education system but also to change the minds of Sri Lankans:

> We must create a Sri Lankan society in which every Sri Lankan will be trilingual and competent to deal in all the three languages. The time has gone when the Sinhala people considered that Sinhala was their language. Every Sinhala citizen of this country must think that Tamil is also his language, every Tamil citizen of this country must think that Sinhala is also his language [...].[97]

The quotation above is from 1991 when Ashraff made a suggestion to the minister of higher education about the status of the Tamil language. Here he refers to the constitution as a means of support for his statement. As early as in 1989, Ashraff expressed similar ideas in an appropriation bill for the ministry of education about a bridge for national unity:

> National unity could be achieved [...] only if all citizens know all the languages spoken by all communities in this country. I suggest a 15-year plan [...] so that if the children who enter the primary grade and over a 15-year period are exposed to all the three languages, Sinhalese, Tamil and English, we could produce in the year 2005 a new generation of Sri Lankan citizens [...].[98]

Ashraff wanted to implement this act in preschool, stating that it is wrong for a child in Sri Lanka to learn only one language.[99] He suggested that the government should take over all preschools so that it could implement this act. As a complement to this educational program, Ashraff gave four suggestions for how to make Sri Lanka more peaceful. In a speech to the minister of education in 1990, the alleged words of the Prophet Muhammad as recorded in hadith literature come in handy: "education and knowledge are the lost treasures of every human being; pick them up wherever you find them".[100] True to his rhetoric, he complemented this reference with references both to a Tamil poet and to Abraham Lincoln, and he continued, transcending the issue of language and approaching common religious values as a basis for national unity, thusly:

---

[96] AP: 1991: 23–4, Civil Procedure Code Amendment Bill. 31/1 1991.

[97] AP: 1991: 280, Appropriation Bill 1992 Minster of Education & Higher Education. 2/12 1991.

[98] AP: 1989: 71, Appropriation Bill to the Ministry of Education, Cultural Affairs and Information. 6/4 1989.

[99] AP: 1990: 81, Tertiary and Vocational Education Bill. 20/2 1990.

[100] AP: 1990: 32, Appropriation Bill 1991 Ministry of Education & Higher Education. 6/12 1990. The source Ashraff used to quote the Prophet Muhammad is unknown.

1. The establishment of a National Code of Ethics. It has to be compiled and students given all encouragement to follow it. 2. Facilities should be provided in all schools for a comparative study of religion. 3. Seminars should be organized for teachers and upper grade students with a view to re-awakening their sense of responsibility by focusing attention on religious tenets and moral values. 4. An Advisory Committee composed of religious dignitaries of all religions should be set up to advise the Hon. Minister and Ministry of Education in all matters connected with the restructuring of society on a moral base.[101]

Hence, there are two aspects related to education and the creation of national unity that the SLMC strives for, according to Ashraff. One is bridging the language gap.[102] Language became an important issue for the SLMC because the government had earlier enforced the Sinhala Only Act (see Chap. 1), making Tamil a secondary language in the country. If Tamil had equal status as an official language throughout the post-colonial period, it would then be easier for Muslims to get government jobs. Ashraff's speeches often referred to Dr. Colvin R. de Silva (1907–1987), a Trotskyist and founder of the first Marxist party in Sri Lanka (Lanka Sama Samaja Party), and his statement "one language, two countries; two languages, one country", meaning that both the Sinhala and Tamil languages should have equal status in the country.[103]

To study the different religions of the country was also then, according to Ashraff, a key to building a peaceful nation. Teachers have a unique role in bridging the gaps among the Sri Lankan people, and for that reason the Sri Lankan government should give top priority to issues like maximum salary and facilities.[104] In the speech referred to above, Ashraff spoke about a new generation that should be exposed to the country's three languages and three religions as a step towards national unity, hence the suggestion for a committee to be created in which representatives of all religions could get together and discuss their common values in order to agree upon basic tenets for a common education.[105]

Ashraff asserted that new generations of Sri Lankans should grow up learning each other's languages. College students should therefore be exposed to the different languages by interacting in the same classrooms. On another occasion, Ashraff used the law colleges as an example and stated that the different language communities rarely spoke to each other.[106] In a parliamentary debate, he accused another member of parliament (Nimal Siripala de Silva, SLFP) of being partisan and supporting only the Sinhala Buddhists; Ashraff thought that this focus on one particular community would lead to the destruction of the nation:

---

[101] AP: 1990: 326–7, Appropriation Bill Ministry of Education & Higher Education. 6/12 1990.

[102] AP: 1990: 82, Tertiary and Vocational Education Bill. 20/2 1990.

[103] AP: 1990: 10, No Confidence in Government. 21/1 1990.

[104] AP: 1991: 280, Appropriation Bill 1992 Minster of Education & Higher Education. 2/12 1991.

[105] AP: 1991: 281, Appropriation Bill 1992 Minster of Education & Higher Education. 2/12 1991.

[106] AP: 1989: 228, Council of Legal Education Ordinance: Rules Adjournment. 7/11 1989.

> We cannot think of saving the Sinhala Buddhists or saving only the Tamils or saving the Muslims only. All of us as Sri Lankans have a duty to think as Sri Lankans and ask the question as to how we are going to save this nation as one unity.[107]

Generally, Ashraff dropped his focus on "Muslims" when addressing the mistakes of the Sinhala Only project that was promoted in the 1950s.[108] In the same speech quoted directly above, Ashraff stressed the importance of all three languages and at the same time also defended English as being important for building a friendly, peaceful, and plural democracy in the nation by bridging other language gaps. In his vision, Sri Lanka should be a trilingual society where English is not only the bridge between Tamil and Sinhalese but also a language that is useful for Sri Lankans going abroad and for international relations.[109] Again, the Qur'an comes in as a justification for this vision. According to Ashraff, the Qur'an teaches the unity of the entire human race and, as a consequence, the unity of the nation of Sri Lanka:

> "Lahu Mafis Samswati Wa Ma fil Arl"
> Everything on the earth, everything in the heaven belongs to Allah the only God. Why I am quoting this is to say that languages are no exception to this universal concept. In the name of languages we shall not differ, in the name of languages we shall not fight [...] In the Holy Koran Allah has stated that he had created people, societies and communities not with the purpose that they fight among themselves but that they understand each other.[110]

The last sentence is a direct quotation from the Qur'an (4:171 and 49:13, English translation by Rashad Khalifa). For Ashraff, there are other ways apart from education through which national unity could be promoted. In an appropriation bill to the minister of sports in 1991, Ashraff referred to the national cricket team:

> [A]nd you deserve to be congratulated for the elaborate arrangements that you are making, and let me pray that Sri Lankan sportsmen and sportswomen will show their colors and through that keep the flag of Sri Lankans flying all over the South Asian region. [...] When you are playing you also inculcate in the young minds certain basic values that would constitute a very disciplined and healthy nation, at least a nation in which people will learn to accept defeat.[111]

While Ashraff claims in the above that it is essential that members of different communities play and train together, he also stresses the potential of sports in the processes of nation-building.

---

[107] AP: 1989: 108, Appropriation Bill 1989 Ministry of Public Administration, Provincial Council and Home Affairs. 10/4 1989.

[108] AP: 1990: 136, Supplementary Supply: Mid-day Meal to School Children. 23/5 1990.

[109] AP: 1991: 280, Appropriation Bill Minster of Education & Higher Education. 2/12 1991. See also AP: 1990: 137.

[110] AP: 1992: 139, Implementation of the Official Language Policy. 4/8 1992.

[111] AP: 1991: 363, Appropriation Bill: Ministry of Sports. 18/12 1991.

Islamic Economics

One sphere in which Muslim politics is most evident when looking at Ashraff's first years in parliament is the world of banking and economic growth. In this sphere, Ashraff actively tried to promote what he saw as a particular Islamic economics. In several speeches, he endorsed the traditional Muslim notion of interest-free banks.[112] Ashraff spoke openly about the economic system in the country as a problem in need of a solution. He said that people could not afford ordinary groceries like sugar and milk, and he urged the leader of the country not to follow what he termed the "capitalist way of America".[113] He furthermore put forward Iran, with its interest-free banking system, as a model and advocated a pilot project, or at least the founding of an institute, to study the possibility of implementing this particular economic system in Sri Lanka:

> We seriously believe that an interest-free economy is the solution – and the only solution – to the economic problems that we are facing today. Very recently I read an article where a researcher has said that the higher the rate of interest the higher the rate of unemployment, and the lower the rate of interest the lower the rate of unemployment. [...] On the other hand, we are left with the socialist, communist thinking. But what happened to the communist world? [...] Like a house of cards, everything is collapsing.[114]

In the discourse on an Islamic financial system, the SLMC leader recurrently referred to the Qur'anic term *riba*, often translated as usury.[115] At other times, his allusions to the scriptures were more specific: in a speech from 1991, he quoted four verses from the Qur'an in order to support his point about to point an Islamic economic system (verses 2:275, 2:276, 2:278, and 3:130, all from Yusuf Ali's English translation.). In addition to referring to the Qur'an, in another speech he mentioned an article (author and name of the article unknown) and stressed that:

> A good moral society cannot be established in Sri Lanka, a Buddhist nation where Lord Buddha himself has prohibited the taking of usury by exploitation. [...] Economic morals are important [...] The prohibition of usury is clearly associated in these verses of charity [...] Usury moreover promotes habits of idleness since the usurer instead of doing any hard work or manual labor becomes like a parasite [...]. Islam sides with labor but its prohibition of usury tries to restore the balance between the two, not allowing the capital to enthrall labor. It is in reference to the honorable place that Islam gives to labor that the Holy Koran says that Allah has permitted trading and forbidden usury.[116]

The reference in this quote is to the commonplace Islamic religious notion of balance and harmony. It is usually related to the Qur'anic imagery of a "pair of scales", *mizan*.[117] Also noteworthy is that similarities with Buddhism in terms of the

---

[112] These ideas were also promoted in the text *Our vision*. See O'Sullivan 1999: 254.

[113] AP: 1990: 23, Debt Recovery Bill. 24/1 1990.

[114] AP: 1990: 25–27, Debt Recovery Bill. 24/1 1990. For another example, see AP: 1991: 119–124.

[115] See Choudhury 2013.

[116] AP: 1990: 27, Debt Recovery Bill. 24/1 1990. For another example, see AP: 1991: 119–124.

[117] Smith 2015.

rejection of usury are again pointed out. In a later speech, Ashraff mentioned the constitution, which states that "the Republic of Sri Lanka shall give to Buddhism the foremost place and accordingly it shall be the duty of the state to protect and foster the Buddha Sasana (teachings from Buddha)".[118] On the same occasion, he emphasized that Sri Lanka, as a Buddhist nation, should follow the way of the Buddha. In a speech the following year, he claimed that the founder of Buddhism presented the same basic ideas that are found in Islam. Later in the speech, he stated that Islam lays down "the rules of the game" (even for business and all kinds of financial activities) and that the "Islamic concept of money and wealth goes hand in hand with the noble teachings of Lord Buddha".[119]

Ashraff continued trying to implement the interest-free system in banks and argued for a way to evaluate it:

> I would like to have economic advisors and economic producers to travel to countries like Iran to observe the society without interest functions. Another country would be Sudan. Sudan is working on coming out of IMF (International Monetary Fund) and [standing] independently of it. Yes, also in Pakistan. We need to find out how such an interest-free function works there and implement the good aspects of this in our country. We need to find out what motive the banks have in giving financial loans to people. At the same time, we need to know when we implement the Islamic interest-free approach where the banks show commitment when they give loans to those who start businesses as opposed to banks that give loans under interest with no commitment to those who borrow the money.[120]

One year later, Ashraff commented upon the introduction of interest-free banks, which at this point had become a reality, and stated that interest-free banks were the dawning of the idea of Islam. He also congratulated the minister of agriculture, Lalith Athulath Mudali (UNP), who introduced these loans to farmers.[121]

Riba is not the only term associated with money and economics that Ashraff selected from the "pool of resources". He also mentioned *zakat,* the compulsory giving of alms that constitutes one of the five pillars of Islam.[122] According to Ashraff, *zakat,* was a compulsory tax with a rate of 2.5% not only on one's income but also on one's wealth.[123] Ashraff focused on the role of *zakat* as an obligation. He cited the Qur'an (unknown translation):

> And in their property is the right of the beggar and those devoid of riches (i.e. the poor). Chapter 7, verse 156. And spend in the path of Allah and do not throw yourselves with your own hands into destruction. Chapter 2, verse 191. O you, who are believers, spend from the pure things that you have earned. Chapter 30, verse 38. You give your relatives his right and

---

[118] The constitution of Sri Lanka, quoted by Ashraff in AP: 1990: 196, Excise Amendment Bill. 5/9 1990.

[119] AP: 1990: 385, Appropriation Bill 1991: Minister of Finance. 21/12 1990.

[120] AP: 1992: 241–2, Turnover Tax Act. 16/12 1992 (translated from Tamil). For similar arguments, see AP: 1992: 15, Peoplization of State Banks. 19/2 1992.

[121] AP: 1991: 120, Supplementary Supply: Agriculture Productivity Villages. 11/7 1991.

[122] See Nanji 2013.

[123] AP: 1992: 41, Finance Amendment Bill 4/3 1992. See also AP: 1992: 116.

to the poor and a wayfarer. Chapter 30, verse 38. O you who believe, spend from what we have given you. Chapter 2, verse 225.[124]

This appropriation bill from 1989 is an example of a time when Ashraff seems to have taken on the role of a religious authority, interpreting the scriptures in relation to concrete issues. When advocating an Islamic policy of the distribution of wealth, he quoted a paragraph from *Shari al- The Islamic Law* by Dr. Abdur Rahman.[125] He claimed that Islam equals poverty alleviation:

> It (Islam) assures that in the process of distribution none of the factors of production exploits the other. The landowners, the laborers and the owners of capital jointly share in their productions. [...] The Holy Prophet and the *Rashidun* Caliphs achieved this goal through prohibiting a very large number of exploitative and unjust techniques in trade and commerce. A study of *Hadith* literature is suggestive of those measures which include disciplinary restrictions in the landlord and the farmer, the employer and the employee and the producer and the trader. Our study on prohibition of *Riba* has explained some of those measures.[126]

Another sphere of activity related to economics where religious terms and symbols are likewise visible in Ashraff's rhetoric is the topic of fraud and how to prevent it. Ashraff argued in a speech to the minister of justice that the teachings of the Qur'an should have a place in laws against frauds; he quoted verse 282 from Sura 2 and stated that there should be witnesses to these fraudulent actions.[127]

Public Morals

Other areas where Muslim politics emerge in Ashraff's speeches are the spheres of ethics, sexuality, and gender relations. In a debate with the minister of tourism, he said that promoting tourism to make profits for Sri Lanka also puts Sri Lankans' "social, cultural, religious and moral values" at risk.[128] One concern that Ashraff had, and where religious references were directly invoked, was male prostitution:

> According to the holy Koran, Allah destroyed nations that were involved in homosexuality [...] This is what the Koran says in this matter: And (we sent) Lut, who said to his people. Will you persist in these indecent acts which no other nation has committed before you? You lust after men instead of women, truly you are a de-generate people (Chapter 7, verse 80) [Yusuf Ali].[129]

[124] AP: 1989: 25, Appropriation Bill. 23/3 1989.
[125] The author of this book is described as a scholar of Islamic law.
[126] AP: 1989: 25, Appropriations Bill. 1989 23/3 1989.
[127] AP: 1992: 203–6, Appropriation Bill 1993: Minister of Justice. 8/9 1992.
[128] AP: 1989: 110, Appropriation Bill to the Ministry of Tourism. 11/4 1989.
[129] AP: 1989: 111, Appropriation Bill to the Ministry of Tourism. 11/4 1989.

The story of Lot (Arabic. Lut) appears in one of the verses in the Qur'an that is referred to in order to argue against homosexuality.[130] At the time of the speech, the issue was a matter of public debate because there was an ongoing discussion about pedophiles coming to the country and engaging in sexual activities with young boys.[131] Homosexuality was also banned in Sri Lanka (as it still is), hence Ashraff's arguments from the religious texts were not in any way controversial in the Sri Lankan context.

In the same speech, he tried to further strengthen his arguments by claiming that this kind of "bad tourism" increased drug use and the spread of diseases such as AIDS in the country. In line with this argument, Ashraff wanted to refuse entry into the country for every tourist that had AIDS in order to secure the safety of the nation.[132] The subject of AIDS is something Ashraff came back to when he defended polygamous marriages as a Muslim right:

> That shows the gravity of the illness and to what extent Sri Lanka as a nation today is vulnerable. Why not make polygamous marriages legal [...] Every male member is going to support my proposal. Female members will also like it because today it is not only the AIDS problem. [...] A more serious problem is prevailing in the North and East. That is the problem of young girls that are unable to find partners for a married life.[133]

AIDS is, according to Ashraff, a threat to the nation, and Islam has the answers: prohibit tourists with AIDS and homosexual tourists that seek prostitutes from entering the country, and allow polygamous marriages. In Ashraff's opinion, polygamous marriages will subdue people's urges for unnecessary sexual contact.[134] Ashraff tried to justify Islamic law for the benefit of the nation in order to gain support from non-Muslim politicians.

"Bad tourism" was something that affected the Sri Lankan family structure, which Ashraff called the unity of society. Foreign money could never hold precedence over the preservation of the moral and cultural values of Sri Lanka.[135] Later on, he continued his proclamations about tourism, condemning the Sri Lankan government for attracting female prostitutes by promoting casinos and gambling.[136] Again, the Buddha came in handy. He spoke about how the Buddha singlehandedly had forbidden gambling and, therefore, Sri Lanka should follow this tradition.

The Buddha, hand in hand with Islam, was also useful when Ashraff turned to another issue related to public morals: the use of alcohol. In a speech to the minister of health, the role of Buddhism in the constitution again played a role in the rhetoric used. Ashraff claimed that liquor had no part to play in Sri Lankan culture:

---

[130] See Rowson 2013.

[131] Miller 2002: note 3.

[132] AP: 1989: 110, Appropriation Bill to the Ministry of Tourism. 11/4 1989.

[133] AP: 1992: 230, Appropriation Bill to the Ministry of Health. 14/12 1992.

[134] AP: 1992: 230, Appropriation Bill to the Ministry of Health. 14/12 1992.

[135] AP: 1989: 111, Appropriation Bill to the Ministry of Tourism. 11/4 1989.

[136] AP: 1989: 329, Appropriation Bill to the Ministry of Tourism 1990. 11/12 1989.

I am a great admirer of Lord Buddha. Lord Buddha had taught good ways of life to humanity. Lord Buddha had stated that human society can be clean. It can be free of corruption if
it can keep away from evil, and one of the great evils identified by Lord Buddha is Liquor
[...] Islam prohibits it [...] and we must tell the nation that we cannot any longer continue
to preach as guardians of the Buddha Sasana and at the same time depend on these distill-
eries to generate income for our country.[137]

One year later, speaking on the same topic, the references to Islam are gone, and
Ashraff again stressed that alcohol should not be allowed, according to Buddhism.[138]

On another issue related to public morals, one more specifically pertaining to
Islam, Ashraff commented upon the fact that the newspaper *Newsweek* had published a picture of the Prophet. Ashraff claimed that:

[T]here it seems to be a pattern universally in insulting the religion of Islam and the Prophet
whom we hold dear to us. [...] The particular issue of the Newsweek should not be allowed
to be circulated in Sri Lanka [...].[139]

In addition to this, he said "it is forbidden to make a portrait of Muhammad".[140]
Ashraff in the above quoted parliamentary speech took on the role of a defender of
Islam and Muslims. The word "we" denotes, in this case, Muslims, and "insulting
the religion of Islam" is the primary phrase.

Islamic Laws

As the distribution of images of the Prophet in public can be seen as a particularly
"Muslim" or "Islamic" issue, so can the matter of Shari'a courts. Ashraff argued
with the minister of justice for the possibility of expansion for the jurisdiction of
these courts:

Today we have our Constitution and we are proud of that as Sri Lankans. Sri Lanka allows
every community to believe in and practice his own faith. We have the Quazi courts, but
their functions are confined only to marriage and divorce and personal matters. But what
about custodial matters? Why not [...] think of setting up the sharia courts so that not only
those aspects but even the other legal aspects [...] can be brought into play.[141]

Ashraff thus cited the constitution of Sri Lanka and brought up the notion that
every community has a right to practice its faith. Therefore, he claimed, Muslims
should be able to deal with legal aspects other than family matters in Shari'a courts.
In the same speech, Malaysia is introduced as a good example of how the integration of Shari'a courts into the legal system can work. It should be noted that although

---

[137] AP: 1990: 196–7, Excise Amendment Bill 5/9 1990. For a similar argument, see AP: 1992: 270,
Appropriation Bill 1992 Minister of Ports and Telecommunications. 29/11 1991.

[138] AP: 1991: 33f Custom Resolution: Import Duties. 19/2 1991.

[139] AP: 1989: 62, Question by private notice. 5/4 1989.

[140] AP: 1989: 62, Question by private notice. 5/4 1989.

[141] AP: 1992: 207, Appropriation Bill: Ministry of Justice. 8/9 1992. For another example, see AP:
1990: 1–12.

"custodial matters" are referred to, it is not specified in detail which laws he wanted to extend to Shari'a courts, except for the statement that Shari'a courts should increase their areas of competence. Ashraff's speech on Shari'a should be seen in context. As was previously mentioned, there was at the time a large public discussion on the issue taking place.[142]

When it comes to changes within existing Muslim family law, he was more specific. He claimed, for example, that there was an abuse of polygamous marriage: men take advantage of it and get divorced easily.[143] He argued that amendments must be made to Muslim family law, stating that "it is the responsibility of the husband to maintain the wife [...] as he gets married to another person".[144]

In regard to another question related to Islamic law, Ashraff spoke on the topic of the adoption. Ashraff again acted as a religious authority, providing a direct interpretation of Islam:

> We are dealing with the newly born Sri Lankan citizens. There will be a time if every Sri Lankan baby is adopted in any of the foreign countries, when they reach the age of majority, when they start thinking on their own [...] As a party, the Sri Lankan Muslim Congress has a duty on this occasion to put forward the Islamic aspect of it. According to Islam, adoption is permitted but when adopting, the child must know who his true, natural parents are.[145]

The debate on whether adoption is permitted by Islamic law or not has been discussed for a long time among religious scholars.[146] Ashraff, however, simply declared that Islam does not prohibit it, as long as the child knows his or her roots. What is important from Ashraff's point of view is that the child knows he or she is a Sri Lankan child and the identity of his or her biological parents. Therefore, he suggested that the adoption of infants should not be permitted. Furthermore, Ashraff also stated in the same speech that "it is a loss for the country when Sri Lankan children are adopted to foreign countries".[147]

Foreign Policy

Islam, directly or indirectly, has a given place when Ashraff made his move from domestic to international politics. One such area is Israel and its role in international politics. In a critical talk on Israel, Ashraff openly protested against the government, claiming that Israel, in different ways, was involved in the civil war in Sri Lanka. He even went so far as to say that the nation was under threat by the Israeli military, which was he said was advising the government at that time. Ashraff was referring

---

[142] See Wagner 1990: 214.

[143] AP: 1992: 208, Appropriation Bill: Ministry of Justice. 8/9 1992.

[144] AP: 1992: 208, Appropriation Bill: Ministry of Justice. 8/9 1992.

[145] AP: 1992: 30–3, Adoption of Children Amendment Bill. 21/2 1992.

[146] See Powers 2013.

[147] AP: 1992: 32, Adoption of Children Amendment Bill. 21/2 1992.

to the Israeli Interests Section (it is rather unclear what type of organization this was), which, following an invitation issued by the Sri Lankan president Jayawardene, was established in 1984 at the American Embassy. Its mission was to give military advice to the Sri Lankan army and train the Sri Lankan police.[148] Traditionally, the Sri Lankan official policy had been pro-Palestinian, so this invitation constituted a major change in strategy. Ashraff claimed that the Israeli Interests Section was undermining the interests of Muslims as a religious group. He furthermore claimed that the Muslim political leaders and the Muslim members of parliament had met with the president to say that they wanted to end the collaboration. In the same speech, he announced that:

> The Israeli Interests Section was opened up in order to curb the militant activities for which we wanted assistance. […] Even after this section was opened the problems remained unresolved. […] There is no justification for keeping the Israeli Interests Section any longer in Sri Lanka.[149]

Ashraff clearly wanted the Israelis out of the country, asserting that the problems had not been resolved and that the Israelis consequently should leave. Israel's presence in Sri Lanka sparked mass protests among Muslims around the country, and in some cases it also led to riots; in the Muslim- dominated town of Kattankudy, the government's army opened fire on a protesting crowd.[150]

In 1990, the government closed the Israeli Interests Section, but the SLMC did not cease its criticism. One and a half years later, Ashraff accused the LTTE of having direct links to Mossad, the Israeli intelligence agency, and expressed his concern that this interference would destabilize the entire country.[151] He claimed that the true reason that made the Sri Lankan government close the Israeli Interests Section was that Mossad actually supported the LTTE. He also pointed out that Muslim countries had great admiration for Sri Lanka's foreign policy towards Israel and that it was for this reason that Mossad was involved with the Tamil Tigers.[152] In this infected climate, Buddhism once again was referred to. Ashraff told the audience a story about the Buddha, a lion (the symbol of the GoSL), a tiger (the symbol of the LTTE), and a wolf (symbolizing Mossad):

> They [the Lion and the Tiger] could not agree on how best the dead carcass of a deer should be shared between them. Therefore they went to a wolf. The wolf said, 'You cannot settle this matter. Let me settle it for you,' and the wolf took the carcass for himself and walked away.[153]

---

[148] O'Sullivan 1999: 95.

[149] AP: 1989: 46, Appropriation Bill to the Ministry of Foreign Affairs. 3/4 1989. See also AP: 1990: 314.

[150] O'Sullivan 1999: 228.

[151] AP: 1990: 261, Public Security Proclamation. 22/11 1990. Ashraff also talks about the CIA, Jews, and Zionists as having a hand in the internal affairs of Sri Lanka. See AP: 1991: 42.

[152] AP: 1991: 216, Public Security Proclamation. 24/10 1991.

[153] AP: 1991: 216, Public Security Proclamation. 24/10 1991.

Ashraff developed his thoughts about Mossad's associations with the LTTE by quoting a Tamil/Muslim newspaper:

The news item says that "at a dinner in Paris one of the LTTE cadre members had stated that they were regularly being paid by the MOSSAD for the only purpose of killing the Muslims in this country. [...] The Sri Lanka Muslim Congress always had this doubt because the Muslim community and the Tamil community [...] for a thousand years have been living in peace [...] But all of a sudden [...] a new development took place in this relationship [...] and the two communities moved further from each other.[154]

In this quote, Ashraff blames the conflict – and hence the attacks on Muslims – on interference from an external force. He subsequently made a plea to the government to look at this seriously. The government then in fact issued a commission to investigate these accusations, but it did not find any evidence that the charges were true.[155]

Taking his arguments about Israel further along a more blatantly anti-Semitic path, Ashraff spoke of Jews, Zionists, and the American CIA as threats to the world-wide Muslim community. He said that in reality, the Gulf War in 1990–1991 was a war between the West and Third World countries.[156] America and its allies were not at all interested in rescuing the Kuwaiti people, he claimed. All they were after was the oil.[157] In addition to this, Ashraff commented upon the situation in Israel and Palestine:

Sir, today if Saddam Hussein walks out of Kuwait, what is the guarantee that America is going to leave the soil of Saudi Arabia? Already our holiest mosque al Aqsa is in the hands of the Jews, in the hands of the Zionists, in the hands of American CIA agents. There is a direct threat to the two holiest of holy places to the Muslim community, namely, holy Mecca and holy Medina Al Sherif where our beloved Prophet is buried.[158]

Ashraff then called the war "a conspiracy against the Muslim world" and proclaimed that rational humans would do anything to condemn it.[159] In his 1991 speech about the Gulf War, Ashraff's views on the Muslim *umma* take a more global approach. "Muslims" no longer only refers to a local, "imagined community" but also to a global *Gemeinschaft*. He moreover criticized the United Nations (UN), as he believed it should have intervened in the conflict between Palestine and Israel like it did in the case of Kuwait. He consequently accused the UN of adopting a double standard. Similarly, he accused the United States of, instead of freeing Kuwait, bombing places that are holy for Muslims:

---

[154] AP: 1992: 215, Public Security Proclamation. 23/7 1992.

[155] O'Sullivan 1999: 309.

[156] The war that took place in 1990–1991 when the United States and its allies attacked Iraq in response to the Iraqi invasion of Kuwait.

[157] AP: 1991: 8, Adjournment Motion: Gulf War. 24/1 1991.

[158] AP: 1991: 12, Adjournment Motion: Gulf War. 24/1 1991.

[159] AP: 1991: 12, Adjournment Motion: Gulf War. 24/1 1991.

But what did America do? Instead of going to Kuwait they went across to Iraq and started
to bombard the holiest places like Karbala. There are hundreds of holy Muslim Saints buried there, and this has shocked the conscience and sentiment of the Muslim world.[160]

As is also the case when he earlier constructed Muslims as a category in the Sri
Lankan context, Ashraff does not mention internal Muslim diversity here either. In
this quote, for instance, he refers to Karbala, which is most holy for Shia Muslims.
He also talks about "saints", which, at least in the Sri Lankan context, is a word used
most often when referring to Sufism. Later that year, Ashraff continued his interest
in the Palestinian uprising and celebrated them as heroes on the fourth anniversary
of the intifada.[161]

The Muslims of India constitute another segment of the population with which
Ashraff identified himself. Commenting upon the events that took place in India in
1992 when the Babri Mosque was destroyed by a Hindu mob, he declared, while
drawing parallels to the militant (Hindu) Tamil attacks on Muslims, that he was
grateful that he lived in a Buddhist country that showed respect for Islamic
principles.[162]

Analysis

What, then, might, from the perspective of Muslim politics, be concluded from the
speeches Ashraff delivered in parliament? First of all, it becomes clear that events
related to the civil war are an important context for the construction of a unified
Muslim community and of the SLMC as its representative. Attacks on "Muslim villages" and "mosques" strengthen the notion of a conflict that affects "Muslims" as
a unified local *umma*. As was the case in the interviews, Ashraff used certain attributes to describe Muslims as poor refugees and above all else as targets of violence
in the local imagined community of "(Sri Lankan) Muslims". Apart from the civil
war, the issue of education in particular and the role of the Arabic language tend to
be important in the construction of "Muslims".[163]

As is often the case with Muslim politics, women, and especially women's clothing, tend to be attributed with symbolic functions. This observation is in line with
the conclusions discussed in previous chapters concerning Muslims being constructed as a category within the SLMC's rhetoric by pointing out unique elements
in language and clothing.

Just like in the interviews with the leading members of the party and the discourse on the history of the party, Ashraff continually repeated in his parliamentary
speeches (for example, in the discussion about the Indo-Sri Lankan Peace Accord)

---

[160] AP: 1991: 13 Adjournment Motion: Gulf War. 24/1 1991.

[161] AP: 1991: 309 Appropriation Bill 1992 Ministry of Plantation Industries. 9/12 1991.

[162] AP: 1992: 227, Appropriation Bill 1993 Minister of Post and Telecommunications (cont'd).
11/12 1992. Translated from Tamil. See also AP: 1992: 190.

[163] Cf. Eickelman and Piscatori 2004: 102.

that Muslims constitute a separate, but internally unified, ethnicity. His approach came as a direct response to the Tamil militant organizations' claims that language – not religion – should form the basis for ethnicity.[164] Part of the creation of Muslims as an ethnicity lies in Ashraff's identification of a specific part of the country as an original "homeland" for Muslims.[165] However, Ashraff's strong emphasis on Muslims as an ethnic group in its own right does not turn into separatist nationalism. *The recognition of a Muslim identity that Ashraff promoted "does not lead to an automatic association with Political Islam inspired to run an own state".[166] In the 1980s, there was actually one group (Hizb-ul-Islam) that sought to establish an independent Islamic republic in Sri Lanka, and it supported the SLMC.[167] At most, the SLMC under Ashraff demanded some form of Muslim administrative autonomy.[168]*

It is clear from the parliamentary speeches examined here that Ashraff was always keen to express his loyalty to the state – and, moreover, his loyalty to Sri Lankan nationalism and national unity. This focus on the nation is evident from his views on education. Most of his suggestions were about how education could foster national unity, particularly through language.[169] Sri Lanka has been a post-colonial society since 1948, and being a post-colonial society has contributed to the belief that Sri Lankans have something in common. Ashraff fully endorsed the view that Sri Lankans have a common past and future.[170]

When Ashraff created a new political party in 2000, the National Unity Alliance (NUA), it was this theme of nationalism that was at the forefront. In creating this new party, Ashraff showed his ultimate rhetorical devotion to the Sri Lankan nation.[171] Ashraff took part in creating a Sri Lankan identity by pointing to the nation's pre-history.[172] There were some references to Islam made in the initial phase of the NUA, but the party soon developed into a wholesale secular party.[173] It did not, however, compete with the SLMC for votes, since it got most of its votes from the Sinhala-speaking community in the Ampara District.[174]

In the way Ashraff expressed his loyalty to the nation, we can detect traces of Muslim politics. He cited verses from the Qur'an in support of the unity of mankind – and, as a consequence, the unity of the Sri Lankans. He selected these verses – and the religious notions they connote – among other possible ones. In the

---

[164] Knoerzer 1998: 152.

[165] There is little doubt that the SLMC had its major support in the eastern part of Sri Lanka. This is clear when viewing voting statistics for the elections of the 1980s (Knoerzer 1998: 152).

[166] *Saravanamuttu* 2010: 15.

[167] O'Sullivan 1999: 256.

[168] Abubakar 2010: 128.

[169] Balibar 2002: 132.

[170] Cf. Anderson 2006: 121.

[171] Balibar 2002: 123.

[172] Balibar 2002: 119.

[173] See National United Alliance n.d.

[174] McGilvray and Raheem 2007: 29.

Qur'an, there are several terms that could be connected to national unity and more to a kind of pluralist acceptance; the most famous term is arguably the notion of *ahl al- kitab* (people of the book), but that term is traditionally associated with Zoroastrianism, Judaism, Christianity, and, in the Indian context, Hinduism.[175] Ashraff chose to be inclusive. This inclusiveness can be seen as a consequence of the fact that his political opponents, the Muslim representatives from the west coast, often accused him of communalism. It should be noted, however, that there is some contradiction between Ashraff's expressed loyalty to the nation and the SLMC's demands for some form of Muslim self-rule in the southeast. On the one hand, Ashraff needed to acknowledge voices that wanted some form of self-governance for Muslims, but, on the other hand, he wanted to stay loyal to the state.

The Muslim politics of Ashraff often include not only references to sacred terminology made by citing scriptures in support of a particular stance but also providing terms and references with extended meaning. This is evident in his use of the word jihad. From the perspective of Islamic tradition as a whole, the term jihad has diverse meanings in diverse contexts.[176] Ashraff related jihad to patience (*sabr*) as a morally superior stance even though his main point was that patience has its limits. He chose to focus on jihad as an individual duty and as a form of self-defense, not as a public, common duty of warfare declared by a legitimate leader. Hence, he did not declare jihad; he merely suggested that the prerequisites for it as an individual duty have been, or may soon be, met.[177] The demands that the government create a separate Muslim army unit may, however, be seen as at least a sort of declaration of what the Qur'an refers to as *nafir 'amm*, that is, war as a collective endeavor.[178]

It has already been noted above how Ashraff associated the politics of the party to the notion of a "middle path". As has been noted, to turn against both Marxism and capitalism and to introduce Islam as a viable third way is something that is not uncommon on the Indian sub-continent nor in the world of Muslim politics.[179] The anti-capitalist focus derives mainly from an anti-imperialist discourse, and the anti-Marxist articulation is based on the conviction that the Left is always militant.[180] Islam is presented as the untested alternative to "failed" communism; this was declared during the midst of the collapse of the Soviet Union and other communist states.

As was the case in the context of the SLMC's official documents, it is in this analysis intriguing to draw some parallels between Ashraff's speeches in parliament and the ideas of Sayyid Abul-A'la Mawdudi. First, there is the notion of the middle path. Like Mawdudi, Ashraff introduced Islam as a political ideology, and it was presented as an alternative to the two dominant ideologies, namely, communism and

[175] See Wilde and McAuliffe 2013.

[176] See Landau-Tasseron 2013.

[177] Lewis 1988: 73.

[178] Despite Ashraff's use of Islamic terms and symbols, some of his opponents consider him as having been an "Islamic fraud". See Farook 2009.

[179] See Eickelman and Piscatori 2004: 43.

[180] Cordier 2010: 482.

capitalism. This idea of Islam as a middle path originates from the Qur'anic term *wasatiyya*. This notion has been used by other Muslim political movements as well.[181]

Ashraff's notions about Islam and economics also closely mirror the ideas of Mawdudi. Like Mawdudi, there are two key concepts that Ashraff wanted to implement in society. The first is *zakat* (alms) as a formal tax from the government to the underprivileged. Like Ashraff, Mawdudi saw this tax as a way for the government to impose *zakat*. The second Islamic economic principle suggested by both Ashraff and Mawdudi is the prohibition of *riba* (usury). However, Mawdudi also suggested a shared risk/profit relationship between customer and bank, something not found in Ashraff's speeches.[182] The similarities are probably not coincidental.

Still, there are also areas of difference between Ashraff's and Mawdudi's thoughts. The issue of citizenship (as noted above) is such a difference. Mawdudi's thoughts were inspired by a vision of an Islamic state in which non-Muslims lived as *dhimmi* under special laws, such as the obligatory payment of protection tax (*jizya*). No such notion is found in Ashraff's rhetoric.

On the basis of what has been outlined and discussed in this chapter, it is possible to enter into a dialogue with previous research and to correct some misunderstandings. For example, O'Sullivan writes about Ashraff's call for jihad as a sign of Muslim militancy in the SLMC.[183] She contrasts this with non-SLMC Muslim politicians in western Sri Lanka who promoted Islam as a peace-loving and tolerant religion.[184] I contest this on the basis that if one wants to understand the SLMC's position on violence, one has to move beyond the use of a particular term to how this term is actually conceptualized in a particular context. The use of the term jihad is not in itself a sign of militancy. O'Sullivan's interpretation could be seen as an over-emphasis of the role of Islam in the SLMC.

At the same time, scholars who argue that religion is exaggerated in the politics of the SLMC have not looked at the whole picture. For example, Klem criticizes O'Sullivan's work, pointing out that she misread the SLMC's "political rhetoric as the ascendancy of Islamist politics".[185] I agree with Klem, but both miss the fact that the SLMC, since its early years, has been conducting thoroughly Muslim politics, albeit not "Islamist" in the sense of advocating the Islamization of state institutions. There is more to Muslim politics than fundamentalism versus secularism.[186] When

---

[181] Mawdudi was not alone among Islamist thinkers in proposing this. See Bellén Soage 2010: 30f; Altuntas 2010; and Mitchell 1969, Chapter VIII.

[182] Ahmed 1985: 107

[183] O'Sullivan 1999: 267.

[184] O'Sullivan 1999: 266.

[185] Klem 2012: 736. This could also be observed in Imtiyaz 2005.

[186] The concepts are extremes and cannot be restricted to any organization in particular. They should be seen as tendencies among organizations. Hjärpe described these concepts in this way: "Secularism and fundamentalism are in opposite to each other when it comes to religion's function in society. The secular sees religion as an individual choice [...] The fundamentalist states that Islam in itself is a social order" Hjärpe 1983: 42.

Spencer claims that the SLMC is not an Islamist party, he is indeed correct, but that does not mean that the SLMC is not into Muslim politics.[187]

Perhaps one should even argue that "Muslim politics" becomes too narrow a focus when approaching the content of Ashraff's speeches. He often transcended the "pool of resources" provided by Islamic tradition and astoundingly used a general sort of "religious politics". This "religious politics" is most evidently incarnated when he referred to the Buddha and Buddhist concepts but also when he in an even more general way refered to values shared by several religions. Especially noteworthy is that when Ashraff spoke about the governmental institutions and how they should respond to events in the war, there is no Muslim politics to be detected; instead, we run into Buddhist concepts. It seems that in an exposed situation, where Muslims are being killed outright and there is a need for help, Muslim politics becomes less important and even unhelpful.[188]

When Ashraff used Islamic "sacred terminology", the lack of its attachment to any issue that could be deemed "controversial" or problematic by the state is typical. For the most part, references to Islam, in terms of beliefs or practices, are in line with views already shared by society at large. Ashraff himself also explicitly and repeatedly discussed compatibility between existing ideals in Sri Lankan and Islamic equivalents. Muslim politics, as presented in Ashraff's speeches, was, with few exceptions, neither radical nor oppositional.

One area in which Muslim politics indeed contributes something substantial in terms of a body politic is economics and the notion of an Islamic banking system as an alternative to the current system and its problems. Still, the suggestions put forward by Ashraff do not "necessarily imply direct confrontation with the regime".[189]

The strong condemnation of Israel and Mossad, in combination with anti-Semitism, is not uncommon in Muslim politics.[190] *The Israel-Palestine conflict can serve as a transnational symbol of Muslim identity that Muslim politicians around the world can use as a strong symbol to strengthen their own position in relation to a general public.*[191] *Using the Israel-Palestine conflict as a symbol for Muslim identity also appears to be the case with Ashraff and the SLMC, and it also holds true for other* examples such as the Gulf War or Salman Rushdie's novel *The Satanic Verses.*[192]

Is the SLMC a Muslim protest movement, and its rhetoric an example of what Eickelman and Piscatori highlight as "protest and bargaining" in Muslim politics? In some regards, I would affirm this. We can see that by referring to Muslims as victims, Ashraff turns the SLMC into a Muslim protest movement, but it is not a protest movement of the sort to which Eickelman and Piscatori refer, namely, a movement that seeks to enforce Islam as the solution to society's problems. It is

[187] Spencer 2012: note 7.
[188] C.f. Eickelman and Piscatori 2004: 126.
[189] Eickelman and Piscatori 2004: 109.
[190] See Eickelman and Piscatori 2004: 13.
[191] Eickelman and Piscatori 2004: 146.
[192] Eickelman and Piscatori 2004: 16. See also Edwards 2009: 103f.

rather a protest that states that the "Muslim voice needs to be heard" and that the party is responsible for delivering it. The SLMC could, moreover, be said to be the result of the objectification of Muslim consciousness, since it tries to implement Islamic ideas in society. This objectification is also spotted in Ashraff's comparisons of Islam to Buddhism. In the case of the SLMC, the approach is eclectic in the sense that it tries to implement Islamic ideals, notions that might in the end turn out to be rather general ones relating to justice, equality, and peace.

References

Primary Sources

Ashraff in Parliament Volume I –1989. Colombo: Dahrussalam Publication. (Ed) Rauff Hakeem (2005).
Ashraff in Parliament Volume II –1990. Colombo: Dahrussalam Publication. (Ed) Rauff Hakeem (2005).
Ashraff in Parliament Volume III – Year 1991. Colombo: Dahrussalam Publication. (Ed) Rauff Hakeem (2006).
Ashraff in Parliament Volume IV – Year 1992. Colombo: Dahrussalam Publication. (Ed) Rauff Hakeem (2006).
National United Alliance (n.d.). Colombo: Dahrussalam Publication.

Literature

Abubakar, Carmen A. 2010. A Never-Ending War and the Struggle for Peace in Southern Philippines. In *Islam and Politics in Southeast Asia*, ed. Johan Saravanamuttu. London/New York: Routledge.
Adams, Charles J. 2015. Maturity. *Encyclopaedia of the Qurʾān*. Brill Online. Retrieved February 23, 2015, from http://referenceworks.brillonline.com/entries/encyclopaedia-of-the-quran/maturity-EQCOM_00115.
Ahmed, Ishtiaq. 1985. *The Concept of an Islamic State: An Analysis of the Ideological Controversy in Pakistan*. Doctoral dissertation, Edsbruk: Department of Political Science, University of Stockholm.
Alexander, Scott C. 2015. Trust and Patience. *Encyclopaedia of the Qurʾān*. Brill Online. Retrieved February 23, 2015, from, http://referenceworks.brillonline.com/entries/encyclopaedia-of-the-quran/trust-and-patience-EQCOM_00209.
Altuntas, Nezahat. 2010. Religious Nationalism in a New Era: A Perspective from Political Islam. *African and Asians Studies* 9: 418–435.
Ameerdeen, Vellaithamby. 2006. *Ethnic Politics of Muslims in Sri Lanka*. Kandy: Center for Minority Studies, Kribs Printers.
Anderson, Benedict. 2006. *Imagined Communities*. London: Verso. First Edition 1983.
Balibar, Étienne. 2002. Nationsformen: Historia och ideology. In *Ras, Nation, Klass*, ed. Etienne Balibar and Immanuel Wallerstein. Uddevalla: Bokförlaget Daidalos AB.

Bearman, P., Th. Bianquis, C.E. Bosworth, E. van Donzel, and W.P. Heinrichs. 2006. Bāli<u>gh</u>. *Encyclopedia of Islam, Second Edition*. Brill Online. Retrieved February 3, 2015, from http://referenceworks.brillonline.com/entries/encyclopaedia-of-islam-2/ba-lig-h-SIM_1143.

Bellén Soage, Ana. 2010. Yusuf Al-Qaradawi: The Muslim Brothers' Favorite Ideological Guide. In *The Muslim Brotherhood: The Organization and Policies of a Global Islamist Movement*, ed. Barry Rubin. New York: Palgrave Macmillan.

Choudhury, Masudul Alam. 2013. Usury. *Encyclopaedia of the Qurʾān*. Brill Online. Retrieved October 23, 2013, from http://referenceworks.brillonline.com/entries/encyclopaedia-of-the-quran/usury-SIM_00438.

Cordier De, Bruno. 2010. Challenges of Social Upliftment and Definition of Identity: A Field Analysis of the Social Service Network of Jammat-e-Islami Hind, Meerut, India. *Journal of Muslim Minority Affairs* 30 (4): 479–500.

De Silva, Nilika, and Faraza Farook. 1999. Ashraff 'talks' with Lord Buddha. *The Sunday Times*. Retrieved July 31, 2015, from http://www.sundaytimes.lk/991128/news3.html..

Edwards, John. 2009. *Language and identity*. New York: Cambridge University Press.

Eickelman, Dale F., and James Piscatori. 2004. *Muslim Politics*. Princeton: Princeton University Press. First edition 1996.

Farook, Latheef. 2009. *Nobody's people: The forgotten plight of Sri Lanka's Muslims*. Colombo: South Asia News Agency.

Glynn, Sarah. 2012. Muslims and the Left: An English Case Studie. *Ethnicities* 2012: 1–22.

Hjärpe, Jan. 1983. *Politisk Islam*. Malmö: Gleerups Förlag.

Imtiyaz, A.R.M. 2005. Violent Muslim Mobilization in Sri Lanka: Some Questions. *Polity* 2 (5 & 6): 14–16.

Klem, Bart. 2012. In *the Wake of War: Eastern Sri Lanka's Political Geography in Transition*. Ph.D. thesis, Zürich: Geographisches Institut.

Knoerzer, Shari. 1998. Transformation of Muslim Political identity. In *Culture and Politics of Identity in Sri Lanka*, ed. Mithran Tiruchelcam and C.S. Dattathreya. Colombo: International Center for Ethnic Studies.

Landau-Tasseron, Ella. 2013. Jihād. *Encyclopaedia of the Qurʾān*. Brill Online. Retrieved October 3, 2013, from http://referenceworks.brillonline.com/entries/encyclopaedia-of-the-quran/jihad-COM_00101.

Lewis, Bernard. 1988. *The Political Language of Islam*. Chicago: Chicago University Press.

McGilvray, Dennis B. 1982. Dutch Burghers and Portuguese Mechanics: Eurasian Ethnicity in Sri Lanka. *Comparative Studies in Society and History* 24 (2): 235–263.

McGilvray, Dennis B., and Mirak Raheem. 2007. Muslim Perspective on the Sri Lankan Conflict. In *Policy Studies*, 41. Washington, DC: East-West Center. Society of Environmental Economics and Policy Studies.

Miller, Jody. 2002. Violence and Coercion in Sri Lanka's Commercial Sex Industry: Intersections of Gender, Sexuality, Culture and the Law. *Violence Against Women* 8 (9): 1045–1074.

Mitchell, R.P. 1969. *The Society of the Muslim Brothers*. London: Oxford University Press.

Nanji, Azim. 2013. Almsgiving. *Encyclopaedia of the Qurʾān*. Brill Online. Retrieved October 28, 2013, from http://referenceworks.brillonline.com/entries/encyclopaedia-of-the-quran/almsgiving-COM_00008.

O'Sullivan. 1999. *Identity and Institution in Ethnic Conflict: The Muslims of Sri Lanka*. Ph.D. thesis, Oxford: Oxford University.

Powers, David S. 2013. Adoption. *Encyclopaedia of Islam, THREE*. Brill Online. Retrieved October 30, 2013, from http://referenceworks.brillonline.com/entries/encyclopaedia-of-islam-3/adoption-SIM_0304.

Rowson, Everett K. 2013. Homosexuality. *Encyclopaedia of the Qurʾān*. Brill Online. Retrieved October 30, 2013, from http://referenceworks.brillonline.com/entries/encyclopaedia-of-the-quran/homosexuality-COM_00085.

Saravanamuttu, Johan. 2010. Introduction. In *Islam and Politics in Southeast Asia*, ed. Johan Saravanamuttu. London/New York: Routledge.

Smith, Jane I. 2015. Eschatology. *Encyclopaedia of the Qurʾān*. Brill Online. Retrieved February 24, 2015, from http://referenceworks.brillonline.com/entries/encyclopaedia-of-the-quran/eschatology-EQCOM_00055.

Spencer, Jonathan. 2012. Performing democracy and violence, agonism and community, politics and not politics in Sri Lanka. *Geoforum, Special Issue, Space, Contestation and the Political* 43 (4): 725–731.

Wagner, Christian. 1990. *Die Muslime Sri Lankas: Eine Volksgruppe im Spannungsfeld des ethnischen Konflikts zwischen Singhalesen und Tamilen*. Freiburg im Breisgau: Arnold-Bergstraesser-Institut.

Wilde, Clare, and Jane Dammen McAuliffe. 2013. Religious pluralism and the Qurʾān. *Encyclopaedia of the Qurʾān*. Brill Online. Retrieved October 29, 2013, from http://referenceworks.brillonline.com/entries/encyclopaedia-of-the-quran/religious-pluralism-and-the-quran-COM_00171.

Chapter 5
Hakeem in Parliament 2006–2011

Abstract This chapter focuses on the current leader Rauff Hakeem's speeches in parliament and elements of Muslim politics in them. As described above, the political conditions were different during the second half of the period that I am investigating in comparison to those that existed during Ashraff's era. This was largely due to the fact that the civil war ended in 2009. Nevertheless, the war was ongoing during the first years of the Hakeem period, and it is also in regard to this topic that we find most of the references to Islam, or, rather, to Muslims. As will be shown, Muslim politics are in practice almost absent from speeches where other topics are addressed.

Keywords Muslim politics · Islam · Muslims · Sri Lanka · Sri Lanka Muslim Congress · Rauff Hakeem · Pragmatic politics · Religion and politics

The Civil War

Tamil Militant Movements

In 2002, during the civil war, the SLMC and the LTTE signed a document that is called *Joint Communiqué of the Liberation Tigers of the Tamil Eelam and the Sri Lanka Muslim Congress*.[1] Despite the cooperative spirit of the document, the SLMC's policy in the parliament towards the Tamil Tigers did not change. Since the

---

[1] This document states that political solutions had been found by the LTTE and the SLMC. The LTTE leader at that time, Prabhakaran (who continued leading the LTTE until his death in 2009), made a public statement saying that the Muslims who had been evicted by the LTTE in 1990 were allowed to resettle in the northern region. The LTTE also agreed to stop collecting money from the Muslims to support their struggle for their own homeland and agreed that when it was time for talks between the government and the LTTE to begin, Muslims would be present as a third party represented by the SLMC. The negotiations between the LTTE and the SLMC were a huge success, as Muslims were recognized as stakeholders in regard to the peace negotiations. Perhaps the most important matter of all, however, was that the LTTE recognized the Muslims as a unique community based on religion, not language. (see Appendix 3) This is also the main argument in the document *Resolution to the conflict in the northern and eastern provinces* n.d.

© Springer Nature Switzerland AG 2019

A. Johansson, *Pragmatic Muslim Politics*,

https://doi.org/10.1007/978-3-030-12789-3_5

signing of the document, Hakeem has in fact several times accused the LTTE and the Karuna faction (a splinter group of the LTTE) of being the instigators of hostilities towards Muslims as a group. In this excerpt from a speech delivered in 2007, Muslims are presented as distinct from Tamils:

> Before this on many occasions, there was forced settlement on the areas belonging to the Muslims in Karpala and these were resolved. [...] I have to keep in mind that perhaps the Karuna faction is trying to sow seeds of discontent or even to threaten the relations between the Muslims and the Tamils as they attempt to show their power or try to increase their presence there.[2]

In general, according to Hakeem, the LTTE is to blame for the hostile situation, and he was vocal in his critique. On occasion, Hakeem referred to a press release that he attributed to the Tamil Tigers that made a direct threat to Muslims in the east. The press release urged Muslims to leave immediately because the east was, according to the Tamil Tigers, Tamil, that is, non-Muslim, territory.[3] Hakeem also has described how Muslims had to flee from militant Tamil groups. He claimed that "Muslims have difficulties coming back to Unichai and Urugamam after the Tamil Tigers forcefully evacuated them" and drew parallels to the expulsion of Muslims from the northern region of Sri Lanka by the LTTE in 1990.[4]

Hakeem's view of the Tamil Tigers is not, however, unitary. Even though he has generally criticized the LTTE, he at least at one point stated that the SLMC supported the LTTE's cause – not their struggle for an independent state but their struggle for minority rights within the nation-state of Sri Lanka.[5] Hakeem has also stressed peaceful coexistence and how this was threatened by religiously motivated violence based on false allegations:

> The news circulating that there were "jihad" organizations within the Muslims, which is much demeaning and without evidence, has whatsoever, no truth. This is something that our universal based rights society has realized very clearly.[6]

It is worth noting that "jihad" in this speech has a thoroughly negative meaning, which is different from the more ambiguous use of the term in the speeches made by Ashraff that were analyzed in the previous chapter. "Jihadi" groups, meaning those engaged in militant religious activism, among Muslims are not present. That is debatable, but they could emerge as a result of a future development: "[at] this late stage... it [the hostile actions of the LTTE] appears that a fertile ground for radical-

---

[2] HA 2007-01-09: 129, Abrogation of the Ceasefire Agreement (translated from Tamil).

[3] HA 2006-11-21: 811, Parliamentary debate, Appropriation Bill, 2007 (translated from Tamil).

[4] HA 2007-01-09: 129, Parliamentary debate, Public Security Proclamation (translated from Tamil) and HA 2007-01-09: 129, Parliamentary debate, Public Security Proclamation (translated from Tamil).

[5] It is not clear in what way the SLMC supports the LTTE. However, earlier statements suggest that the SLMC does not support a separate Tamil country but instead supports the rights of the Tamil people, and that the SLMC opposes the EU's banning of the LTTE; see HA 2006-08-07.

[6] HA 2006-06-21: 1602, Parliamentary debate, Massacre at Kebithigollewa (translated from Tamil).

ization is being created among Muslims as a result of this neglect".[7] This statement should be contrasted with what Hakeem had said earlier that year when he denied that Muslim victims of hostilities were prepared to use weapons in their own struggle. There were earlier reports from 2002–2003 in Tamil-language media on one particular group, the "Osama Front", which was said to be active in Mutur.[8] In 2006, allegations about another group once again came from the LTTE's leadership. There had been reports about young, armed Muslims in Muslim-dominated towns and violence between different groups of Muslims.

In his speeches, Hakeem has stressed the self-image of the SLMC as the sole representative voice of Sri Lankan Muslims in general, based on the results of democratic elections. It is in this light that one should see his insistence on speaking up against what he viewed as injustices experienced by Muslims in the country and the importance of events that transpired during the civil war. This Muslim community is, according to Hakeem, caught in the crossfire between the government and the Tamil Tigers and is distinct from both.[9]

Hakeem has in speeches extended his public sympathies beyond Muslims, however, and has also touched up the suffering of what is construed as other distinct communities, that is, the Sinhala and Tamil.[10] The distinction he has drawn between Tamils as a community on the one hand and Tamil militants on the other is a clear one. The civilian members of the two communities are both parts of the Sri Lankan nation, but the militant LTTE fighters have no place in it.[11] Even though Hakeem has admitted in his speeches that all communities are suffering, the focus is slightly different in those cases where when he described acts of violence committed against Muslims. The attacks on Muslims are frequently described as especially cruel, directed towards innocent, defenseless people who were killed while performing innocent actions, often religious ones, such as praying or visiting mosques.[12] His descriptions of such acts of violence often include more explicit details, as can be seen in the following:

> [T]he armed cadres of the LTTE separated young and able-bodied men from women, children and the elderly. Some of the cadres were seen beating the women, the children and the elderly, who chose to plead on behalf of the detained men.[13]

---

[7] HA 2006-11-07: 2917, Parliamentary debate, Public Security Proclamations.

[8] McGilvray and Raheem 2007: 42.

[9] For example, see: HA 2006-08-11: 2579, Parliamentary debate, Question Public Security Proclamation, HA 2006-10-19: 367, Parliamentary debate, De-Merger of Northern and Eastern Provinces: Stated by Hon. Rauff Hakeem.

[10] HA 2007-01-09: 126, Parliamentary debate, Public Security Proclamation.

[11] HA 2006-05-26: 739, Parliamentary debate, The Current Situation Faced by Tamil Civilian Population in the North-East (translated from Tamil).

[12] See HA 2006-11-21: 812, Parliamentary debate, Appropriation Bill, 2007 (translated from Tamil).

[13] HA 2006-08-08: 58, Parliamentary debate, Question by Private Notice: Grave injustice Caused to the Civilians of Mutur.

Moreover, when Hakeem has described the LTTE's violence, he has provided exact numbers of Muslim families killed and evicted as well as details of the misery experienced by Muslims.[14] Also, in regard to the refugee situation, Hakeem has explicitly focused on the plight of Muslim refugees. On one occasion, Hakeem stated that it was the Tamil Tigers' tactic to displace this segment of the population in order to draw Muslims as a community into the conflict.[15] In another speech, Hakeem compared the circumstances faced by Muslims to ethnic cleansing in Africa, asking: "Is the LTTE contributing towards the Eastern Muslim homelands becoming a Rwanda and Burundi? We certainly are bleeding [...]".[16] In the same speech, he claimed that Sri Lanka has one of the largest populations of *Muslim internally displaced persons* (IDP's) in the world:

> Sir, of the entire world Muslim population of more than 1.5 billion, half the population lives as minorities in other countries with predominant non-Muslim majorities. Today, Sri Lanka has achieved a dubious record of being a country with the largest Muslim IDP population in any non-Muslim country with the eviction of the Mutur Muslims.[17]

Nevertheless, the SLMC, by way of Hakeem's statements, presented itself as a responsible political party that addressed the conflict in a general, and not partisan, manner and that wished for a "durable and dignified peace that would be acceptable to all communities through negotiations".[18]

Also while criticizing the LTTE, he has said that the organization needs to know that Muslims as a community are not targeting the Tamil Tigers.[19] In many speeches, Hakeem has been harsh in his criticism of the LTTE and other Tamil militant movements. In one speech, he stated that the Tamil Tigers murder people and drove Muslims away from areas to which they have a historical claim.[20] In another speech, he went so far as to call the LTTE terrorists and say that they should be condemned by the international community in general.[21] In 2009, when the war was over and the government had defeated the LTTE, Hakeem congratulated the president, saying:

> [W]e are meeting for the first time after His Excellency the President addressed Parliament following the remarkable success he, as the Commander-in-Chief, had in the war in this country. [...] The Muslims in this country have all the more reason to rejoice at the prospect of an end to the war in this country since they have suffered immensely for the past several decades. [...] Polybius, the Greek Historian who is known for his ideas of political balance

---

[14] HA 2006-07-06: 2282, Parliamentary debate, Public Security Proclamation (translated from Tamil).

[15] HA 2006-08-08: 123, Parliamentary debate, Provision of Relief for Displaced People of Mutur (translated from Tamil).

[16] HA 2006-08-11: 371, Parliamentary debate, Public Security Proclamation.

[17] HA 2006-08-11: 368, Parliamentary debate, Public Security Proclamation.

[18] HA 2006-08-08: 60, Parliamentary debate, Question by Private Notice: Grave Injustice Caused to the Civilians of Mutur.

[19] HA 2006-07-06: 2282, Parliamentary debate, Public Security Proclamation (translated from Tamil).

[20] HA 2006-08-11: 369, Parliamentary debate, Public Security Proclamation.

[21] HA 2008-08-06: 2725, Parliamentary debate, Public Security Proclamation.

in the government which was later used in Montesquieu's "The Spirit of the Laws" and the drafting of the United States Constitution, once said, I quote "Those who know how to win are much more numerous than those who know how to make proper use of their victories". [...] Our Motherland [is] a truly united country. We, the Muslims pledge our wholehearted support to any honorable move forward based on mutual respect and understanding [...].[22]

In the intense last moments of the civil war, the SLMC officially supported the government and its final battle against the LTTE. Hakeem argued then that the LTTE and its allies are the enemies not only of Muslims but also of the nation as a whole. Consequently, the day they were defeated was a day to rejoice.[23]

The Government

Before giving his wholehearted support to the government, Hakeem, like Ashraff before him, criticized not only the LTTE and the different Tamil factions but also the government army and police. They had not lived up to their responsibilities of pro-tecting citizens who wound up getting caught in the crossfire in the conflict between the LTTE and the Sri Lankan government, a group he saw as primarily consisting of Muslims.[24] As the "spokesperson" for Muslims, a self-proclaimed role that we have seen the SLMC take from its inception, Hakeem's duty became safeguarding the material interests that were specific to that particular group, for example, mosques.[25] In one speech, Hakeem criticized the government for, through not acknowledging them as a distinct group, forcing Muslims to choose sides in the ongoing conflict, something they, according to him, would prefer not to do:

> It (the government) advocates the Bush doctrine "Either you are with the enemy or with us." This means "Either you are with us the government or with the Tigers. Even the Muslim politicians from the government seem to say this to us.[26]

Hakeem thus seems here to be torn between supporting the government and criti-cizing its role in the conflict with the LTTE. On some occasions, he implicitly did the latter, for example, by stating that the government was responsible for killing *civilian*s when he on one occasion referred to "an artillery attack which targeted this checkpoint" and which "according to scores of eyewitnesses, resulted in the death of some civilians".[27] Sometimes, he has even equated the government with the LTTE for not taking responsibility for the suffering and killing of civilians:

---

[22] HA 2009-05-26: 68–9, Parliamentary debate, University of Vocational Technology Act: Order.

[23] HA 2009-05-26: 69, Parliamentary debate, University of Vocational Technology Act: Order.

[24] HA 2007-01-09: 129, Parliamentary debate, Public Security Proclamation.

[25] HA 2008-09-24: 992, Parliamentary debate, National Housing Development Authority (Special Provisions) Bill.

[26] HA 2007-01-10: 212, Parliamentary debate, Peace Process and Current Situation Pertaining to Tamil Civilian Population in the North-East (translated from Tamil).

[27] HA 2006-08-08: 58, Parliamentary debate, Question by Private Notice: Grave Injustice Caused to the Civilians of Mutur.

All peace-loving people of Sri Lanka have come to realize that both the Government and the LTTE continue to make sanctimonious pronouncements supposedly with the objective of respecting the humanitarian needs of the people.[28]

Hakeem has also criticized some of the members of parliament for not taking seriously those Hindu Tamil members of parliament who advocate *satyagraha* (the Hindu principle of non-violence):

[T]he Tamil Coalition party in its early stage [...] engaged and staged peaceful satyagraha. [...] In recent times that approach as a course of action has changed due to recent political impact and they have resorted to violence. That is something in our time we need to ponder about, yet the government has shown no interest in such a peaceful struggle for satyagraha. In this house there have been demonstrations, uprisings and disruptions. We are now observing that the government has gone to the extent where perhaps it might show interest only to wild demonstrations in the way or perhaps confusions in the house.[29]

Like Ashraff before him, then, it has not been unusual for Hakeem to use references to other religious traditions than Islam in an appreciative manner. Similarly, on those occasions when he has stated that war is not the answer to the country's problems, he has quoted both Benjamin Franklin ("There never was a good war or a bad peace") and Cicero ("An unjust peace is better than a just war").[30]

It is noteworthy that Hakeem, when he has spoken of the victims of the civil war, does not limit himself to Muslims. In regard to the terms of the Ceasefire Agreement, Hakeem has stated that after the attacks in Mutur in 2006, it was the government's duty to guarantee that civilians were safe. He moreover has claimed that the government needed to look over the Ceasefire Agreement in order to protect the innocent.[31] According to Hakeem, then, the government has a responsibility to protect civilians, and he consequently has accused it several times of failing to do so, especially in the northeast.[32] He has also blamed the government for ruthless artillery attacks on civilians.[33] We might then conclude that when he has spoken to the government, Hakeem has tended to formulate his rhetoric around the people of Sri Lanka in general, not around Muslims in particular.[34] Occasionally, Muslims are pointed out in his speeches as a particular group among the victims of the events that occurred in Mutur:

---

[28] HA 2006-08-08: 59, Parliamentary debate, Question by Private Notice: Grave Injustice Caused to the Civilians of Mutur.

[29] HA 2006-09-28: 1904, Parliamentary debate, Question by Private Notice (translated from Tamil).

[30] HA 2006-06-21: 1601, Parliamentary debate, Massacre at Kebithigollewa and HA 2007-06-07: 1122, Parliamentary debate, Evictions of Tamils from Lodges in Colombo (translated from Tamil).

[31] HA 2006-08-08: 59, Parliamentary debate Question by Private Notice: Grave injustice Caused to the Civilians of Mutur.

[32] HA 2006-08-08: 123, Parliamentary debate, Provision of Relief for Displaced People of Mutur (translated from Tamil).

[33] HA 2006-08-08: 124, Parliamentary debate, Provision of Relief for Displaced People of Mutur (translated from Tamil).

[34] HA 2006-08-08: 124, Parliamentary debate, Provision of Relief for Displaced People of Mutur (translated from Tamil).

The Ceasefire Agreement that has resulted in the forced eviction of Muslims from areas of their traditional habitation and systematic destruction of the political and economic power of the Muslims of the Northern and the Eastern Provinces.[35]

Hakeem has also blamed the government for depriving Muslims of a representative voice in the peace talks, and he continued to air additional grievances in parliament.[36] Even though references are to Muslims as victims of discrimination and oppression, the frequent attention that both Hakeem and Ashraff have paid and paid to the east coast as a geographical area limits the actual composition of that particular group.

Government representatives responded to Hakeem's criticism by stating that Muslims would have their say within the government. The government's promise was, however, not enough for Hakeem and the SLMC, who demanded that Muslims should be treated as a distinct third party at the peace talks, alongside the Tamils and Sinhalese. That Muslims should be part of the peace negotiations was also included in the agreement with the LTTE from 2002, which clearly gave the role of representing Muslims to the SLMC:

I know, people would refer to the Ceasefire Agreement and say, "The Ceasefire Agreement is strictly between the LTTE and the Government. The Muslims have no role to play and these are issues which can only be resolved if both parties agree." In that regard I must emphasize here that both the LTTE and the Government at different points in time, in bilateral discussions and agreements which have been signed with the Sri Lanka Muslim Congress, have recognized the fact that as a matter of right we should be allowed to participate with a separate delegation in the peace talks.[37]

In 2007, in a parliamentary debate concerning local authorities, Hakeem criticized the symbols on the flag that the government wanted to erect in the eastern part of the country: a lion, an eagle, and a fish. The problem for Hakeem was that the lion, a symbol closely associated with Buddhism, would, according to him, make the flag questionable in the eyes of Muslims in the east. The government should, according to him, look for an appropriate Muslim symbol instead.[38]

To avoid repeating what happened in 1990, when Muslim inhabitants in the north were expelled by the LTTE, Hakeem has stressed how important it was that the Muslims who were displaced would be allowed to return to their land and what he has presented as their traditional territory. He stated in one debate that "the government should relocate the Muslims as well as the Tamils to their lands [...]".[39] In another one, Hakeem, making specific reference to religious considerations, claimed that it was important that Muslims would be able to go back to Mutur and "reclaim the bodies, to claim our rights as Muslims in offering Islamic rites to the dead

---

[35] HA 2006-08-08: 60, Parliamentary debate, Question by Private Notice: Grave injustice Caused to the Civilians of Mutur.

[36] HA 2006-06-21: 1531, Parliamentary debate, Appropriation Bill, 2007.

[37] HA 2006-02-01: 132–5, Parliamentary debate, Geneva Conventions Bill.

[38] HA 2007-07-19: 428, Parliamentary debate, Local Authorities (Special Provisions) Bill (translated from Tamil).

[39] HA 2007-06-06: 936, Parliamentary debate, Public Security Proclamation.

bodies".[40] Hakeem has also asserted that Muslims would not want the peace agreement between the government and the LTTE to be taken lightly. Instead of talking, they should stop the war immediately. Moreover, Hakeem has expressed his fear that the government's bombing of the LTTE was pointless and would only lead to increased support for Tamil militants.[41] In another speech, Hakeem verbally attacked some of the parliamentary members, especially those in the government, who did not want to take part in the minute of silence for civilians killed in areas dominated by Tamil-speaking Hindus, saying that this showed how polarized the country was. The SLMC, on the other hand, wished to join in the condolences and thus did what any respectable party in Sri Lanka should do for the sake of the nation:

> This is very unprecedented in the precincts of this House. This perhaps shows how polarized we are, as a nation. If we cannot for a very solemn and sad reason come together in expressing our grief and condolences for the dead, how can we call ourselves a nation? What right have we got to say that we are a nation of decent individuals?[42]

One of the major subjects of importance for Hakeem had been the question of the state of emergency (which ended in 2011). He has clearly stated that he did not like the way that the government and its institutions enforced the state of emergency.[43] Hakeem has also voiced in many speeches his view that the state of emergency was a way for the government to deny the democratic rights of the other political parties, especially in the case of the election in the eastern part of the country.[44] He has also accused the government of using the communal conflict, which involved violence between Hindu Tamils and Muslims, as an excuse to continue holding onto power there.[45] He has moreover stated that the government lacked credibility:

> In this country, the successive governments have used for their own ends the emergency rule historically. It appears to me that the government does not seem to bring the code of conduct to ministers who have exceeded their powers during emergency rule. These ministers tend to accuse newspapers that expose the government's wrongdoings as newspapers working for terrorists groups.[46]

Hakeem's criticism of government actions during the state of emergency contains other elements as well. For example, he has claimed that government supporters had made threats against both members of the SLMC and Muslims who were not members of the party, especially on the east coast. Exactly who these supporters

[40] HA 2006-08-08: 125, Parliamentary debate, Provision of Relief for Displaced People of Mutur (translated from Tamil).

[41] HA 2006-08-10: 188, Parliamentary debate, Humanitarian Crisis Triggered by the Ongoing Hostilities.

[42] HA 2006-06-21: 1601, Parliamentary debate, Massacre at Kebithigollewa.

[43] HA 2007-01-09: 126, Parliamentary debate, Public Security Proclamation.

[44] HA 2008-02-26: 749, Parliamentary debate, Public Security Proclamation.

[45] HA 2008-02-26: 755, Parliamentary debate, Public Security Proclamation, (translated from Tamil).

[46] HA 2009-10-08: 172, Parliamentary debate, Public Security Proclamation, (translated from Tamil).

were is unclear.[47] Hakeem has furthermore referred to instances of people being abducted by men driving white vans, supposedly members of government security forces.[48] Hakeem has also asserted that the current government is "building up armed gangs for their own political purposes. People supporting the government, they also get hold of innocent people, abduct them and torture them".[49] In spite of these events, the SLMC would not back down:

> Today, these thugs have come to our candidates' houses to destroy properties and threaten us. But, we are not the minority Muslims who will back off from this destruction. The thugs want us to look to the other side while they engaged in wanton destruction. Tomorrow is the election and we are not going to let these people rob us of our human rights and the right to vote.[50]

It was not only politicians who were threatened, according to Hakeem. These government supporters, or thugs, had also threatened Muslims during the performance of prayers in mosques. Hakeem stated to the parliamentary audience in 2008 that:

> In one mosque after the prayer session, as the believers were on their way home, the thugs confronted the believers and issued the threat that they should vote for the government and not any other party.[51]

Although Hakeem has stated that it was the government's fault that the state of emergency was a failure in the country, he was also harsh in his criticism of the police force's actions. When commenting upon one event in Alutgama in the south-west, where Muslim-owned shops had been attacked and targeted by thugs, Hakeem stated that the Muslim inhabitants no longer had any confidence in the police, and he claimed that the police and the armed forces had not done anything to stop the mob.[52] Another time, he also accused the police of not investigating certain activist groups (for example, the Karuna faction) and indicated that some would escape punishment because it was pointless to even report their crimes.[53] Hakeem has also said that the police are supposed to be the upholders of the law, but in order to be credible more minorities should be included in its ranks.[54] On another occasion, when a number of Muslim teachers had been assaulted, Hakeem pointed out that police should have been more helpful because "being the Ramadan period, obviously Muslims are terribly perturbed and I must say here that the people of the area

---

[47] HA 2006-05-26: 741, Parliamentary debate, The Current Situation Faced by Tamil Civilian Population in the North-East (translated from Tamil).

[48] There were a lot of reports in the media regarding these events. See, for example, BBC 2012.

[49] HA 2008-08-06: 2726–7, Parliamentary debate, Public Security Proclamation.

[50] HA 2008-08-06: 3185, Parliamentary debate, Sabaragamuwa and North Central Provincial Council Elections.

[51] HA 2008-02-26: 754, Parliamentary debate, Public Security Proclamation (translated from Tamil).

[52] HA 2006-02-01: 132–5, Parliamentary debate, Committee on Public Petitions.

[53] HA 2007-01-09: 129, Parliamentary debate, Public Security Proclamation.

[54] HA 2006-02-01: 13, Parliamentary debate, Committee on Public Petitions and HA 2007-07-19: 429, Parliamentary debate, Local Authorities (Special Provisions) Bill (translated from Tamil).

are blaming the police for not taking timely action".[55] In regard to another incident, the police were given the blame for mismanaging evidence:

> The local police messed up all the available material and evidence in the crime scene. They never preserved anything. There are eyewitnesses who saw vital clues in the crime scene and subsequently, when they went to the scene, none of those objects were available [...] before the Magistrate and for forensic examination itself.[56]

In another debate in May 2006, Hakeem spoke about the fishermen's need for help from the government. Even though Hakeem referred in this case to fishermen in general, he identified these mainly as Muslims. Sometimes, however, non-Muslims are also included, for example, when he pointed out that the Sinhalese fishermen could still go to work whereas the non-Sinhalese fishermen could not. In a later debate in June 2006, he stated: that.

> [Regarding the] security situation in the north-east, it is not an understatement to say that the ones who are most affected in the coastal area now are none other than the innocent fishermen and their community. I assert strongly that the Minister should consider the plight of the fishermen who are affected by the sea blockade imposed on them. [...] The fishermen particularly affected are those in the Trikonamalai area who are not able to fish because of the ban of laying fishing nets in those coastal areas, thus affecting their daily lives. I would like to request that we need to make alternative arrangements for those fishermen [...] I would assert that the government should at least provide food and other basic needs to those 8,000 fishermen and their families whom we have to rescue from the severe hardships they are going through. [...].[57]

The northeast province's merger remained an important topic for Hakeem and the SLMC until the province was divided into two on December 31, 2006. Hakeem, like Ashraff before him did, has spoken about the Indo-Sri Lanka Peace Accord and how the government did not consult with Muslims regarding the merger, and he made a similar point when discussing the exclusion of Muslims from the negotiations on the separation of the northeast province in 2006. According to Hakeem, Muslims should have a primary role as a separate minority group in politics in the northeast with the SLMC as its political representative.[58] Later, he stated that:

> We the Muslims would not accept at all the union of the North-east sector unconditionally and this is something that the leadership of the Tamil National Coalition party is aware of. We are aware that without proper consultation with the minorities in the North-east sector the court's ruling of the separation of the North-east could bring serious consequences. We cannot deal with this issue without taking into account the wellbeing of the Muslims. We can only consider after we have looked into the injustices of the Muslims who live under the

---

[55] HA 2008-09-24: 992, Parliamentary debate, National Housing Development Authority (Special Provisions) Bill.

[56] HA 2008-02-07: 854, Parliamentary debate, Commissions of Inquiry (Amendment) Bill.

[57] HA 2006-06-20: 1316–19, Parliamentary debate, Fisheries and Aquatic Resources (Amendment) Bill (translated from Tamil). See also HA 2006-05-26: 741, Parliamentary debate, The Current Situation Faced by Tamil Civilian Population in the North-East (translated from Tamil).

[58] HA 2006-11-07: 2914, Parliamentary debate, Public Security Proclamations (translated from Tamil) and HA 2006-11-21: 812, Parliamentary debate, Appropriation Bill, 2007 (translated from Tamil).

union of the North-east sector. Due to this, under the leadership of R. Sambanthan and the leadership of the Sri Lanka Muslim Congress Party we have discussed together some issues that affect us, wholeheartedly, after sharing this together we agreed that we would then approach the government for further discussion.[59]

When Hakeem has addressed what he views as the main problems faced by the Muslim population, he not only has directed his remarks towards at the government but also to members of the international community, such as the Norwegian government, the Independent International Commission (undefined), and the Human Rights Commission.[60] The demand was mainly for protection, but various references to the idea of an autonomous, self-governing region for Muslims (MSGR) in the southeast have occasionally recurred.[61]

Additional Issues

The matters of the state of the nation and of nation-building play a central role in Hakeem's speeches. In them, suggestions are made for the development of the nation. He has also used India as a model for the idea of a just distribution of resources to different provinces in the country.[62] In his role as minister of post and telecommunications/minister of justice, he had to deal with issues of national, rather than communal, interest.[63] Hence, in many of his parliamentary speeches, often delivered in Sinhala, there are no specific references to Muslims as a separate group.

Hakeem's approach in parliament is in many respects pragmatic, even explicitly so, as, for example, in a comment about the eighteenth amendment, which gave more power to the president[64]:

> We, the Sri Lanka Muslim Congress, did ponder and reflect upon this predicament and we have taken a very pragmatic decision to support his administration in the national interest, which concluded a very difficult military expedition and which for all purposes, was looked upon very pessimistically by many, including ourselves on the other side. I must be very

---

[59] HA 2007-01-10: 210, Parliamentary debate, Peace Process and Current Situation Pertaining to Tamil Civilian Population in the North-East (translated from Tamil).

[60] See HA 2006-09-27: 1621, Letter to the president that was included in the HA record, HA 2007-09-18: 125–6, Parliamentary debate, Investigation Into Death of Tamil Civilians by Aerial Bombardment and Multi-Barrel Rocket Fire, (translated from Tamil), and HA 2006-05-26: 740, Parliamentary debate, The Current Situation Faced by Tamil Civilian Population in the North-East (translated from Tamil).

[61] Ameerdeen 2006: 211.

[62] HA 2010-07-01: 401, Appropriation Bill 2010.

[63] For example, see HA 2007-12-05: 2399, Appropriation Bill 2008, HA 2007-03-06: 1232f, Sale of Sri Lankan Telecom Share (translated from Sinhala), HA 2007-03-06: 1195f, National Construction Association of Sri Lanka (Incorporation) Bill (translated from Sinhala), HA 2010-12-06: 1390f, Age Limit for Admission to Sri Lankan Law College, HA 2010-12-04: 1178f, Appropriation Bill 2011, and HA 2011-10-06: 130f, National Police Academy Bill.

[64] Eighteenth amendment to the constitution of Sri Lanka, retrieved 2014-02-08.

frank and open about my convictions as a politician. [...] Today we have to look at things much more pragmatically; we have to look at this issue with an eye on serious reconciliation. [...] In that, I am sure the Sri Lanka Muslim Congress in taking this decision, we have very carefully looked at the need to play a pragmatic role and also have a serious introspection about our own ideology in working with an administration which pursues a program of actions which is aimed at post-conflict development and reconciliation. I am sure His Excellency the President and his administration would pay heed to the concerns that would be raised by us, and I am sure we have the independence to talk about the grievances of our community, as well as of all the rest who feel marginalized.[65]

In several of Hakeem's speeches, other areas in regard to which Muslims needed special attention that were not related to the civil war are identified. For example, Muslims, according to Hakeem, experience injustices within the educational system.[66] He therefore has demanded that the government look into the situation:

The grievances of the Muslim community are such that many schools – I do not think they can call many schools as leading schools – there are perhaps some schools which have a certain level of standard, but then except for a few, many schools do not fall within this category. The grievances of the Muslims are such that they have faced many difficulties. One recent case was when the Principal of Ramanadan Ladies' College refused admission for Muslim students from Batticaloa and other areas who had attained the Government stipulated cut-off mark for the Grade Five Scholarship. These students had scored, as the Hon. Minister of Education said, 176 marks that make them eligible to enter these schools. Finally police complaints had been lodged on various pretexts preventing parents from going to the school. This has become such an issue where unnecessary ethnic tension is created as a result of imposing admission policies which have been decided on certain criteria by the Ministry of Education.[67]

Unlike Ashraff, Hakeem has rarely addressed international issues. On one such occasion in 2010, Hakeem took the opportunity to criticize Israel's blockade against Gaza as well as Egypt's policy on border crossing:

I must also state as a Leader of a Muslim political party, that in a sense I am ashamed at the way in which Egypt has been behaving of late, crossing the so-called Rafah Border Crossing which has been closed in order to support and aid and assist the Israeli blockade. Because of the fall-out of this incident, in order to avoid domestic uprisings, they have immediately announced that they are re-opening the Rafah Border Crossing but this is in order, just to placate the public sentiments for the time being. It will not be long before the Egyptians, again under pressure from the Americans and the Israelis, will go back to closing the borders, heaping the hardships and increasing the misery of these people in the Gaza Strip.[68]

Hakeem thus at least once has made an explicit reference to himself as a *Muslim* political leader. Together with the references to the trials and tribulations of Muslims in Sri Lanka – and the SLMC as the sole political body addressing these grievances – this constitutes nearly the sum total of Hakeem's official references to religion, even to religions other than Islam. Unlike the case of Ashraff, such issues as

---

[65] HA 2010-11-26: 869–72, Appropriation Bill 2011.
[66] See also HA 2008-08-06: 2728, Public Security Proclamation.
[67] HA 2007-08-08: 1030, Parliamentary debate, Government's New Policy on Admission of Students to Grade One.
[68] HA 2010-06-09: 320, Attack on Aid Flotilla by Zionist Israeli Commandos.

Buddhism's compatibility with Islam are rarely addressed in the parliamentary speeches made by Hakeem that are examined here. He has, however, in regard to the suffering of civilians, occasionally talked about the fact that Sri Lanka is a predominantly Buddhist country and that they thus should follow the true values of the Buddha, which are to foster compassion and empathy towards people who suffer.[69] Other than these few examples, references to religious beliefs and practices are absent from Hakeem's speeches.[70]

Analysis

In approaching Hakeem's parliamentary speeches from the viewpoint of Muslim politics, the most conspicuous feature is its absence. There are, in practice, almost no examples of the use of an Islamic "pool of resources". One may then ask if the demand for a(n) (undefined) Muslim symbol on the flag for the eastern province should be considered an example of Muslim politics. It depends upon which type of symbol Hakeem had in mind, and this is not specified. When I confronted Hakeem with the lack of Muslim politics in his speeches, he said the following:

> OK, I don't quote the Qur'an and the Sunna, but occasionally I refer to the Qur'an and various other things […] I am careful in a multiethnic society, that even Mr. Ashraff in the latter part of his political career, even attempted to rebrand the SLMC, under a new […] name, which has its own rationale. He founded the National Unity Alliance […] We had a discussion on reinventing the idea so we don't impose the Muslim element or the Muslim factor, and to rebrand in such a way that it would be more acceptable and also attract the non-Muslims to the political movement, and we will try to be a little more diverse in our composition.[71]

Hence, the main reason given is one of pragmatic considerations. Explicit references to Islam may alienate the audience in parliament as well as limit the scope of potential voters. It appears as if the specifically Muslim identity of the party is more of a burden than a resource for the current leadership. Hakeem's official denial of the existence of any militant jihadism in Sri Lanka may be understood in this light.[72] As a matter of fact, there do exist activist radical reformist (Salafist) movements on the island of Sri Lanka that, as mentioned earlier, have destroyed Sufi shrines.[73] The strong denial of the existence of such activism from the side of Hakeem is under-

---

[69] HA 2007-07-19: 430, Parliamentary debate, Local Authorities (Special Provisions) Bill. The theme of ending the war has been a subject for Hakeem all throughout the last period. For an example just before the end of the war, see HA 2008-09-09: 175–81, Parliamentary debate Public Security Proclamation (translated from Tamil).

[70] At one time, Hakeem was asked in parliament about the Qur'an and Muslim personal law, but he did not answer. HA 2006-09-28: 1912, Parliamentary debate, Muslim Marriage and Divorce (Amendment) Bill.

[71] Rauff Hakeem, 2013-02-24.

[72] Cf. Mercado 2008.

[73] See McGilvray and Raheem 2007.

standable. The government has been harsh in its military campaigns against the LTTE and similar movements, and it is reasonable to assume that it would be equally harsh against militant movements among Muslims.

The term "Muslim" in the name of the party should not be understood as being related to a set of religious beliefs and practices but instead as a reference to the notion of Muslims constituting a distinct community. This can be seen in the way Hakeem has described the "unified" community of Muslims. As was the case with the interviews and with Ashraff's speeches, there are certain attributes that come to the fore in SLMC discourse on Muslims. Muslims in Sri Lanka are, in the words of Hakeem, refugees, powerless, and peaceful victims of the aggression of others. This focus on a distinct community without relation to a set of religious beliefs is a process that can also be seen in other contexts, such as, for example, in the case of India and Pakistan in the years after independence when religious leaders accentuated the "Islamic identity to distinguish themselves from the Hindu majority" and in the case of Bosnia: "Bosnian Muslimness is largely the result of competing Serbian and Croat nationalism and such externally defined notions of ethnicity [...]".[74] As in the case of the views of informants presented in the previous chapter, in Hakeem's definition of Muslims, there appears to be little "behind the ethnic marker".

Hakeem is well aware of the aspirations of the distinct Muslim minority group and that demands for autonomy can lead to discrimination in society at large, where people in general take the side of the ruling government against the SLMC. This could lead to the identification of Muslim politics with terror and Islamization.[75] One of the suggestions that the SLMC has proposed in the past (and still does) is the creation of a Muslim self-governing region (MSGR), which is explained as a "territorial power base and a point of leverage to ensure Muslim concerns will be adequately addressed [...]".[76] The SLMC's proposals today are even more inclusive and not only concentrated on the southeast region; the proposal aims to include Muslim-dominated areas in the northeast as a part of an MSGR. Using the category of unified Muslims in the manner Hakeem does makes it easier to "press claims of greater recognition of Muslim rights".[77] The vision of the MSGR has, however, won very little understanding and support from the Sinhala and the Tamil political leadership.[78] The SLMC nevertheless holds onto these visions that also appear to have some backing, as can be seen in relation to a group of students who declared that Muslims are a separate ethnic identity and that the southeastern part of Sri Lanka is their homeland.[79] The so-called Oluvil Declaration, presented in 2003, may be viewed as the expression of a minor student organization sending out a message, but

---

[74] Eickelman and Piscatori 2004: 82, 103.

[75] Abubakar 2010: 142.

[76] McGilvray and Raheem 2007: 26.

[77] Eickelman and Piscatori 2004: 106.

[78] McGilvray and Raheem 2007: 27.

[79] McGilvray and Raheem 2007: 41.

the declaration was proclaimed before an audience of 60,000 people.[80] The demand for a self-governing region seems indeed to have support among potential Muslim voters, and this is arguably the main reason why the SLMC still has such a demand on its agenda.

The SLMC has been in and out of the alliance with the government as a minority party since 1994. The necessary forming of coalitions with other political parties turns the SLMC in a pragmatic direction, which reduces the possibility of putting forward religiously based claims.[81] As we have seen, Hakeem has sometimes stated that, as a Muslim political leader, he needs to cater to the interests of Muslims. In the case of the SLMC, religion is downplayed in favor of getting something out of the collaboration with the government while at the same time trying to show the SLMC's religious messages to the voters.[82] The downplayed use of religion is also visible in the vague formulations of Islamic guidelines and other ideological formulations as well.[83]

If we compare Hakeem's speeches with those of Ashraff, we can thus distinguish a significant difference when it comes to the frequency of the use of the Islamic "pool of resources", that is, of religious terms, themes, and references. Instead, Hakeem makes use of motifs and symbols taken from everything from Greek historians to the U.S. Constitution. Hakeem nevertheless continues to stress that the SLMC represents Muslim interests, albeit not necessarily religious ones.

References

Primary Sources

Interviews with Named Informants

Rauff Hakeem, 2013-02-23, 2013-02-24.

---

[80] This declaration contains five principles: "One – Muslim autonomy must be ensured in any federal solution. Two – Muslims are entitled to their equitable share in all resources for development. Three – The Muslim political leadership must unite. Four – Muslims must be represented as a separate entity at peace talks. Five – The final political settlement must have the consent of the Muslims". See Jeyaraj 2003, McGilvray and Raheem 2007: 41, and Fazal 2012: 173.

[81] Cf. Demker 1998: 154.

[82] Demker 1998: 167.

[83] Brown and Hamzawy 2010: 3–4.

Parliamentary Speeches

Speeches from Rauff Hakeem between 2006 and 2011. Retrieved from the Hansard archive online from 2011–2013.

Literature

Abubakar, Carmen A. 2010. A Never-Ending War and the Struggle for Peace in Southern Philippines. In *Islam and Politics in Southeast Asia*, ed. Johan Saravanamuttu. London/New York: Routledge.

Ameerdeen, Vellaithamby. 2006. *Ethnic Politics of Muslims in Sri Lanka*. Kandy: Center for Minority Studies, Kribs Printers.

BBC. 2012. White van 'terrorises' Jaffna. *BBC Sinhala*. Retrieved November 20, 2012 from http://www.bbc.co.uk/sinhala/news/story/2007/03/070323_jaffna_batticaloa.shtml.

Brown, Nathan J., and Amr Hamzawy. 2010. *Between Religion and Politics*. Washington, DC: Carnegie Endowment for International Peace.

Demker, Marie. 1998. *Religion och Politik*. Den europeiska kristdemokratins dilemma. Stockholm: SNS förlag.

Eickelman, Dale F., and James Piscatori. 2004. *Muslim Politics*. Princeton: Princeton University Press. First edition 1996.

Eighteenth amendment to the constitution of Sri Lanka. Retrieved February 8, 2014., from http://www.priu.gov.lk/Cons/1978Constitution/18th%20Amendment%20Act(E).pdf.

Fazal, Tanweer. 2012. Minorities and Their Nationalism(s): The Terms of a Discourse in South Asia. *South Asian History and Culture* 3 (2): 163–176.

Jeyaraj, D.B.S. 2003. Oluvil Declaration Proclaims Advent of Muslim Thesam. *Sunday Leader*. Retrieved February 6, 2014 from: http://www.thesundayleader.lk/archive/20030209/issues.htm.

McGilvray, Dennis B., and Mirak Raheem. 2007. Muslim Perspective on the Sri Lankan Conflict. In *Policy Studies*, 41. Washington, DC: East-West Center. Society of Environmental Economics and Policy Studies.

Mercado, Eliseo R. 2008. The Effect of 9/11 on Mindanao Muslims and the Mindanao Peace Process. In *Asian Islam in the 21st Century*, ed. John L. Espositio, John O. Voll, and Osman Bakar. New York: Oxford University Press.

Chapter 6
Concluding Remarks – Pragmatic Muslim Politics

Abstract The last chapter of this book presents conclusions regarding the use of religious symbols by the Sri Lankan Muslim Congress based upon the previous chapters. It argues that the use of religious symbols by the party is pragmatic. It is a fail-safe strategy the SLMC uses. This chapter also draws parallels to other countries in Southeast Asian and South Asia where Muslim political parties exit.

Keywords Muslim politics · Islam · Muslims · Sri Lanka · Sri Lanka Muslim Congress · Pragmatic politics · Religion and politics

A basic claim underlying this book is that earlier research on the SLMC has not adequately dealt with the role of Muslim politics in the party, that is, how its representatives have discursively used the "pool of resources" that is Islamic tradition in terms of references to beliefs, practices, and a "sacred terminology". A thorough analysis of this area has been the primary aim of the book. A somewhat surprising general conclusion that may be drawn is that, in sum, Muslim politics is rather peripheral. Use is made of the "pool of resources", but the references to Islam as a religious tradition are scarce. While searching for Islam "behind the ethnic marker", I have been forced to conclude that there is, in fact, little of it.

I argue therefore that the Muslim politics of the SLMC is basically *pragmatic*. The concept "pragmatic politics" has been subject to considerable academic debate.[1] This has in some cases been used interchangeably with *Realpolitik* and could be conceptualized in this way:

> [A] loss minimizing strategy or 'fail-safe' – a way of conducting politics which, though it may occasionally mean getting a sub-optimal result, will minimize the catastrophes that would happen were a 'best-case scenario' regularly to be relied on.[2]

---

[1] There are of course many definitions of and theoretical frameworks for Realpolitik or, as I prefer to call it, pragmatic politics. For other examples, see Wayman and Diehl 1994, Johnston 2008, and Festenstein 1997.

[2] Robertson 2004: 420.

© Springer Nature Switzerland AG 2019
A. Johansson, *Pragmatic Muslim Politics*,
https://doi.org/10.1007/978-3-030-12789-3_6

"Pragmatic politics" can be seen as the direct opposite of politics that is ideology driven and utopian. This fits well with what has been observed in the case of the SLMC. The main use in the party of references to Islam as a religious tradition has been to delimitate Muslims as a specific group in the political context of post-colonial Sri Lanka. While there were some initial attempts, particularly during the time of Ashraff, to put forward specific "Islamic" solutions to social problems, with direct references to the scriptures particularly in the economic field, few, if any, such attempts can be seen today.

Throughout this book, there is one theme that is recurrent in all my data: representatives of the SLMC portray themselves as spokesmen for all Sri Lankan Muslims. In texts, parliamentary speeches, and in the interviews, the image of Muslims as an indivisible, distinct ethnic category with common experiences and common interests emerges. This is an imagined community, with little real foundation. This is something that the political Muslim elite has done before, and, in the vein of Qadri Ismail in his article "Unmooring Identity", I would like reiterate the following questions: What is a Sri Lankan Muslim? Is it an individual defined by religion or ethnicity? Ismail's answer to the latter question is neither.[3] My answer is: it depends upon the individual doing the defining, and for what purposes. The discourse among members of the SLMC is an attempt to achieve hegemony in the larger discourse on who is a Muslim in Sri Lanka and, ultimately, who represents Muslims. In this, the SLMC utilizes what has been termed "the objectification of Muslim consciousness" (as discussed in previous chapters) but also the situation of internal conflict between groups.

This attempt at achieving hegemony to speak for the country's Muslims can explain the vagueness in the party's Muslim politics. References to key Islamic concepts or to the scriptures are often vague and left without further elaboration, for example, in official documents and parliamentary speeches, particularly those of the late leader Ashraff. Such references are mainly used as ethnic markers in a vague manner. The vagueness is necessary in order for these references to function as part of Muslim politics directed towards a general, but internally divided, Muslim public. The most important terms and symbols in SLMC's are not, as could be expected, following Eickelman and Piscatori, religious terminology and symbolism. They are descriptions of what the Muslims as a community are affected by: they are poor, refugees, and victims of violence. The religious terminology is certainly there, but the words used are in the discourse lacking any clearly defined meaning. In this construction of Sri Lankan Muslims, certain elements become problematic, particularly the fact that Sri Lankan Muslims are diverse. Here, we also find groups directly affected by poverty and inter-group violence (for example, Malays). Likewise, concepts such as "Tamil–speaking minorities" are something that "disturbs" the discourse on creating Muslims as an ethnic category that strives for hegemony.

In the constitution of the party, it is stated that the Qur'an and the hadiths are the supreme guidelines for the SLMC's political decision-making. This is an example of the imprecise manner in which references to Islamic tradition are made. What

---

[3] See Ismail 1995: 80f.

exactly in these scriptures is to be respected is left undefined, and this makes it possible for the leadership to make interpretations in whatever ways that suit them. From the side of the receivers of this discourse, there is an important emotional element to be considered. The party's use of references to certain elements in Islamic religious tradition triggers feelings of belonging. These elements have to be well-known among the public, albeit not necessarily understood. Among these are formulations written in Arabic script, such as the profession of faith, or symbols such the crescent.

The discursive practice preferred by the SLMC, when it comes to the role of references to Islamic tradition, is pragmatic in the sense that it seeks to get maximum power at minimum risk. For example, the internal Muslim conflict between Sufis and reformists regarding the veneration of saints is avoided altogether even though it is highly relevant to many Muslims in Sri Lanka. Risk avoidance need not only be seen in relation to a Muslim audience of potential voters but can also be detected in relation to non-Muslims and to persons within the state apparatus who may be skeptical to the party. Hence, the SLMC avoids using terminology or symbols that could be used in order to brand the party as extremist.

One of the documents analyzed does, however, appear to have less of a pragmatic character, namely, *Code of Conduct*, which specifies what is expected, in terms of religious beliefs and practices, from members of the SLMC. The list of requirements, such as following the five pillars of Islam, displaying a particular ethics, and avoiding prohibited behavior, is explicit and detailed. The way in which this document differs from both other forms of public documents and public rhetoric prompts the question as to its purpose. It appears to have little practical use, since there is no system for policing whether members indeed abide by what they have signed when entering the party. It would appear that the role of *Code of Conduct* is again symbolic; it states what a Muslim in general ought to believe and do at least ideally in a manner that is more about creating a sense of "us" than outlining a set of binding requirements. In general, I detect a gap between the official document's statements of supreme guidelines and its decreased visibility in both interviews and in parliamentary speeches. The Muslim politics of the SLMC seems to depend upon context.

Code of Conduct is an "internal" document, and my analysis shows that, internally, in the discourse of the SLMC, Muslim politics is somewhat more conspicuous and concerns such things as, for example, how the party is to be run. In external communication, however, this aspect is toned down, and instead there are recurring examples where references to the ideals of the nation and common national identity and the integrity of the nation are more central. One example is to be found in sweeping statements that position the party as striving to "preserve and ensure the Independence of the Judiciary" even when discussing the role of Shari'a. When verses from the Qur'an are quoted, they stand alongside slogans focusing on the nation, such as "we are all Sri Lankan".

My material shows that the imprecise, de-contexualized, and vague use of references to Islamic tradition, in terms of a sacred terminology or of religious symbols, opens up for an internal struggle and critique within the party. For example, in the constitution of the SLMC, references are made to the Qur'an and the hadiths, which are said to be the supreme guidelines of the party, but it is left unspecified what this entails in practice. This invites some members of the high command to criticize the leadership, demanding a politics that is more "Islamic".

There exists a potential for religious conflicts built into the party structure of the SLMC because of different figures of authority. On the one hand, there is the leader's unique role in having the final say in party affairs, and, on the other hand, there is the existence of a body of religious scholars, which is formally given the role of ensuring that whatever the party decides is in line with Islam. The religious scholars of the party are said to be "the police" in the decision-making process. In reality, they appear to have little influence, and their role is mainly symbolic. They provide an aura of sacred authority, but in fact it is the leader, in line with how the principle of *shura* is interpreted, that always makes the final decision. Thus, paradoxically, religious scholars can be marginalized in the decision-making process with the help of a principle selected from the "pool of resources" and interpreted in a suitable manner.

What is particularly noteworthy in the discourse of the SLMC is that, apart from *Code of Conduct,* there is little reference made to Islamic religious tradition when the central group of "Muslims", that is, those the party claims to represent, is defined. Instead, Muslims are defined in other ways, primarily as victims either of aggression or of governmental neglect. They constitute a group that is "poor" and that consists of "victims" and "refugees". Most of all, however, they are a group defined by what they are not: Tamils (that is, Tamil-speaking non-Muslims) or Sinhala. The leading members of the SLMC delimitate Muslims by referring to "others" who are not Muslims. Muslims are not a separate category in the official Sri Lankan census of different ethnic groups. It is a category created and nurtured by the SLMC, inclusive and vague, and hence useful for the mobilization of a diverse group of potential voters.

During the Ashraff period, references to Islam as a religious tradition and citing the Qur'an and hadith-literature occur in the political discourse directed towards non-Muslims in parliament. Islam is presented as something that might contribute to solving problems in society. It is significant that in Ashraff's speeches when references to elements from the Islamic tradition are made, it is often done in a manner that equates Islam with other religious traditions, especially Buddhism. This is to be interpreted in line with the general pragmatic stance adopted by the SLMC, given the fact that the majority in parliament are Buddhists, but it is also a concrete example of an interpretation where an element selected from the "pool of resources" is redefined in a new context. One clear example of this is when Ashraff suggested the implementation of interest-free banks (*riba*) and cites the Buddha's views on usury. The frequent comparison of Islam with other religions and the contextualized Islamic ideas that are presented are good examples of how a pragmatic minority party tries to be realistic when implementing Islamic ideas in the policies of the nation.

One important observation made in this book is that while there existed elements of Muslim politics (in Eickelman and Piscatori's understanding of the term) in the parliamentary speeches delivered during Ashraff's time, this appears to have disappeared under the current leadership.

There is no indication of the current leaders suggesting any Islamic norms, values, and practices as solutions to societal problems. Even the "sacred terminology" has vanished. All that is left are traces of the ethnic dimension of Muslims in Sri Lanka as a distinct group and of the SLMC as the group's political representative.

What lessons may then be learned from the analysis of the SLMC and its Muslim politics that is presented in this book? What new fields of research has it opened up? I suggest that one such area is the study of what can be termed "non-Islamist" political activism related to Islam. There are quite a few examples of this in the region, that is, South Asia and Southeast Asia. The common shared context is that of acting as representatives of Muslims in a minority situation.

Political scientist Paul R. Brass discusses "elites" in *Ethnicity and Nationalism: Theory and Comparison* (1991) when he analyzes Muslim (and Hindu) political organizations in India. These organizations are, as is the case with the SLMC, run by an elite claiming to represent a particular group in society. He notes that this elite uses symbols important for their supporters but in a pragmatic way: "The symbols used to create a political identity also can be shifted to adjust to political circumstances and the limitations imposed by state authorities [...] could be triggered by a dramatic social change".[4]

Another interesting example in the context of India is the Jamaat-e-Islami Hind (JIH). Even though it has Islamist roots and initially demanded the Islamization of society and the creation of an Islamic state as a means to this, the organization changed into becoming a defender of the secular state.[5] The support for the secular ideal was based on that it was the best institution for the preservation of minority cultures. The JIH came to focus on education and the social elevation of the community that it claimed to represent. The public image promoted by the organization is that of being a supporter of human rights, a promoter of democratic values, and an opponent of political and economic colonization.[6] The way in which key religious terms are conceptualized displays close similarity with what can be found in the case of the SLMC. For example, the term jihad is later used by the Students Islamic Movement of India (SIMI), affiliated with the JIH, as a defensive war justified by anti-Muslim riots. The SIMI claimed that "it is the role of the state in the mistreatment of its citizens that sets the discourse of jihad in motion [...] and it is a manifestation of an exclusive undemocratic politics".[7] This line of reasoning can be found in Ashraff's speeches in parliament having to do with the protection of Muslims in Sri Lanka. Furthermore, just like Ashraff did, the JIH promotes Islam as a peaceful religion, emphasizing that the Prophet Muhammad was *rahmatul lil*

---

[4] Brass 1991: 17, 25–6.

[5] By "secular", Ahmad argues that a state that does not represent any religion treats all religions equally and does not forbid citizens from practicing their faith. Ahmad 2009: 8. See also Ahmad 2003.

[6] Cordier 2010: 482.

[7] Ahmad 2009: 164,166.

alamin (a mercy to mankind) and arguing that he did not advocate war.[8] Additionally, the JIH promotes common human values (for all communities), the prevention of communalism and cultural aggression, the purification of the national society, and support for the demands for Muslim personal law and religious education.[9]

In Singapore, a Muslim organization called the Islamic Religious Council of Singapore (IRCS) has tried to promote an ideal Singaporean Muslim identity. Ten key notions have been presented, and these are quite similar to the principles of the SLMC's constitution.[10]

In the case of Nepal, we find similar examples. Religious studies scholar Megan Adamson Sijapati (2011) argues that: "To brand Muslim movements in Nepal 'Islamist' would be inapt" because Islamism indicates that their goal is to Islamize the whole nation".[11] In Nepal, political organizations, even in those cases where Muslims form the majority, are staunch supporters of pluralist politics.[12]

The examples above are all from South and Southeast Asia and even if there examples in these regions when Muslims minorities have taken up arms these democratic approaches may indicate a more general tendency in political activism related to Islam in multi-cultural, multi-ethnic, or multi-religious settings where Muslims are in the minority.[13]

Eickelman and Piscatori define Islamist movements as essentially protest movements. And, indeed, the ideology of the leading members of the SLMC displays elements of protest. In contrast to Islamist parties, the SLMC, however, lacks the aspiration to infuse Islam in society at large. We are here thus dealing with a protest movement of a different kind. The purpose of the elements of protest within SLMC discourse is simply to make sure that the group the party claims to represent, and in effect creates, is recognized as consisting of citizens having equal rights in the context of the post-colonial nation-state of Sri Lanka. With the aid of a (in terms of votes) loss-minimizing strategy, the leaders of the SLMC pragmatically aim to unify all Muslims on the island.

Previous research has approached the SLMC as a religious party aiming ideologically to infuse Islamic values, standards, and regulations into Sri Lankan politics. Habitually, this kind of research forgets the elementary insight that words such as "jihad", even though part of a conventional "sacred terminology", do not have a

---

[8] Ahmad 2009: 164.

[9] Ahmad 2009: 205–6. This is not unique to a minority situation. For example, this relationship between different religious groups and nationalism is not exceptional in any way. Esposito and Voll (1996) give an example of the Muslim Brotherhood in Sudan, which rearticulated Islamic positions on non-Muslims living within an Islamic society to legitimize them as Sudanese citizens.

[10] Islamic Religious Council of Singapore, quoted in Steiner 2011: 125. See also Mutalib 2005, 2010. The pluralist idea is not in any way uncommon in Islamic political history; for example, in Indonesia, Nahdatul Ulama was "committed to the idea of a pluralist, democratic and nonsectarian Indonesia". See Eickelman and Piscatori 2004: 55.

[11] Adamson Sijapati 2011: 5.

[12] See Hefner 2000: 7.

[13] See Nilsen 2012 and Taya 2010, for some examples regarding violent Muslim organization in the regions.

fixed meaning. If we analyze the internal and external discourse of the SLMC without taking the flexibility of semantics and interpretation into consideration, we risk overemphasizing the role of religion within the party.

As Eickelman and Piscatori have convincingly argued, there has been a tendency among "orientalist" scholars to see Muslim political organizations as static, non-rational, and hostile to religious coexistence.[14] Because of this clichéd picture of political parties that in one or another way invokes Islam, it is crucial to analyze how religious terminology and symbols are invested with meaning in particular contexts; in the case of the SLMC, the overall significant context is the multi-religious Sri Lankan society in which Muslims constitute a minority, and political mobilization within the existing democratic system therefore needs to be pragmatic.

Equally important to question is the research that simply dismisses the SLMC as a non-religious party. If we do not analyze religion thoroughly in parties that explicitly refer to holy texts and religious prescriptions, what, then, are we left with? It appears as if scholars feel an urge to label Muslim parties such as the SLMC as either Islamist or non-religious, as if Muslim parties could not occupy a moderate position. The fact that moderate, pragmatic Muslim parties, such as the SLMC, do not want to infuse Islam in society at large should not, on the other hand, make us ignore the very real effects (for instance, attitudes towards homosexuals or peace ideals) of the use of religious notions and ideas. Political parties that advocate pragmatic Muslim politics are as worthy a subject for investigation as Islamist parties are, and they need to be examined equally thoroughly in their own right.

References

Adamson Sijapati, Megan. 2011. *Islamic Revival in Nepal*. New York: Routledge.

Ahmad, Zafar. 2003. *Future of Islam in South Asia*. Delhi: Autopress.

Ahmad, Irfan. 2009. *Islamism and Democracy in India*. Princeton: Princeton University Press.

Brass, P.R. 1991. *Ethnicity and Nationalism: Theory and Comparison*. New Delhi: Sage Publications.

Cordier De, Bruno. 2010. Challenges of Social Upliftment and Definition of Identity: A Field Analysis of the Social Service Network of Jammat-e-Islami Hind, Meerut, India. *Journal of Muslim Minority Affairs* 30 (4): 479–500.

Eickelman, Dale F., and James Piscatori. 2004. *Muslim Politics*. Princeton: Princeton University Press. First edition 1996.

Esposito, John L., and John O. Voll. 1996. *Islam and Democracy*. New York: Oxford University Press.

Festenstein, Matthew. 1997. *Pragmatism & Political Theory*. Cambridge: Polity Press.

Hefner, Robert W. 2000. *Civil Islam. Muslims and Democratization in Indonesia*. Princeton: Princeton University Press.

Ismail, Qadri. 1995. Unmooring Identity: The Antinomies of Elite Muslim Self-Representation in Modern Sri Lanka. In *Unmaking the Nation: The Politics of Identity and History in Modern Sri Lanka*, ed. Pradeep Jeganathan and Qadri Ismail. Colombo: Social Scientists' Association.

---

[14] Eickelman and Piscatori 2004: 56.

Johnston, Douglas. 2008. *Faith-Based Diplomacy: Trumping Realpolitik*. New York: Oxford University Press.

Mutalib, Hussin. 2005. Singapore Muslims: The Quest for Identity in a Modern City-State. *Journal of Muslim Minority Affairs* 25 (1): 53–72.

———. 2010. Authoritarian Democracy and the Minority Muslim Polity in Singapore. In *Islam and Politics in Southeast Asia*, ed. Johan Saravanamuttu. New York: Routledge.

Nilsen, Marte. 2012. *Negotiating Thainess: Religious and National Identities in Thailand's Southern Conflict*. Ph.D. thesis, Lund Studies in History of Religions, Lund University, Sweden.

Robertson, David. 2004. *The Routledge Dictionary of Politics*. London: Routledge.

Steiner, Kerstin. 2011. Religion and Politics in Singapore: Matters of National Identity and Security? A Case Study of the Muslim Minority in a Secular State. *Osaka University Law Review* 58: 107–134.

Taya, Shamsuddin L. 2010. The Politicization of Ethnic Sentiments in the Southern Philippines: The Case of the Bangsamoro. *Journal of Muslim Minority Affairs* 30 (1): 19–34.

Wayman, Frank Whelon, and Paul Francis Diehl. 1994. *Reconstructing Realpolitik*. Michigan: University of Michigan Press.

Appendices

Appendix 1: Brief Introduction to Informants

A.L.M. Kaleel joined the SLMC in 1984 and is a high command member. His position in the party is the president of the Majlis-e-Shura (since 2000) and he is a religious scholar (Moulavi). He is based in Colombo.

Tuan Nazeer has been a member of the party since the beginning of 2000. He is not a high command member. He was the propaganda minister of the party in 2006 dealing with different media. At present he is the media manager for the chairman of the party, Basheer S. Dawood. My questions to Tuan Nazeer were not the same as those to high command members as my interview with him was based on how the SLMC deals with the media.

Hasen Ali is a member of the high command and was one of the first members of the party. Besides being the General Secretary, Ali is also a member of the parliament and is a well-known face in Sri Lankan politics. He has a master's degree in engineering from Saudi Arabia, but works full time in the organization of the SLMC.

H.M.M. Ilyas is a member of the high command and his role in the SLMC is the representative of the Ulema Congress. He joined the party in 1988 when he ran in the local election. He is based in Deltota, in the Kandy district.

M.G.M. Rizvie is not a member of the high command. He is the secretary of the national organizer Shafeek Rajabdeen and the coordinator of minister of justice and party leader Rauff Hakeem. He is also a member of the central committee and my interview with him concerned the SLMC's organization.

Rauff Hakeem is a member of the high command and the leader of the party. He is at the moment the minister of justice and has had more ministerial portfolios in the government. He joined the party in 1987, and became the General Secretary in 1992 and the leader of the party in 2001 when the late leader Ashraff died. He is originally from Kandy but lives in Colombo.

© Springer Nature Switzerland AG 2019
A. Johansson, *Pragmatic Muslim Politics*,
https://doi.org/10.1007/978-3-030-12789-3

Shafeek Rajabdeen is a member of the Western Province – Provincial Council and the Colombo Chief Organizer of the SLMC. Rajabdeen has been in the Western Province – Provincial Council from 1999 to the present time. Before he joined politics he and his father had a construction company where he worked for 30 years. He is also the current president of the Moors Sports Club, which is one of the oldest Muslim sports clubs in the country. My interview with Rajabdeen took place there. He is now in his fifties and has a wife and children.

S.H. Athambawa is not a member of the high command or the party. However, he is a religious scholar and was one of the advisers of the late leader M.H.M. Ashraff, and he has written a biography about Ashraff. My interview with him concerned Ashraff's religious aspects and the history of Ashraff's political background.

S.L.M. Hanifa is a member of the high command and a member of the municipal council in Akkaraipattu. He is also a religious scholar (Moulavi) and he joined the SLMC in 2009.

Sithy Rifaya is the leader of the Ladies Congress, which is one of the SLMC's affiliate bodies. Refaya is in her late fifties and married. She has also been involved in politics for a long time. Before she joined the SLMC she was a part of the United National Party (UNP) until 2001. She also used to work at the Ministry of Labour from 1968 to 1981, she worked mostly with questions regarding trade. After that she worked at the Direction of Muslim Affairs and she represented Sri Lanka at the first convention for Muslim women, held in the Philippines. According to Rifaya, she joined the SLMC after being disappointed with the UNP for not letting her be part of the leadership. This made her want to join the SLMC, but she was also affected by how the SLMC was attacked by media and other parties. She is now a managing director of her family's company, Confidence Travels, which helps people from Sri Lanka to work in the Middle East.

HC Member 1 has been a member of the party since the mid 1980s. He is based in the eastern part of Sri Lanka.

HC Member 2 started out in the party in the mid 1990s and has since then contested in different elections. He lives in the eastern part of Sri Lanka.

HC member 3 is a member of the high command. He joined the SLMC in the 2000s. Since then he has had different positions in the party.

HC member 4 joined the SLMC in the late 1990s and he has contested for them several times. He lives in the eastern part of Sri Lanka.

HC member 5 joined the party in the mid 1980s and has contested for the party several times in the eastern part of the country.

HC member 6 has been with the party since the 1980s and has contested for the party in the western part of Sri Lanka.

HC member 7 joined the SLMC in the 1980s and has been active in elections since then.

HC member 8 has been in the party since the mid 1980s and has contested for them in the eastern part of Sri Lanka.

HC member 9 joined the party in the 1980s. He has contested for the party and been a part of the provincial council in the eastern part of Sri Lanka.

HC member 10 joined the party in the 1990s and has contested for the party in the eastern part of Sri Lanka.

HC member 11 joined the party in the 2000s and has contested for the party in the eastern part of Sri Lanka.

HC member 12 has been a member since the 1990s. He lives in the western part of Sri Lanka.

HC member 13 has been a member since the early 1990s and has contested for the party in the western part of the country.

HC member 14 has been in the party since the beginning and has contested on the east cost for the party.

HC member 15 joined the party in the 2000s and has contested for the party in the eastern part of the country.

HC member 16 has worked on different levels in the parties since the 1990s and has contested for them in the western part of the country.

HC member 17 has been a member of the party since the early 1990s and contested several times for the party.

HC member 18 has been with the party since the early 1980s and has contested on different levels since the beginning.

HC member 19 has been with the party since the mid 1980s and has contested for the party since then. He lives on the east coast.

HC member 20 has been a member of the party since the 1980s and lives on the east coast of the country.

HC member 21 has been associated with the party since the early 1980s and contested under the tree banner several times. He lives in the eastern part of Sri Lanka.

HC member 22 has been in the party since the mid 1990s and has contested for the party on the west coast.

HC member 23 joined the SLMC in the mid 1980s and has contested for the party since the 1990s. He lives on the west coast.

Appendix 2: Letter of Appointment

ශ්‍රී ලංකා මුස්ලිම් කොංග්‍රස්
ஸ்ரீ லங்கா முஸ்லிம் காங்கிரஸ்
Sri Lanka Muslim Congress

12th December 2011

Mr. Mohamed Riaz Cafoor
151/B6/1, Maligawatte Place
Colombo 10

Dear Brother,

Assalaamu Alaikum.

<u>LETTER OF APPOINTMENT AS AREA/BRANCH ORGANISER - 2012.</u>

I am pleased to inform that, you are appointed as the Area/Branch
Organiser for NHS Flats, Maligawatta Place / Apple Watta / Jayantha
Weerasekera Mawatha of Colombo North Electorate in Colombo District
with effect from today.

You are hereby requested to abide by and act in accordance with the
provisions of the Constitution, Code of conduct and the decisions of the Sri
Lanka Muslim Congress in the discharge of your duties.

Please note that your appointment to the above post is valid for one year
from 01st January 2012.

Thank you.

Yours faithfully,

Shafeek Rajabdeen J.P
National Organizer
Colombo District Organizer

Shafeek Rajabdeen J.P
Former Member of Parliament
National Organizer
Sri Lanka Muslim Congress

Shafeek Rajabdeen MP
National Organizer
1B/1B5 A, Evergreen Park, Centre Road,
Muhandiram Dabare Mawatha,
Colombo 05, Sri Lanka.

Office : "Dharussalam"
31, Vauxhall Lane,
Colombo 2, Sri Lanka.

Office Tel : +94 11 2508385
Res   : +94 11 2592330
Fax   : +94 11 2808419

SLMC Off : +94 11 2436752
Fax   : +94 11 4717720
Mobile   : +94 77 7760025
E-mail : shafeekrajabdeen@hotmail.com

Appendix 3: Memorandum of Understanding Between the SLMC and the LTTE

Joint Communiqué of the Liberation Tigers of Tamil Eelam and the Sri Lanka Muslim Congress

The discussion between the Liberation Tigers of Tamil Eelam and the Sri Lanka Muslim Congress that took place today (13.04.2002) were friendly and constructive.

The venue was the Political Headquarters of the Liberation Tigers of Tamil Eelam in Kilinochchi and the discussions lasted for three hours. National Leader Mr Veluppillai Prabhakaran, Political Advisor Anton Balasingham, Political Wing Leader S.P. Tamilchelvan, Batticaloa-Ampara District Commander Colonel Karuna, Trincomalee District Commander Colonel Paduman, Mrs Adele Balasingham represented the LTTE. National Leader Rauff Hakeem, Chairman Athuaullah, Senior Deputy Leader Dr Uthuma Lébbe, Deputy Leader Mohideen Abdul Cader, Secretary for Policy Dissemination Bazeer Seghu Dawood, Deputy Chairman Masoor Noordeen and Additional Secretary for Policy Dissemination Mazoor Moulana represented the SLMC.

In this meeting solutions were found for significant practical problems faced by the Muslims of the North and the East. Leader Prabhakaran made a public request asking the Muslims displaced from Jaffna and Vanni to resettle in their areas. It was decided to establish a joint committee with representatives from the LTTE and the SLMC to create the environment conducive to such resettlement. It was also decided that proper conditions must be created for the resettlement of Muslims in several small villages in the Eastern Province.

It was agreed that the uncultivated agricultural lands belonging to the Muslims of the North and the East must again be utilized by them for cultivation purposes.

The LTTE agreed to discontinue with immediate effect the practice of collecting money from the Muslims to support the struggle. It was decided that the LTTE and the SLMC must appoint a representative each with a view to discussing the problems faced by the Muslims in the various districts in the North and East with Senior Commanders of the LTTE and to consolidate Tamil-Muslim relations.

It was decided to continue these high-level meetings.

It was agreed that when negotiations start between the government and the LTTE, the representatives of the Muslim Congress would contribute to the negotiations as a separate party on behalf of the Muslims.

It was also agreed that the basic political issues of the Muslims of the North and the East must be approached on a principled basis and to have continuous negotiations in order to preserve their distinct political and cultural identity.

It was also decided that since the Muslim Congress enjoys the support of the majority of the Muslims, all negotiations concerning the issues of the Muslims of the North and East must be conducted with the Muslim Congress.

Sgd. V Prabhakaran   Sgd. Rauff Hakeem
National Leader   National Leader
Liberation Tigers of Tamil Eelam   Sri Lanka Muslim Congress

Appendix 4: Ba'ya

AFFIDAVIT

I,..of..
...., being a Muslim do hereby sincerely, solemnly and truly declare and affirm as follows:-

I am the affirmant above named;

I state that I am a member of the Sri Lanka Muslim Congress (SLMC);

I state that I have been elected as a Member of the .... on behalf of the SLMC.

I state that I have signed a pledge *inter alia* declaring allegiance to the Sri Lanka Muslim Congress and its Leadership.

I also state that I have also entered into an agreement with the Sri Lanka Muslim Congress:

I state that upon taking oaths as a Member of .... I become a member of the People's Representatives' Committee of the Sri Lanka Muslim Congress in terms of the provisions of the Constitution of the Sri Lanka Muslim Congress;

I also state that I am liable to be expelled from the Sri Lanka Muslim Congress in the event of violation of the pledge and/or the undertaking given in the Agreement dated ....

I state that I signed the pledge and entered into the agreement referred to above voluntarily and further state that this was done with the earnest hope and belief of safeguarding the interest of the Sri Lanka Muslim Congress and its members.

The foregoing was read over and explained

to the affirmant above named and after

having understood the same signed in my

presence in Colombo on this 2011

Before me

Justice of the Peace

AGREEMENT

Agreement between Sri Lanka Muslim Congress, a political Party recognized under the provisions of Parliamentary Elections Act No.1 of 1981 and having its registered office at "Daarussalaam" No. 51, Vauxhall Lane, Colombo 2.

And

....a member of the Sri Lanka Muslim Congress.

Witnesses as follows:

Mr .... is a Member of the Sri Lanka Muslim Congress.

It is specifically agreed between the parties that the appointment of .... as a Member of the .... is subject to the decision of the High Command of the Sri Lanka Muslim Congress dated ....

The Parties specifically agree that the pledge of loyalty and the Affidavit affirmed to by ....shall form part and parcel of the agreement.

....specifically agrees to abide by and respect the Constitution, Code of Conduct and all decisions of the Sri Lanka Muslim Congress; and,

.... specifically agrees that any refusal and/or failure to honour all or any of the pledges or undertakings in the agreement with the Sri Lanka Muslim Congress is a serious violation of the Party Discipline and in such an eventuality it is expressly agreed that .... is liable to be expelled from the Sri Lanka Muslim Congress summarily.

Signed on this .... in ....

....

(name of the Nominee)

Secretary General

Sri Lanka Muslim Congress

PLEDGE

I , ...as Member of Sri Lanka Muslim Congress do hereby agree and undertake to:

Abide by and defend the Constitution and the Code of Conduct of the Sri Lanka Muslim Congress and respect all decisions of the Sri Lanka Muslim Congress; and

Abide by and respect all decisions and directives issued by the Leader of the Sri Lanka Muslim Congress; and

Resign from membership of .... if nominated, as and when directed to do so by the Sri Lanka Muslim Congress; and

Identify myself as a member of the Sri Lanka Muslim Congress at all times and defend and propagate the policies and decisions of the Sri Lanka Muslim Congress.

In the event of being elected, I state, that I will at all times conform to the decisions of the Party conveyed through the Leader of the Sri Lanka Muslim Congress, will stand with the Party and at no time and under no circumstances will defy the Party and its decisions conveyed through the said leader of the Party.

Submit myself to disciplinary control of the Sri Lanka Muslim Congress.

I also specifically state that I am aware of the decision of the High Command of the Sri Lanka Muslim Congress dated .... and state that I agree to abide by the said decision of the High Command and enter into an Agreement with the Sri Lanka Muslim Congress stipulating the terms and conditions   of   my   candidature   to   be   nominated   to   the   Membership   of   the .... under the Sri Lanka Muslim Congress.

I also specifically agree and state that I am liable to be expelled from the Sri Lanka Muslim Congress in the event of violation of all or any one of pledge referred to above.

                    ....

Witnesses

1   ....

2   ....

Date:......................

Appendix 5: Invitation to the 23 Delegates' Conference

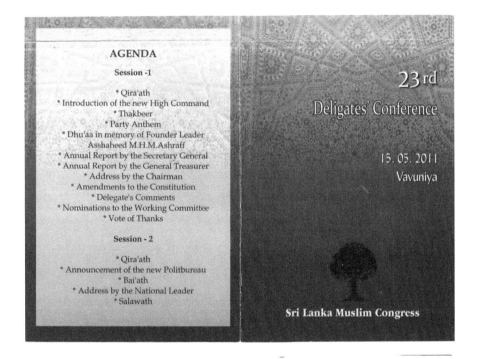

AGENDA

Session -1

* Qira'ath
* Introduction of the new High Command
* Thakbeer
* Party Anthem
* Dhu'aa in memory of Founder Leader
  Asshaheed M.H.M.Ashraff
* Annual Report by the Secretary General
* Annual Report by the General Treasurer
* Address by the Chairman
* Amendments to the Constitution
* Delegate's Comments
* Nominations to the Working Committee
* Vote of Thanks

Session - 2

* Qira'ath
* Announcement of the new Politbureau
* Bai'ath
* Address by the National Leader
* Salawath

23rd
Deligates' Conference

15. 05. 2011
Vavuniya

Sri Lanka Muslim Congress

The High Command
of the
Sri Lanka Muslim Congress
invites

....

to participate
at the

23rd Delegates' Conference

to be held on
Sunday the 15th May 2011
at 2.00 p.m at the

New Town Hall
Vavuniya

Shareek Rajabdeen JP
Fmr Member of Parliament
National Organizer
Sri Lanka Muslim Congress

"Dharussalam"
51,Vauxhall Lane,
Colombo- 02.   Tel/Fax: 011-2436752

Please bring this invitation with you